FUTURE
RIGHT

FUTURE RIGHT

FORGING A NEW REPUBLICAN MAJORITY

DONALD T. CRITCHLOW

St. Martin's Press
New York

www.stmartins.com

Library of Congress Cataloging-in-Publication Data

Names: Critchlow, Donald T., 1948– author.

Title: Future right : forging a new Republican majority / Donald Critchlow.

Description: First edition. | New York : St. Martin's Press, [2016] | Includes bibliographical references and index.

Identifiers: LCCN 2015050149| ISBN 9781250087584 (hardcover) | ISBN 9781250087591 (e-book)

Subjects: LCSH: Republican Party (U.S. : 1854–) | Party affiliation—United States. | Conservatism—United States.

Classification: LCC JK2356 .C733 2016 | DDC 324.2734—dc23

LC record available at http://lccn.loc.gov/2015050149

Our books may be purchased in bulk for promotional, educational, or business use. Please contact your local bookseller or the Macmillan Corporate and Premium Sales Department at 1-800-221-7945, extension 5442, or by e-mail at MacmillanSpecialMarkets@macmillan.com.

First Edition: May 2016

10 9 8 7 6 5 4 3 2 1

CONTENTS

To Senator Jon Kyl and Steve Twist,
Arizona Republicans,
whom I consider good friends

ACKNOWLEDGMENTS

THOSE FEW READERS WHO SCRUTINIZE ACKNOWLEDGMENTS WILL have to forgive me for not offering a perfunctory list of everyone who has made even the slightest contribution to this book, from passing conversation to moral support. Instead, I want to list those people who actually made serious contributions to this book as readers and researchers.

First, I want to thank three friends who read the manuscript at various stages and offered criticisms that were as critical as any anonymous reader for a press. In particular, William Rorabaugh, whom I have known since we were graduate students in History at the University of California, Berkeley, brought his immense knowledge and keen eye to the manuscript; Gregory Schneider brought his knowledge of Republican politics to the penultimate draft; and Irv Gellman offered advice on the entire project from inception to completion.

Four students at Arizona State University, while not agreeing necessarily with the intention of the book, ferreted out much of the data I've used. These researchers include Mikaela Colby, James Potts, Cody Bendix, and Jerry Schumacher.

In addition, I want to thank literary agent Alexander Hoyt for his help in developing this project and securing a press for the book, and Karen Wolny, my editor at St. Martin's Press, who saw the value in this project. Allow me to thank the superb editorial staff at St. Martin's Press, including Laura Apperson, Alan Bradshaw and Meenakshi Venkat, who saved me from even more mistakes that might have been found in this book. Roxane Barwick helped with copyediting and indexing the book.

While understanding that acknowledgments to spouses can be formulaic, my wife, Patricia, read many drafts of the manuscript and provided astute criticism, and I deeply appreciate her intelligence and support. Although they did not contribute in any way to the book, other than my hope that they will become part of the future Republican majority, my grandchildren—Andrew, Alexander, and Joshua—like seeing their names in print, so I will list them as a matter of perfunctory acknowledgment, so as not to betray tradition totally.

FUTURE
RIGHT

INTRODUCTION

CAN REPUBLICANS FORGE A NEW MAJORITY PARTY? THE ANSWER TO this question is an emphatic Yes. This book explores how this is possible, but it's not a certainty. Fortune plays a great role in politics, from selecting good candidates to campaign slipups, the mood of the electorate, and events beyond the control of politicians. Still, the conditions are there for Republicans to emerge as the dominant party of the future.

How is this to be accomplished? *Future Right* makes a twofold argument for creating a new Republican majority. The first argument is based on social and economic trends. The second argument is about political strategy, which focuses on the critical voter blocs necessary for a majoritarian party: women, minority, youth, older, middle-class, and religious voters.

The assumption that demographics favor Democrats as the party of the future is wrong. The Democratic base, an uneasy coalition of women, minorities, and young voters, is vulnerable to a Republican takeover. A close look at survey data shows that these groups are not uniformly liberal on many issues today, and in the future, as more women, minorities, and young enter the middle class, they will find Democratic Party identity politics both stale and inadequate.

Demographics alone are not political destiny, and socioeconomic trends are transforming the identity categories of race, gender, and youth—which provides a rich opportunity for conservatives to create a new majority. Conservatives will need imagination and political acumen if they are to win over voters from these constituencies.

Democrats are quick to point out that whites, the base of the Republican Party, will be in the minority by mid-century. Current minority voters—Hispanics, blacks, and Asian Americans—are voting overwhelmingly Democratic, and as young minorities reach voting age, they will only enlarge Democratic rolls. Young female voters are already voting Democratic, and there is no reason to foresee these voters aligning themselves with a graying, slowly dying Republican Party. Millennial voters overwhelmingly vote Democratic. They are progressives and see the Republican Party as the past, not the future.

The Left and its allies in the Democratic Party will continue to talk about the war on women, racism, and income inequality. It makes for good campaign rhetoric that beguiles their supporters into embracing policies and programs that imprison single unwed mothers in poverty, foster racism, and encourage the rhetoric of class warfare. The fact of the matter is that the older shibboleth categories of race and gender are changing as racial and ethnic intermarriage creates new Americans. More women are going to college than ever before, leaving school to become lawyers, doctors, and business professionals. Women have become corporate managers, executives, and leaders in their professions. The older rhetoric of the Left is clichéd and does not represent the new American Dream that is being created.

While left-wing media pundits and politicians foresee the demise of conservatism in America, social trends favor a revived conservative movement. The Left confidently believes that changing demographics mean the slow death of conservatism; the reality is that if conservatives play it right, they can take advantage of these trends and win in 2016 and future elections. A seismic shift is coming in American society and culture, one that makes possible the creation of a new conservative majority.

In the last two presidential elections, Republicans lost minorities, young women, and youth in overwhelming numbers. Behind the reality of current voting patterns, which doubtless present a gloomy outlook for the Republican Party, there are trends that should not be overlooked. These social and economic trends reveal two major results: the meaning of race and the role of women in society are changing dramatically; and the retirement of the boomer generation, mostly white, will create new opportunities in the knowledge-based economy for racial and ethnic minorities, women, and the young. As the foundation of older identity politics is eroded by these trends, and as minority groups, women, and the young find opportunities in the new economy, becoming well-paid professionals, managers, and CEOs, their current vague concerns about social justice will give way to the real problems of how their taxes are spent; the size of government; economic growth; reducing the national debt; and national security. These issues play to the strength of the Republican Party.

As the old categories of race and gender break down, conservatives are well placed to send a message that invites average people to "Imagine the New America." This message should be articulated by diverse voices that project an optimistic future as they tell of their successes in the land of opportunity and how conservatism represents the creators of the future. This message should be less issue-oriented and instead aimed at the average American voter fed up with the stale, divisive politics of the past.

A quick preview of some of these trends suggests how conservatives can take advantage of this new world.

Race: America is changing ethnically, and the old politics of race is going to be different in the future. Why? The answer is simple: intermarriage. Already Asian Americans are intermarrying with whites at a rate of more than 50 percent; Hispanic Americans are doing so at 35 percent; and African Americans are doing so at 15 percent. The children of these intermarriages tend to marry whites.[1] The reconfiguring of race in America can be an advantage for conservatives who can win Hispanic and Asian Americans who rise financially and successfully in the twenty-first century. The conservative message should stress rewarding success and that taxes are wasted on big government.

Demographic trends show that race is being reconfigured. This transformation is occurring at striking speed, but old ideas about race will remain as culture lags behind social trends. The key to political success for conservatives will be an intermediate strategy of taking advantage of social and economic disparities that will occur among minorities, especially Hispanics, by breaking their long-standing ties to Democrats and the Left.

Asian Americans are at the top of the academic achievement heap. They have tilted Democratic in their voting, especially among the young. This voting pattern is a reversal from the late 1960s, when Asian Americans voted Republican. In many localities Democrats have been much better at candidate recruitment. The Asian-American vote can be regained by giving Asian-American leaders a key seat at the conservative table and by promoting Asian-American success stories—not as an example of one race's success, but of Americans' success.

A similar strategy can be employed by conservatives to win Hispanic voters. A strong entrepreneurial ethos is found within the Hispanic community, combined with a large and growing segment relying on government assistance. Yet even as dependency has grown, most Hispanics consider themselves white, and most live, as shown by the latest census reports, in nonsegregated, racially and income-mixed neighborhoods. At the same time, Hispanics in California have challenged black gerrymandered districts. Conservatives need to break this unfavorable black-brown alliance by integrating Hispanic conservatives into the larger political movement.

African Americans are the least likely to benefit as a group from the social trends that are emerging. The tangled relationship of black leaders and politicians with the Democratic Party cannot be easily broken. What can be broken, however, is their complete lock on the black vote. The entire black vote cannot and will not be won by conservatives. If a segment of black voters, however, can be won to the Republican-conservative side, it will have significant political consequences. This can be accomplished not by trying to compete with the Democrats and the Left for handout programs, but by a campaign revolving around a single theme: what have the Democrats done for you lately? Self-serving Democrats line the pockets of their Wall Street supporters and party lobbyists while ignoring the plight of the poor. Voters, whether they be Hispanic, black, or white, are sick of the established political class not addressing problems of poor or no employment, bad schools, and unsafe neighborhoods. This can be a winning argument, if conservatives can show that they are sick of the political class as well.

★　★　★　★　★

Women: Debates over gender inequality are not going to be the same in twenty years. Why? Baby boomers, those born in the years 1946–64, account for 60 percent of the workforce today. The boomer exodus will create huge new opportunities for women and ethnic minority groups. In the future, women will be running corporate America and will be leaders in business and politics. Conservatives should applaud successful women.

Today more women and Hispanics are going to college. This education will allow them to rise socioeconomically. As they begin to pay more taxes, see government waste, and observe rising dependency from those left behind who did not take advantage of opportunities, they will be open to a conservative message of smaller government, tax reform, less welfare dependency, and traditional family values. To overcome the progressive advantage in the political arena, Republicans need to break the hold the Democratic Party has on career-minded women, who will benefit in the new American economy.

At the same time, Republicans need to show that they understand the problems of women who are being left behind in this new economy. Many of these women are black and Hispanic; many are single mothers; and most are poorly educated for the new workplace. As Arthur C. Brooks shows in *The Conservative Heart: How to Build a Fairer, Happier and More Prosperous America* (2015), Republicans should embrace real social justice for the poor and articulate real ways that poor women and single mothers can share in the American Dream.

As Brooks argues, political rebellion expresses anger. Yet anger in itself does not win voters, especially new voters to a party seeking majoritarian status.

The languages of individual responsibility and compassion are not mutually exclusive. Many of the poor have made bad choices in their lives, including drug and alcohol addiction, dropping out of school, having children out of wedlock, and being trapped in abusive situations. These bad choices were often made in bad environments that made it easy to take the wrong path. Most poor women in general, and single mothers in particular, want a better life for themselves and their children. Life on welfare, food stamps, unemployment benefits, and subsidized housing is gruesome for these women and their children. The task of Republicans is to show that they understand the problems of poor women and want to offer a realistic path out of poverty for them.

Republicans have narrowed the gender gap in recent elections, especially in 2014. White women, single and married, are voting Republican. Minority women, aspiring and poverty-stricken, can also be won to the Republican Party through a conservative agenda that promotes true social justice, equal opportunity, and real choice in individuals' lives.

★　★　★　★　★

Youth: In 1860, Republicans under Abraham Lincoln overwhelmingly won the youth vote by standing as a party of reform. Republicans tapped into discontent among the youth at that time by disassociating themselves from the tired politics of the past. This lesson of the past is a lesson for the future.

Republican presidential candidates in 2008 (John McCain) and in 2012 (Mitt Romney) lost the youth vote by wide margins. Republican candidates did better in some statewide elections among young white voters, but the age gap remains greater for Republicans than the gender gap. Although Barack Obama and media pundits made much of the youth vote in these elections, actual turnout among young voters, 18–25 years old, increased only a couple of percentage points in 2008. Furthermore, there is strong evidence that those just reaching voting age are leaning more Republican. Nevertheless, Republicans face a young voting population that leans heavily Democratic.

It is easy to read too much into these surveys and past voting behavior on the part of youth. While distrustful of corporations and Wall Street, young voters are more favorable toward small business than older voters. Many, close to a majority, favor privatization of Social Security. Presented with issues that concern them, young voters express the same concerns as do all voters: they are most focused on jobs and the economy, education, and healthcare. On social issues, they are divided. While many young voters support gay marriage, they are about evenly divided on abortion. Like most Americans, they believe abortion is a constitutional right, but they do not want "abortion-on-demand." They favor abortion with exemptions to save the life of the mother and in the cases of rape and incest. *Future Right* explores why this shift on abortion has occurred among young voters and also shows that many millennials are deeply religious. The myth that young voters are uniformly progressive and deeply secular is belied by survey data. Furthermore, the great advantage that Republicans have in the long run is that they have a strong base of younger candidates, who are just beginning their careers in local and state government.

BEYOND POLITICS: OBSTACLES FOR THE NATION

The state of the economy looms as the most profound issue facing the nation. Economic growth through a free market economy promotes opportunity, advancement, and prosperity for all citizens. Today the ratio of people receiving some sort of government assistance—welfare, Social Security, housing subsidies, and food stamps, excluding veteran benefits—stands at a ratio of 1.7 to 1. This cannot be sustained as the baby-boomer generation retires and larger numbers of eligible workers drop out of the workforce.

Over the last five years there has been an explosion of food stamps, disability enrollment, Medicaid expansion, and welfare rule relaxation. At the same time, America is confronted with a crisis in Social Security and Medicare costs as the baby-boomer generation retires. This creates the conditions for financial calamity, as well as severe generational conflict. President Obama's economic policies might have contributed to a less than vigorous recovery, but the American economy is undergoing a profound transition that has created its own dynamic. Although American manufacturing remains a sizeable portion of the GDP, manufacturing jobs have declined because of increased productivity through advanced technology. In contrast, incomes for knowledge workers—those with computer and quantitative skills—have risen. Goods-producing workers—those old industrial jobs that helped create a vibrant middle class in the mid-twentieth century—have seen their incomes remain stagnant or decline over the last thirty years. Fewer workers are producing more. Rhetoric by politicians, labor leaders, and pundits that America needs to bring industrial jobs back to the United States sounds good, but the reality is that manufacturing jobs are not going to return to the scale of the past. Not every student is going to have the aptitude or incentive to become a highly skilled knowledge worker. This does not mean, however, that we should create a society of a few people working, paying taxes, and supporting a large class of people dependent on welfare and entitlements. A prosperous economy creates opportunities for everyone.

Americans faced with low economic growth and stagnant wages are confronted further by political gridlock in Washington. Politicians seem completely incapable of offering viable solutions to mounting budget deficits and national debt, entitlement reform, failed public education, high unemployment and low participation in the labor force, the breakdown of the traditional family, and myriad other problems that are mired in partisan quagmire. Past experience shows that most of the issues facing the country can be solved only by a growing economy and the revitalization of civic involvement by average Americans at the community, state, and national levels. More government, more federal programs, and more bureaucratic control from Washington, D.C., will not solve our problems. An active and engaged citizenry creates an environment in which citizens address problems through self-organization.

Yet even while the active electorate has become more ideological and polarized, most Americans are not voting and are disengaged from politics. *Future Right* examines the rise of ideological politics within a context of declining voter participation and a general decline in civic involvement and civic literacy. Large numbers of citizens have retreated into "petty and vulgar pleasures"—a phrase first coined in the nineteenth century by Alexis de Tocqueville.

Knowledge about current political issues and an understanding of democratic institutions have fallen precipitously among the young, as civics is no longer taught (or learned) in high schools or colleges. Voter participation in America has declined over the last century, while voter distrust of government continues to rise. Young Americans are especially cynical about politics. While the media likes to talk about the youth vote in the 2008 and 2012 presidential elections, voter participation between the ages of 18 and 25 has *not* risen. Recent scandals in the IRS, the NSA, the EPA, and the State Department reveal a government that has become all-powerful, politicized, and rampant with cover-ups. Washington is run by unionized bureaucracies, making agencies both highly politicized and ineffective.

This incompetence and corruption have fostered cynicism within the electorate, and they reinforce a perspective that government is not the solution. Instead of encouraging self-organization and community involvement—what economist F. A. Hayek called "spontaneous order—politicians promote a belief that average Americans cannot solve their problems on their own.

Certainly many people will benefit from the demographic and economic changes that are coming. But unless we as a democratic people and our elected officials awaken to a political and social culture in disorder, the only consequence will be a democracy under threat. These problems cannot be solved solely by government, new programs, and increased spending.

If only a select few have the educational and training skills to benefit from changes that are occurring, socioeconomic divisions will intensify. Better-off women will be pitted against women left behind; ethnic divisions (including Hispanics against African Americans) will deepen; and tension's between the rich and the poor and those who work and those who remain dependent on government will escalate.

There is also the matter of race. Although intermarriage rates, especially among Hispanics and Asians, show that a new race of Americans is being created, African Americans are intermarrying at a lower rate (approximately 15 percent). Moreover, unlike Hispanics and Asians, African Americans live in less economically and ethnically integrated neighborhoods. Even more problematic, 72 percent of black Americans are raised in single-parent homes. They are more likely to be unmarried than other Americans. Moreover, close to 49 percent of black children under six years of age live in poverty. One consequence is that the percentage of blacks in poverty has gone up from 23 percent in 2000 to 28 percent today, although some of this rise can be attributed to the federal government's changing definition of what counts as poverty.

While many African Americans continue to experience poverty and a devastating breakdown in family culture—contributing to neighborhoods characterized by crime, murder, gang culture, high rates of incarceration for black males, and abysmally low rates of educational attainment—black Americans continue to vote Democratic, even though the Democratic Party and the party's black officeholders on the national, state, and local levels have done little to address the deep problems of black communities.

Democratic strategists tout that twenty-seven of the largest cities voted Democratic in 2012. Some of these cities, such as Houston, appear to be fortresses in deeply red states. The urban base that Democrats have erected is itself fragile. For all the talk of reurbanization, most Americans (70 to 80 percent) live in lower-density suburban areas.[2] In metropolitan regions with more than 500,000 people, roughly 153 million live in suburbs, while only 60 million live in core cities. This means that more than twice as many Americans live in suburbs than in metropolitan cities. While a few affluent older people have moved downtown, where they have joined young and middle-aged white-collar professionals, the vast majority of the urban population is made up of the impoverished. The actual population growth in American cities has come largely from poorer people, many of them recent immigrants. Today, 38 percent of New Yorkers are foreign born, and other large cities are similar. The urban poor live mostly in Democratic-controlled cities.

Lacking jobs, living in gang-ridden, drug-infested neighborhoods, and sending their children to bad schools that have not been improved by teacher unions, the urban poor continue to vote Democratic, albeit in decreasing numbers as turnout for city elections reaches pathetic depths. Many of these votes come from city employees and their families. They are barely holding on while everything is crumbling around them. Anger and violence have ensued, but the Democratic Party's case for representing the poor must confront the reality that things are not getting better in urban America.

Democratic Party policies have arguably exacerbated conditions by encouraging dependency. Furthermore, national spokesmen for the black community, such as Jesse Jackson, Al Sharpton, and Van Jones, just to name a few, demagogically play the race card to feather their own and their friends' nests, while leaving black brothers and sisters living in abject poverty and crime, with no futures. Cracking the black vote will not be easy for Republicans, but if some headway is not made in this significant voting bloc, Democrats will continue to enjoy electoral advantages in presidential elections as well as in key states.

OBSTACLES TO A REPUBLICAN MAJORITY

Obama won in 2008 with a more than 7 percent margin in the popular vote. Many media pundits and Democratic Party enthusiasts greeted Obama's election as the beginning of a new political era, one dominated by the Left, and the end of what had been a conservative ascendancy. The Republican Party was seen to be in permanent decline. Reality soon caught up with these predictions when Republicans regained the House in the 2010 midterm elections. Obama won reelection in 2012, but with a thin margin in the popular vote. The 2014 midterms, when Republicans swept Congress, put the final stake into the Democratic dream that Republicans were headed toward the dustbin of history.

Republicans made a comeback, but on the national level they faced their own grim reality, both in the immediate future and in the long term. Yet things might not be as grim as they at first appear. Political analyst Nate Silver shows that a small swing in the popular vote of

5 percent in 2016 could swing the election to Republicans.[3] In 2012, when Obama won the popular vote against Romney by 3.9 points, he won 330 electoral votes. In 2008, Obama won the popular vote against McCain by 7.3 points and won 365 electoral votes. Silver's point is that small percentages in the popular vote magnify Electoral College votes. If Romney, Silver notes, had won the popular vote by the same margin that Obama had, 3.9 points, and this swing was distributed uniformly across the states, Obama would have lost Minnesota, Pennsylvania, Wisconsin, as well as Colorado, Florida, Iowa, Nevada, New Hampshire, Ohio, and Virginia. A small swing in the popular vote in a few states in favor of Republicans will mean the collapse of the Democratic "Blue Wall" in the Electoral College.

It would have taken only small changes in some states for Romney to have won the election. Silver calculates that if Obama had lost the popular vote by just 1 percent, Romney would have won the Electoral College 279–259. Running his numbers in May 2015, Silver concluded that there is a 50–50 chance for either a Democrat or Republican to win the White House in 2016.

Republicans have a strong base in the electorate, although it might not be large enough at this point to carry the election for them. White voters—the middle class, married men and women, and older voters—constitute the Republican base. White voters made up 76.3 percent of voters in 2008 and 2012. Although the proportion of white voters in the total electorate is declining, winning the white vote is important for both parties. After deserting the Republican ticket in 2008, affluent voters returned to the Republican column in 2012. While Republicans might have a problem with young and nonwhite voters, Democrats are presented with a problem of winning back white middle-class voters. White middle-class voters were critical in winning the House and the Senate for Republicans in the 2014 midterms. Moreover, voters 45 years of age and older voted for Mitt Romney in 2012. These voters made up 54 percent of the electorate in 2012 and 67 percent in 2014.

Not only have Republicans retaken the white middle-class vote, they are winning the white working-class vote. In states that will be critical for a Republican victory in 2016, such as Florida, the 2014 election offers Republicans hope. In the governor's race in Florida, Democratic candidate Charlie Crist lost whites without college degrees by 32 percent to 61 percent. In Virginia's U.S. Senate race, the Democratic incumbent lost whites without college degrees by 30 percent to 68 percent, even though he narrowly won the election.

In addition, Republicans have a strong base among evangelical Protestants, who voted for Romney in large numbers in 2012 and proved critical in winning the midterm elections for Republicans in 2014. The evangelical Christian vote is a critical bloc in the Republican base. In presidential primaries, evangelical Christians constitute on average 40 percent of the vote in primary states. In some southern states, evangelical voters made up 50 percent of the electorate in 2012. Even in northern states such as Minnesota, the evangelical vote constitutes more than 20 percent of the general electorate. Obviously, Republicans cannot ignore these voters.

Romney won the Catholic vote. Added to the religious vote are Jewish voters, who are still aligned with Democrats. Romney cut into the Jewish vote in 2012. The Jewish vote remains only a small fraction of the overall electorate, but in some key battleground states, such as Florida, it is important.

The Republican base—white, older, and religious voters—has not been enough to win the White House. Moreover, each of these blocs is making up a declining share of the overall electorate. These voters turn out in large numbers, however, and are informed. The issue facing Republicans is whether these constituent blocs can be expanded, and whether doing so will alienate other voters. Some Republican strategists maintain that the white working-class vote and the evangelical vote can be expanded by mobilizing these blocs to register and getting them to the polls. This strategy is debatable, since it often assumes that white working-class people and evangelical Christians who are not voting can be persuaded to vote Republican in the future. Perhaps so, but often winning or expanding one bloc of voters alienates another bloc. This does not mean that Republicans should not try to enlarge the white working-class vote or the evangelical Christian vote. It does mean, though, that some voters might be repelled by issues that concern these blocs. For example, millennial voters are more secular and are progressive on issues such as gay marriage.

Republicans should not backtrack, however, on core principles. That would potentially alienate the base. What is important to keep in mind is that (1) the Democratic base, composed of young, minority, and secular voters, is not uniformly liberal on every issue, and (2) across the board, American voters' highest concerns are the economy, job creation, education, healthcare, and national security. These issues impart an advantage to Republicans. In addition, Democrats are in trouble with white, middle-class, older, and religious voters. Obama won many of these voters in 2008, but Democratic presidential candidates cannot count on repeating his success.

Republicans have a strong base, and if they can expand it and cut into the Democratic base, they can win in the immediate future. Given social trends, they can even become a majority party. In all likelihood, there will not be large swings within the electorate, but a slight change in the popular vote can create landslides.

Over the last six years, Republicans have built a roster of young candidates who appeal to the future and not the past. Four of the candidates who vied for the 2016 Republican presidential nomination—Senator Marco Rubio, Senator Ted Cruz, Governor Scott Walker, and Governor Bobby Jindal—were in their forties. In midterm elections in 2010 and 2014, Republicans won more than seventy Democratic-held seats in the U.S House and fifteen seats in the U.S. Senate. On the state level, Republican presence on the bench is even deeper. Today Republicans are governors of thirty-one states, compared to eighteen Democrats and one Independent. In 2010–2014, Republicans won control of about 1,000 Democratic-held state legislative seats. While this leaves more seats to defend on the national and state levels, it is the foundation for the future.[4]

Republicans face an increasingly ideologically divided electorate, with about 40 percent in each party self-identifying as "liberal" or "conservative." In confronting an ideologically driven electorate, Republicans are going to find it difficult to persuade voters who are Democrats or identify as Democratic-leaning to switch parties. Of course, political beliefs can change abruptly in the midst of a national crisis or serious economic downturn. The 1970s are a case in point. When Richard Nixon, who had won in a clear landslide in 1972, resigned from the presidency in the midst of the Watergate scandal in 1974, Democrats swept the midterm elections that year and then retook the White House with Jimmy Carter, until then an unknown one-term governor from Georgia. After Watergate, fewer than 20 percent of the American electorate considered themselves Republicans. Many saw Republicans going the way of the long-forgotten Whig Party that collapsed in the middle nineteenth century. Stagflation in the late 1970s and the inability of the Carter administration to address runaway inflation combined with high unemployment enabled Republicans, led by Ronald Reagan, to reverse Republican fortunes in 1980. He defeated Carter in a landslide.

Voters' beliefs can change over time. Wealth, marriage, children, and age can change not only people's perspectives about life in general but their political outlook as well.

In fact, the view that political beliefs can change over time is the underlying premise of this book. At present, though, Republicans are faced with the problem of how to win or at least cut into a largely ideologically driven electorate that views opponents as devils incarnate (at worst) and fools (at best).

The older rhetoric of the Left is stale and does not sync with the new American Dream that is being created. Conservative Republicans have a future. This book uses "conservative" and "Republican" interchangeably, with an understanding that not all conservatives are Republican and not all Republicans are conservative. The Republican Party since Ronald Reagan has become the voice of conservatism, even though this voice might vacillate or equivocate and has been unprincipled at times. At present, however, there are only two viable political parties in the game, representing two different visions for America's future—the Democratic Party and the Republican Party.

The Democratic vision is one of the past: a failed, dependent nation, facing fiscal and financial crisis, propelled by budget deficits and national debt. Resistant to meaningful reform, Democrats call for more money to be spent on programs that have failed. Theirs is a dismal future of growing income inequality, relegating the urban poor to decaying cities, high unemployment, and lives without hope for them or their children. They offer a divided America, race against race, rich against poor, women against men, the young against the old, urban dwellers against suburbanites, those wanting to preserve the status quo against those seeking solutions for real-world problems in the twenty-first century.

The Republican Party vision can be one of restoring the American Dream through job creation; advantaging the new middle class of minorities, women, and the young; protecting the elderly on Social Security through serious reform; and addressing the needs of single mothers and their children, newly arrived immigrants, and all Americans who understand the exceptional nature of America's great experiment in self-government. If it is to become a majority party, the Republican Party should stand as a representative of a united people proud of their nation and its place in the world, its values, and its future.

1

WOMEN

WHILE REPUBLICANS HAVE MADE GREAT GAINS AMONG FEMALE
white voters, the gender gap has grown among nonwhite female voters
and younger female voters. Democrats have encouraged this gap by accusing Republicans of waging a "war on women." If the GOP is to become a majority party, Republicans need to overcome the gender identity
politics that has played so well for Democrats. How is this to be done?

- The changing role of women in the American economy and
  the workplace will make identity politics increasingly dated.
  As more women graduate from college with undergraduate and
  advanced degrees, which they are already doing, they will make
  tremendous advances in the workplace.
- These advances will be accelerated as the boomer generation
  retires. Labor scarcity will create a demand for female workers
  with higher educational attainment.
- Already the gender gap is closing as white women, especially
  married women, are voting Republican.
- After the disasters in the 2012 elections, Republicans have
  learned how to handle Democratic "war on women" attacks.

The Democratic mantra of a "war on women" belies the fact that women are not uniform in their voting patterns or in their socio-economic status. Republicans continue to fare well among married women, although this demographic group is dwindling given the decline of marriage in America. Democrats have fared well with single women in the past. But as more young women enter college, attain good jobs, rise in the ranks, and begin to replace retiring white male baby boomers, the female vote is going to be up for grabs. Socioeconomic differences among women will prove to be a greater factor in voting than gender.

As women in the twenty-first century make huge gains in the workplace and increase their wealth and status, the "war on women" charge will ring increasingly hollow. The women's vote is going to become increasingly parsed by socioeconomic status and not necessarily dominated by specific "women's issues."

Even today, the "war on women" accusation does not always play well with female voters. It has not worked with married women, and it backfired in the 2014 midterm elections. Pandering did not work because voters—male and female—were more concerned about the economy and jobs, education, healthcare, and, let's be frank, candidate competency. For example, in the Texas governor's race, Wendy Davis, who had gained national attention for her anti-abortion filibuster in the state senate, was thumped by her Republican opponent, Greg Abbott. In his victory speech, Abbott said to Texas voters, "You voted for hope over fear—for unity over division."[1]

A similar story of misfire came in the Colorado U.S. Senate race in 2014. Mark Udall, the incumbent U.S. senator, made "the war on women" theme a cornerstone of his campaign. Polling showed that few voters thought Udall's theme was important, and those who did were already strong Democrats. By campaigning this way, Udall alienated Independents, who were key to the vote. He lost to Cory Gardner, an evangelical Christian who espoused "family values." The "war on women" strategy also failed in Senate races in Kentucky and North Carolina, and it reached absurd heights in the race for the U.S. Senate seat in Iowa when Democrat Bruce Braley accused his Republican opponent, military veteran Joni Ernst, of being anti-woman.

Talk of "gendered America" and the conflict between white male privilege and women dominates current liberal political rhetoric today. Democrats might be behind the curve on this issue, however, if social trends are any indication. "Gendered America" is breaking down as women become increasingly divided into the married and the unmarried; the educated and the undereducated; and those women who fit into the new global economy and those who do not.

The key to Republicans winning the female vote is keeping and extending their base of married and single white women voters, while not inflaming those women who give high priority to reproductive rights and abortion issues with fiery language that has the unintended consequence of turning them out on Election Day. Republicans can win female voters—white, nonwhite, single, and married—on the economic issues. As with males, both white and nonwhite women are concerned about jobs and the economy. Many women, especially nonwhite women, consider women's issues a high priority in voting. These women's issues include legalized abortion, federal funding and access to contraception, equal pay for women, and equal opportunity.

The Democratic "war on women" strategy uses these issues to mobilize women. This strategy worked in 2012, but it failed in the 2014 midterm elections because Republican candidates did not fall into the trap and instead shifted the debate to the economy, healthcare, and national security. As women move up the economic ladder, gender issues will remain but will become less important than issues that play to Republican strengths—the economy, making government more efficient, and ensuring a strong national defense.

A LOOK AT THE NEW REPUBLICAN WOMAN

Jessica P., a tall, attractive woman in her late thirties, serves as vice president of governmental relations for a major energy company. Her career projects a model for women in the coming decades. Born in Brazil and raised in Honduras, she came to America when she was fifteen years old. Her first language was Portuguese, but she worked hard at learning English. Later she hired a speech therapist to overcome her accent. She graduated from college with a degree in Portuguese and a minor in economics. "After college," she observes, "I did not have much in the way of job skills. I took the first job I could get."

Her first job was in customer service. "I worked many jobs in this area. Often I was making coffee for bosses." Her first step up came when she got to head a team in the call center. "It gave me frontline experience that I carried into the rest of my career." After this post, she moved into government relations. "In college," she says, "I was not terribly interested in politics. Just slightly. In college, I was not paying too much attention to who voted." In her new job, she became interested in and began to learn about business and government.

Jessica's skills led her to take a job as a lobbyist for the state chamber of commerce, and then she worked for a public interest firm. Her first direct involvement in a political campaign came in 2008, when she went to work for John McCain's presidential effort. After McCain lost, she returned to the energy company where she had begun her career. She worked with charitable, public interest, and urban groups. In 2010 she moved to government affairs, where she became the youngest VP in her company's history. As she was moving up the corporate ladder, she married, had three children, and divorced. She makes time for her children, often freeing Saturdays to make sure she can attend school events.

She realizes her good fortune. She is thankful for the support from male colleagues who have helped advance her career. They appreciated, she observes, her hard work. She is adamant in her belief that hard work pays off, but that women need to be given opportunities to succeed. "Too many men," she said, "don't understand the issues of women having a career and trying to raise a family at the same time."

She is deeply involved in Republican politics. One of her major concerns is that Republicans are not bringing young women into the party as candidates or voters. She believes that the major focus for the Republican Party to attract women should be on returning dignity to individuals. To do this, she argues, the party should return to core issues about the importance of opportunity and work. "We should celebrate all work. Not everyone can go to college. But all jobs have dignity. Republicans tend to disparage certain kinds of jobs. Not everyone is middle class or rich. What Republicans should praise is that every job has dignity and going to a job and doing a full day's work brings dignity to the individual."

Democrats, she maintains, treat women as if they cannot think for themselves. Women need to be encouraged to think for themselves, and Republicans cannot appear to be just a party of "old white guys talking about birth control. This turns people off.

"As a single mom in the workforce," she adds, "I want my children to make sure that they have choices. I want them to have choice as to where they go to school, where they go to college, and I want to make sure I can afford them." For Hispanic women, "it is all about family. They are family focused. Work is about bettering their own lives and bettering the lives of their children." They want choice and opportunities. "The Hispanic women I know," she says, "want jobs and they fear government assistance. They want dignity."

Jessica is convinced that if Republicans are going to succeed in winning Hispanics and women to the party, the party needs to speak with a different voice. It is not just the message, but the messenger. Hispanics and women need to be brought to the table, but Republicans cannot do this if white men tell women what to believe on birth control, abortion, and gay marriage. While Jessica has no interest in running for office, she believes Republicans need women to emerge as leaders in the party. But these female candidates, she notes, should be prepared to have the press ask them questions about their families and their children, and for pundits to make snide comments about their dress and makeup.

She concludes that the best thing that can happen to the party is for new leadership to step forward. We have huge challenges ahead of us as a nation, she believes. The party needs to focus on core issues. "We have spent too much time explaining," she says, "telling people what we are against as a party. Let's tell them what we are for." Talk of family values, she notes, is important, but many women don't have kids. Republicans need leaders who understand and can speak for the new generation. "Americans are an optimistic people. They believe in

American exceptionalism. They love this country. They are concerned about national security and they want opportunities and dignity as individuals. This should be our message. Offering choice, real dignity, real opportunity for all Americans."

Jessica expresses the view of a woman who has built a career, risen in the corporate ranks, but struggled to achieve what she has. Although she would not describe herself as a feminist, there is no doubt that her opinions are shaped largely by her role as a woman in a corporate world, as a single woman, and as a woman concerned with career advancement, her children, and the state of the nation and the world. She emphasizes the importance of "choice" that extends beyond birth control, abortion, or whom one marries. Her view of choice is expansive. It includes school choice, career choice, job choice, and choice in how one achieves economic well-being.

GENDERED AMERICA: PAST AND FUTURE

Gender politics is not new to America. Social issues related to contraception and reproductive rights have intensified political polarization in today's politics. The role of women in American politics is also by no means new. In antebellum America, women were actively engaged in public life, serving on local community and school boards and working as active reformers in the temperance and abolition movements. European visitors to pre–Civil War America, male and female alike, commented on the privileged status and independence of American women. While noting that women did not have the right to vote in America, Alexis de Tocqueville observed in the second volume of *Democracy in America* (1840), "I have recorded so many considerable achievements of Americans, if anyone asks me what I think the chief cause of the singular prosperity and growing power of this people, I should answer that it is due to the superiority of their women."

After a long struggle, women achieved the right to vote with the passage of the Nineteenth Amendment in 1920. Further progress toward equality came in the 1960s and 1970s with the enactment of the Equal Pay Act (1963) and Title VII of the Civil Rights Act (1964);

equal opportunity found expression in the Equal Employment Act (1972); educational opportunity for women was ensured by Title IX of the Education Amendment Act (1972); a woman's right to abortion became a constitutional right with the Supreme Court's decision in *Roe v. Wade* (1973); and credit protection for women was further guaranteed in the Depository Institution Amendment Act of 1974.

With clear advancements for women—but by no means have all issues been resolved—American politics remains full of talk about "the war on women" and women's inequality. Much of this rhetoric has come over the abortion issue, but the imputation is that great social inequality continues to exist. While not denying gender inequality, the picture of women's status today and in the future indicates great benefits for many women and growing inequality for others.

By the end of the first decade of the twenty-first century, women accounted for nearly half the workforce in America. This trend toward greater female participation in the workforce coincided with increased educational achievement as more and more women entered and graduated from college.[2]

The future will present great opportunities for women for a simple reason: labor scarcity created by the retirement of white male baby boomers and the slow rate of population growth, even with immigration. In every area—management, law, medicine, education—the demand for skilled knowledge workers, combined with labor scarcity, is going to open doors for women in unprecedented ways. Complaints about unequal pay, closed doors in certain occupations, and glass ceilings are going to by drowned out by the rush of women becoming middle managers, CEOs of large corporations, doctors, lawyers, judges, and U.S. senators. As American society experiences this unprecedented social transformation, those political parties that welcome and adjust to these changes by representing the "new American woman" will benefit. Successful candidates will have to carefully appeal to the successful woman, while addressing the concerns of women left behind in an economy reliant on skilled knowledge workers.

Educated women will be the greatest beneficiaries of a changed workforce, just as white males benefited in a booming post–World War

II economy. Many in the white workforce are now retiring, and there won't be enough white males to replace them. White male privilege will be replaced by female workers "privileged" to have received post–high school, college, and postgraduate educations.

Baby boomers, those born in the years 1946–64, account for a large part of the workforce today. They number about 48 million full-time workers in a total workforce of 134 million. Boomer retirement will have a disproportionate impact on the top tier of the workforce. When today's baby boomers retire, new opportunities will be created for ethnic minorities and young women. Women in particular should gain from the boomer exodus, but so should minority groups. Whites, male and female, comprise about 62 percent of the age group just entering the workforce. This opens the door to well-educated minority groups to find opportunities for occupational and professional advancement.

Labor scarcity will characterize the new economy. Not only are there not enough white males to replace the current white male workforce, but the birthrate is not enough to replace the existing workforce. Falling marriage rates and later-age marriage have contributed to declining population growth.[3] The overall birthrate is the lowest in American history, falling to 63.2 births per 1,000 women of childbearing age. This is down from the peak in 1957 of 122.7 births per 1,000 women of childbearing age. In just the period between 2007 and 2010, the overall birthrate fell 8 percent, with the largest drop, of 14 percent, among foreign-born immigrant women. Mexican immigrant birthrates dropped an extraordinary 23 percent.

The decline in fertility rates means declining rates of population growth. The fertility rate needed to maintain the current U.S. population is 2.1 children born per woman of childbearing age. Today the fertility rate is 1.9 children and falling. This decline in the rate of population growth has major implications for the economy, investment markets, and Social Security and Medicare, which rely on young workers paying taxes to support them.

Education and income are decisive factors in how people vote. It is evident that there will be increasing divisions among women voters, and these divisions will be more evident among Hispanics and African Americans, as minority women advance financially and socially.

Declining population growth will mean fewer available workers in the future. Labor scarcity, historically, has resulted in higher wages and technological innovation. In the late nineteenth century, as the economy boomed and the demand for labor rose even as immigrants flooded into the country, real wages and technology increased to make for more efficient production. Today, America remains a technological leader. Computers, machine tools, and robots provide cognitive and manual tasks once performed by low-skilled labor. The number of U.S. manufacturing jobs has declined as a proportion of the workforce, while the number of highly skilled jobs has increased. Global competition has also encouraged technical innovation. Technological exports from the United States as a percentage of total exports trail only those of Korea and Ireland.

Labor scarcity and the demand for technological innovation will place a premium on an educated and highly trained workforce. Today about 50 percent of high school graduates are attending college, although overall only 20 percent of Americans have college degrees.

More women are attending and graduating from college than ever before in American history. College used to be for young, white, affluent men. This is no longer the case. Not only are more women than men attending college, but the typical university classroom today has increasing numbers of minority students. Women now make up 57 percent of college students, an exponential gain from the 40 percent in the 1970s.[4] This increase was especially marked by young white women entering college, but Hispanic and black women are attending in increasing numbers as well. About 70 percent of white women enroll in college immediately after high school graduation, compared to about 62 percent of young white men. The number of young black women entering college increased to 69 percent of those who graduated from high school. The gender gap in higher education is pronounced. A higher percentage of females—white, Hispanic, and African American—is going to school than of males.[5]

Today more Hispanic women are enrolling as full-time students in colleges and aspiring to doctoral degrees than ever before. Hispanic women are completing high school at higher rates (73 percent) than their male Hispanic counterparts (63 percent). Approximately a third (31 percent) of college-age Hispanic women are enrolled in college, while just a fifth (20 percent) of eligible college-age Hispanic males are attending college full-time. Thirty years ago, Hispanics made up about 1.2 percent of first-year college students. Today they make up 8.2 percent, and if community college is included, the percentage rises to 11 percent. Many of these Hispanic students, especially females, aspire to be doctors, lawyers, or PhDs.

Female college students are majoring in professional fields such as healthcare, public administration, and psychology. Science, technology, engineering, and math majors among women are increasing. In 2012, 40–45 percent of math, statistics, and physical science degrees were awarded to women. The majority of biology degrees (58 percent) were earned by women. The major areas where women are falling short are computer science and engineering, majors still dominated by males, but women are not just the majority of education or humanities majors anymore.[6]

The increasing number of college-educated workers entering the workplace has narrowed the wage gap between men and women. From 1979 through 2009, wages for women rose from 62 percent to 80 percent of men's wages. For younger women, 25–35 years old, the gap narrowed to 90 percent, suggesting that the wage gap will continue to narrow as wages equalize for older cohorts. Moreover, women are entering the workforce with stronger credentials, which will further equalize wages. Not only has the gap narrowed; the trend is toward wage equality.[7]

The future looks good for many American women. Already, more American women than men have master's degrees or higher. Among those 25 and older, 10.6 million U.S. women have master's degrees or higher, compared to 10.5 million men. Women still remain below men in MBA schools (about 35 percent) and in law and medical schools (about 47 and 48 percent), but it's worth noting that more women than men are attending law school at the University of California, Berkeley, and more women than men are attending medical school at Emory and the University of North Carolina. At most medical schools, women make up close to 50 percent of the students.

In the private sector, women are playing an increasing role as professionals and managers. Women still are found working as registered nurses, dental assistants, cashiers, and elementary and middle school teachers. The majority of pharmacists and accountants are women. Yet today close to a majority of life scientists, mathematicians, and statisticians are women. A third of physicians, lawyers, and judges are women. A quarter of computer programmers are women.[8] Some of these women are finding new roles as managers and CEOs. Although a survey by the *Wall Street Journal* of sixty leading American corporations found that only 14 percent of corporate executive committee members were women and few women were CEOs, nearly 140,000 women in these companies have already made it to mid-level management—about one-third of the women professionals in these organizations. Only a few have become vice presidents, senior vice presidents, or members of the C-suite, but as the number of female mid-level managers increases and white male boomer executives retire, women will shatter the corporate glass ceiling. In the 1980s, few women pursued advanced degrees, particularly MBAs, which lead to top corporate jobs, but this is no longer true. It is easy to predict growing numbers of female CEOs in the coming decades.

★ ★ ★ ★ ★

Are we entering the "Century of the American Woman"? Trends suggest that college-educated women, in general, will be wealthier, more powerful, and more competitive than men. It's difficult to see how this won't be the case with the retirement of male boomers, the high educational advancement of women, and a scarce labor market for highly trained workers. In this new age, the Democratic chant of a "war on women" will appeal to fewer and fewer women. The appeal will be to those women left behind in the new economy. Their interest will be less on feminist discourse than on real jobs, education for their children, and opportunity. If Republicans can play to their strengths, they will be able to claim that if there was ever a "war on women"—itself arguable—they "won the war" because they are the party of reform, a party that looked to the future.

Much like race in America, the category of gender is going to change in the future. In the meantime, Republicans face a serious problem of winning single women to their side. Republicans are winning the battle for the married women vote, but the party is getting trounced in the single women vote. Over 30 percent of single mothers are Hispanic; 28 percent are black. Single mothers are likely to be younger, less educated, and poorer.

In this new economy that will find a place for educated women, single mothers, who remain less educated, are likely to remain poor, as will their children when they become adults.

The social consequences of out-of-wedlock births are well documented. Children of single mothers tend to perform poorly in school and fail to graduate from high school. Many are prone to alcohol and drug abuse and find themselves stuck in poverty. The American family might be in transition and new family arrangements emerging, but right now out-of-wedlock births present a major social problem in the United States.

Furthermore, there is a correlation between the kind of family one is raised in and how one later votes. Voters raised in single-parent households tend to vote Democratic or not to vote at all. Given the high rate of out-of-wedlock births and the decreasing birthrate for two-parent families, the likelihood of a large number of voters becoming Democrats is high. This is a future problem for Republicans, but one that should be dealt with now. Creating a majority party entails sustaining majority status.

Republicans should remain steadfast in their support of the traditional family. Children raised in two-parent households are better off. At the same time, Republicans need to project to all voters that they understand the problems faced by single parents. Simply telling single mothers that two-parent families work better, albeit true, does not address their immediate needs or win votes. Not only should Republicans show that they understand and sympathize with the problems faced by single mothers, they need to support policies that help address these problems. Democrats think in terms of enlarging entitlement programs. Republicans should promote educational reforms that provide access for poor single mothers and families to public and private magnet and charter schools. Republicans should espouse the creation of voluntary mediating institutions—parenting, anti-gang, youth, drug-rehabilitation, and prison-reentry programs. George W. Bush began this effort in his presidency. His opponents attacked him for ignoring the separation of church and state because many of the programs were church-based. Republicans can learn from these mistakes, but if the entitlement state is going to be reformed, they need to offer alternatives. Just talking about family values, downsizing the government, and lowering taxes is not enough for a party seeking majority status and claiming to be a party of reform.[9]

HOW THE DEMOCRATS CAPTURED THE WOMEN'S VOTE

The gender gap for Republicans is formidable. In 2014, well over a third of women identified themselves as Democrats and over 50 percent leaned Democratic.[10] This compares to less than a quarter of women who identified themselves as Republicans and about a third who leaned Republican. This gap breaks down, as GOP strategists know, along racial and marital lines. But even here, Republican support is soft. A little over a fourth of women (28 percent) strongly identify as Republican. This is only 1 percent more than married women who declare themselves Democrats (27 percent). Where the Republicans have strength among married women. Here, the GOP does well, as close to half of these women "lean Republican" (48 percent), 7 points above married women who "lean Democratic" (41 percent).

Married women, especially those with children, are more financially stable and less dependent on government. Married women tend to be white, affluent, and older, fitting neatly into the cohort of Republican voters who are college educated and earning more than $50,000 a year. Whatever advantage Republicans have with married women, however, is countered by their lack of support among single women. Unmarried women are decidedly Democratic or leaning that way, giving their party a 35-point (64 percent to 29 percent) advantage over their rivals.[11]

Republicans now face a march across Death Valley if they are going to win women to their side. Women in 2012 voted overwhelmingly for Barack Obama (55 percent) over his challenger, Mitt Romney (44 percent). Men favored Romney, 52 percent to 45 percent. This seems to indicate a gender-divided nation, except upon a closer look, the gender vote is varied: Romney won 53 percent of married women. Among white women, Romney won with an impressive 14 percent advantage over Obama, winning 56 percent to 42 percent. By winning the married women vote and the single white women vote, Romney narrowed the overall gender gap in these categories. Where he lost, though, was in the nonwhite female vote and the nonwhite single women vote. Only 31 percent of nonwhite single women voted for him, while Obama extended his share of the nonwhite vote.

Obama's attack campaign, the "war on women," worked with single and nonwhite voters.[12] Obama won 69 percent of single women voters and carried 76 percent of the Latina vote and 96 percent of the black women vote. They turned out for him in large numbers, and their share of the vote was larger. In 2012, nearly 60 percent of female voters were married and they preferred Romney. On the other hand, black and Latina women are disproportionately represented among unmarried female voters, and they favored Obama by a two-to-one majority. Furthermore, many of the nonwhite women are young, and they voted for Obama. Nonetheless, Romney won young white voters by 7 points, 51 percent to 44 percent. This was somewhat consoling news for Romney, but given the steady increase in nonwhite voters, male and female, Republicans could not jump for joy. Keeping and extending the white vote proved essential for Republicans in the 2014 midterms, but in the long run this vote won't be enough by itself to win the White House or blue or purple states.

Married women have voted Republican in every presidential election since 1980, with the notable exception of 1996, when they went for Bill Clinton by 4 points. Romney can take solace of sorts that he won 2 percent more white women than McCain, the Republican presidential candidate in 2008. Solace, though, is what losers take to make themselves feel better.

Romney narrowed the gender gap by winning white married women. The key to Obama's success with women was single non-white women. Given that women were the majority of voters across the country, the women's vote proved critical to both campaigns. Of course, women, whether married or single, cast their votes for a variety of reasons. A female voter can wear any number of hats. She might be a mother concerned with a candidate's stance on education; a Hispanic concerned with immigration; or an unemployed worker concerned with the economy. Whatever their motivation, the result was that Obama maintained the gender gap over Romney by 11 points because of the increased minority vote due to the influx of Hispanic and African-American women. Obama's support among white women declined in 2012, and the gap between female white voters was still larger than it was for Clinton in his reelection campaign in 1996.[13]

Obama's success among women did not equal his 2008 performance, when he had a 14-point advantage over John McCain. Still, it was an impressive victory. Romney's improvement among white married women mirrored the general shift of white male voters to the Republican column. Pundits suggested that Romney's business background might have been more appealing to men than women, and that women found Obama's stress on maintaining the social safety net, raising taxes on the wealthy, support of abortion rights, and insistence on healthcare coverage for contraception more appealing.

The Obama administration has carefully constructed an image that he is sympathetic to women, with the president appearing before women's groups, relating anecdotes about his relationship with his mother, appointing large numbers of women, and proposing laws promoted as helping women. To some extent, Obama was forced to adopt this strategy in order to woo women who were furious with him for defeating Hillary Clinton in 2008.

Overall, women told pollsters that their major concern was the economy, as it was for men as well. Even for women with children younger than eighteen, the economy was their primary concern.

Contraception and abortion lagged far behind in what drove women to vote for Obama. Yet behind "It's the economy, stupid" lies a more important motivation. Romney was simply trounced by voters who told pollsters that Obama "cares about people like me." Romney won among those who were concerned with "leadership" and "vision," but Obama projected an image of caring about women.[14]

The economy proved important to Obama's victory. He won on this issue not because of specific economic proposals, but because voters thought that Obama's heart was in the right place when it came to caring about their economic anxieties. Image is important, but image extends beyond just "I feel your pain" rhetoric. Candidates construct narratives that include more than specific economic programs and policy goals. Obama constructed a narrative that placed Romney on the defensive through negative and positive campaigning. On the negative side (positive for Obama) was a concerted attack that Romney was rich, the son of a wealthy family, and a ruthless investor out to make profits at the expense of the working men and women of America. Romney's financial success, his good looks, and his quiet, reserved manner were turned against him. Romney did not help himself by telling donors at a fund-raiser, secretly recorded by Jimmy Carter's grandson and later released by the left-wing magazine *Mother Jones*, that 47 percent of the population is made up of people who believe they are "victims" and who are "dependent on government." What appeared to be continuous harping about tax cuts reinforced an image that Romney cared only about the wealthy and Wall Street.

Obama's support for federal funding of contraception and abortion might have turned off evangelical Protestants, traditional Catholics, Mormons, and orthodox Jews, but many voters, especially single women, concluded that Obama was concerned about the poor and understood their problems. These voters might not have agreed with specific Democratic programs, but they related to Obama as a caring and compassionate leader. Married women were concerned most about the economy. So were single women, but they regarded social issues such as pay equity, woman's healthcare, and reproductive rights as equally important. As Rose Rios, a forty-year-old registered Republican in New

Jersey, told Reuters, "Republicans are so far right. They do not represent the views of . . . independent women."[15]

The Obama campaign hammered Romney on his record on women's issues. Romney's counter that his campaign had "binders" of women to join his administration if he won appeared bureaucratic and condescending. To some, it sounded like binders of porn photos; to others, it sounded like the binders somehow contained women. The impression was dehumanizing. Romney's opposition to abortion and federal insurance coverage for contraception appealed to his pro-life supporters and could be supported by a conservative. The problem was Romney's articulation of these positions, which sometimes appeared opportunistic and driven by partisanship. Obama's narrative that Romney was anti-woman was reinforced by Missouri senatorial candidate Todd Aiken, an evangelical Christian who had to apologize to voters for talking about occasions for "legitimate rape." Aiken refused to step down after the outrage caused by his remarks, even as Republicans across the country, including Romney, tried to distance themselves from him. Aiken's supporters in Missouri accused the Republican establishment and the media of trying to dictate to voters what was acceptable Republicanism. Aiken's opponent, Democratic incumbent senator Claire McCaskill, whose poll numbers were low before the hullabaloo that followed Aiken's rape comments, won easily.

Meanwhile, other Republican candidates looked as though they had graduated from the same school of how to lose an election by putting your foot in your mouth. Richard Mourdock, the Republican senatorial candidate in Indiana, declared that "life is that gift from God that I think even when life begins in that horrible situation of rape, that it is something that God intended to happen." In Pennsylvania, a Republican senatorial candidate, Tom Smith, compared rape to unwed motherhood.[16]

Having gone through a brutal primary to win the Republican nomination, which had forced him to the right on issues of immigration and abortion, Romney now had to distance himself from the right in his own party. It was a no-win position. The Republican Right accused him of being the establishment candidate, while the Democrats attacked him as the nominee of a right-wing, anti-woman extremist party. Republican candidates such as Aiken, Mourdock, and Smith not only helped bring Romney down, they fell themselves. Aiken lost to McCaskill in Missouri by close to 25 points; Mourdock in Indiana lost by close to 6 points; and Smith lost to Bob Casey, Jr., a pro-life Democrat, by 9 points. Even after their losses, they refused to admit their mistakes. In his postelection book, with the cumbersome but to-the-point title *Firing Back: Taking on the Party Bosses and the Media Elite to Protect Our Faith and Freedom* (2014), Aiken set his sights on the GOP establishment for having cost him the election. He named names: party strategist Karl Rove and Senate Republicans Mitch McConnell, John Cornyn, John McCain, and Lindsey Graham. Aiken said that he made a mistake in apologizing for remarks that had been misportrayed by the press.

The problem for these Republican candidates was not just projecting the wrong image to attract Independent female swing voters, but a problem of real substance and actual strategy. Conservative Republicans know that the pro-life vote is important. This vote is found among traditional Roman Catholics, evangelical Protestants, and Mormons and is a strong base for conservative candidates. These voters need to become active campaign workers and turn out on Election Day.

Usually it won't take much convincing to rally these voters to the cause. So why bring up an issue such as "rape"? Why fall into the trap of answering a question about rape and conception when asked by a not-too-friendly reporter or Democratic opponent? A Republican pro-life candidate ought to say, "Too many serial rapists are being let go by liberal judges. And any parent, relative, or kin member who rapes a girl in their family should be sent to prison. Let's put the emphasis on the perpetrator of these crimes and talk about what it means to really protect our women and our children. Let's talk about kids growing up in single-parent homes, about mothers struggling just to get by, and about what we are going to do to better their lives."

Of course, this won't satisfy a reporter or a rival candidate if they get a follow-up question. At this point, a conservative can respond, "Making choices about life and death, and deciding about an abortion, is one of the toughest problems a woman, especially a young girl, can make. This is what counselors and family are for. I don't believe this is a decision that should be made by government bureaucrats. I don't believe in federal funding of abortions. We can debate whether abortion is right or wrong. These kinds of moral debates are what make this country great. Let's keep the federal government out of it. Let private insurers decide about funding and individuals and families about the decision itself. What my campaign is about is creating economic opportunities for all Americans, married and single women. Let's talk about jobs and reviving the economy. This will benefit us all."

Reproductive rights present a problem for both Democrats and Republicans. The American public is divided on the issue. Polling on abortion can be extremely misleading, depending on how questions are asked. Nonetheless, there has been a significant shift on the abortion issue, as more Americans have trended toward pro-life positions that restrict late-term abortions.[17] In 1973, most Americans identified themselves as pro-choice. As late as 1995, only 33 percent of Americans identified themselves as pro-life. By 2009, however, Gallup found that 51 percent identified themselves as pro-life, 2 percent more than those identifying themselves as pro-choice.

This trend in attitudes is inevitably reflected in voting. A Rasmussen poll conducted in 2014 showed that 46 percent of adults were likely to vote pro-life, while only 43 percent were likely to vote pro-choice. While these numbers indicate a divided electorate on the abortion issue, the trend toward pro-life positions has increased. Surveys show that many Americans still support abortion when a woman's health is in serious danger, or in pregnancies caused by rape or involving serious birth defects. Support for an abortion when a family is too poor, a married woman does not want more children, or when a woman wants an abortion for "any reason," however, has declined dramatically. Furthermore, support for restricting late-term abortions has grown, especially among women—the very bloc that Democrats need. A Quinnipiac poll and a subsequent *Washington Post* poll in 2013 showed that men and women supported laws restricting abortion after twenty-two weeks of gestation. Particularly worrisome for pro-choice Democrats is that these polls showed a majority of women (60 percent, compared to 51 percent of males) supporting a ban on late-term abortions.

What political strategists from both parties drew from these polls was that the abortion issue could be a double-edged sword. Without careful articulation of the issues, the other side might be inflamed. Democrats therefore needed to craft a message that painted Republican opponents as extremists who wanted to ban all abortions, deprive women of access to contraceptives, and leave them unprotected in the workplace and at home with abusive husbands.

These polls should have suggested to Republicans that electoral success lay in more than just projecting an appealing image, but in a strategy that did not rest on playing defense on wedge issues. This meant turning attacks around and placing their Democratic opponents on the defensive on job creation, government spending, healthcare, education, and national security. Economic issues cut across gender and marital-status lines. In 2012, Republicans seemed to see married women as caring only about economic issues, while single women were concerned with birth control and abortion.[18]

Obama won every swing state in 2012. Female voters were critical in these states. In Florida, Obama beat Romney with female voters 53 percent to 46 percent; in Ohio he took 58 percent to Romney's 42 percent; and in New Hampshire he won 56 to 43. The female vote in North Carolina was 51 to 49, but Romney was trounced by female voters in Virginia, Wisconsin, and Iowa by an average of 10 points.[19] In these states, Obama targeted women voters on the social issues, while Romney talked about female owners of small businesses. Romney emphasized economic issues, but he did not convince most female voters that he wasn't just talking about upper-tier high-wage earners.

Surveys on abortion and social issues can be misleading. A Gallup survey conducted shortly before the election in twelve key swing states found that among registered voters, women considered abortion (39 percent) the most important issue in the election. For registered male voters, Gallup found that jobs (38 percent) and the economy (37 percent) were the most important issues.[20] This poll suggested that men were concerned about the economy and women were concerned about abortion and contraception. A closer look at the poll, however, reveals that women were just as concerned about economic and job issues. When combined, answers about "jobs" and "the economy" showed that 35 percent of women were concerned about these issues. Simply to conclude that women were only or mostly concerned about contraception and abortion is simply wrong. The Romney campaign correctly focused on jobs and the economy, but he did not convince female voters that he had their interests at heart.

Yet even the claim that Romney lost by failing to secure the female vote can be overstated. He won the white female vote pretty solidly. More white women voted for Romney than voted for Obama by well over 50 percent. This was not as high a margin as among white males, with Romney crushing Obama 62 percent to 35 percent. Still, Romney won a higher percentage of the white female vote than did George W. Bush in 2004 or John McCain in 2008.[21] Romney took an impressive 56 percent of the white female vote, compared to Obama's 42 percent. This feat widened the white female gap in the favor of Republicans to 14 points.

The white female vote makes up a smaller proportion of the overall electorate than it once did. Where Obama won the female vote was among nonwhite women. He did so with enormous majorities (96 percent) of the black female vote and 66 percent of women of other races. These nonwhite females account for about one in six voters. This proved to be a key element in Obama's victory. Romney made clear progress in increasing the white female vote for Republicans. If he had exhibited similar strength among minority voters, especially Hispanics, the gender gap would have been narrowed—in fact, overcome. Romney took just 23 percent of the female Hispanic vote, 7 points less than McCain got in 2008 (30 percent) and 10 points less than the 33 percent that George W. Bush received in 2004.

In looking at this female white vote for Romney, the obvious question is "Why?" Why did white females who went to the polls go with Romney? The answer can be boiled down to three factors: income, age, and religion. Romney won in families making over $100,000 a year. Obama won in families making less. The second factor is age.

Older whites tend to turn out at higher rates than minority voters and tend to vote Republican. Finally, most white women and white men are churchgoing Christians, and this group is strongly Republican.[22]

This is all good news for Republicans. As women get older and become wealthier, they just might turn Republican if the pattern holds. Of course, they are not going to get whiter. The white electorate is decreasing. Yet if intermarriage increases, voting along racial lines might become less categorical.

The immediate problem for Republicans is convincing female voters that the GOP is not their enemy. The midterm elections of 2014 suggest one path to success.

HOW THE REPUBLICANS COUNTERED
THE "WAR ON WOMEN"

Democrats entered the 2014 midterms faced with a recently elected second-term president whose public support had dwindled since his re-election two years earlier. The party in power usually doesn't fare well in midterm elections, but Democrats had high hopes of keeping the Senate, and some wishful thinkers even had hopes of cutting into the Republican-controlled House of Representatives. Polls showed even less popular support for Congress than for the president.

Democrats were certain in 2014 that the "war on women" strategy could be reemployed. They were convinced that with a good lineup of candidates and the Republican record on women's issues, they could put Republicans back in their place. Republicans, they believed, seemed to be deaf to criticism of their "anti-woman" agenda. In the House, Republicans pushed through a bill that was perceived as weakening the Violence Against Women Act by omitting protections for gay, Native American, student, and immigrant abuse victims. In seven Republican-controlled state legislatures, measures were enacted banning late-term abortions. Republicans in Congress pushed unsuccessfully against a Democratic-controlled Senate for the elimination of funding for Planned Parenthood. Congressional Republicans refused to support Obama's proposals for updating and bolstering the 1963 Equal Pay Act.

The *New York Times* editorialized that Republicans were conducting a "Campaign against Women."[23] MSNBC reported that GOP lawmakers were escalating their "war on women." MSNBC's Geoffrey Cowley reported that "by all indications, defeat [in 2012] has only hardened the party's resolve to drive a diverse, modern democracy back to the pre-feminist past."[24]

Isabel Sawhill, a Brookings Institution scholar and fervid advocate of contraception accessibility as the most effective means of reducing poverty and inequality in America, joined the chorus saying that Republicans were on the wrong side of the gender gap. She maintained that by failing to support mandated contraception accessibility, Republican Senate candidates Cory Gardner in Colorado and Thom Tillis in North Carolina, as well as other Republican pro-life candidates, were cynically trying to exploit economic issues while backtracking on their extremist positions on abortion and contraception. She argued that accessibility to contraception was a real economic issue and was "key to reducing poverty and inequality and improving social mobility in the U.S."[25]

Sawhill's warning that conservative pro-life Republicans were going to face another 2012 debacle with women was bolstered by other pre-election reports. Jennifer Rubin, a right-leaning reporter for the *Washington Post*, warned that the GOP had a serious problem with women. Looking at the 2012 election results and pre-2014 polling, she noted, accurately, "The image of the fiery, ferocious conservative warrior that the right-wing media applauds is precisely the type that turns off women voters who aren't already hard Republicans."[26] With pre-election surveys showing women as concerned with reproductive rights and accessibility to contraception as with the economy, Democrats thought they could batter their opponents on these issues.

In state after state, though, the Democratic campaign to rally their female base failed—in blue states, purple states, and red states. Not only did the "war on women" theme have a hollow echo among the general public, but the attack fired up the Republican base. These failed campaigns provide lessons for the future.

Democrats looked like they had a strong lineup of female candidates, including Kay Hagan in North Carolina, a state won by Obama in 2012; Michelle Nunn, the daughter of a popular Democratic senator; Alison Lundergan Grimes, running against the vulnerable Senate minority leader Mitch McConnell; and Wendy Davis, who looked like she might step into the Texas governor's mansion after having gained national publicity for her anti-abortion filibuster a year before. Democrats had hopes that incumbent Mary Landrieu might squeak by in her race to maintain her U.S. Senate seat in Louisiana.

In these state campaigns, Democrats sought to distance themselves from Obama's unpopular Affordable Care Act by going on the offensive with the "war on women" theme. It had worked in 2012 and there was an expectation that it would work in 2014, benefiting Democratic male and female candidates while placing Republicans, whatever their gender, on the defensive. The strategy failed. Republicans took both the Senate and the House, won key gubernatorial contests, and deepened their control of state legislatures.

PURPLE LESSONS: COLORADO AND IOWA

The Colorado race for U.S. Senate presents a case study of how Democrats failed in a swing state. Confronted with Cory Gardner, the Republican nominee for the U.S. Senate, incumbent Senator Mark Udall launched a TV ad campaign that warned that his opponent wanted to take Colorado women backward. The spots accused Gardner of waging an "eight-year crusade that would ban birth control." One spot featured a female gynecologist and obstetrician complaining that Gardner sponsored hard anti-abortion laws. Ob-gyn Dr. Eliza Buyers slammed Gardner, saying he was "wrong to make abortion illegal and just as wrong not to tell the truth about it."[27] National feminist organizations joined in the attack. NARAL Pro-Choice America released an ad depicting Gardner as anti-woman and anti-man. The ad showed a man in a dystopian, condom-free future declaring, "Cory Gardner banned birth control. And now, it's all on us guys. You can't find a condom anywhere."[28]

The problem with this attack was that Gardner nearly a year earlier had retracted his support for a pro-life "personhood" state initiative that recognized human life at conception. Gardner pushed for legalizing over-the-counter contraceptives. Gardner supporters began to deride Udall as "Senator Uterus" for trying to make the campaign only about abortion.

On Election Day, Gardner won by one of the narrowest margins in any Senate race in state history. Udall won the battle for the women's vote, 52 percent to 44 percent, a clear 8-point favorite. Gardner swept the male vote with an overwhelming 56 percent to 39 percent. Udall failed to turn out enough women, and he did not inspire the Hispanic vote that had gone overwhelmingly for Obama two years earlier.

If the "war on women" worked for Democrats in 2012, why not use it in the U.S. Senate race in Iowa, even though the Republican candidate, Joni Ernst, was a Harley-Davidson-riding Army veteran? Ernst projected a political persona as a Washington outsider and a reformer. After winning the Republican nomination for the U.S. Senate in a tough primary race, she took the offensive immediately, predicting that "soon we'll be hearing about the war on women." As an Iraq war veteran she declared, "I've been to war. I've seen the sacrifices our men and women in uniform make every day to defend our freedoms. If Democrats start throwing around a 'war,' they better be doing it to honor those men and women."

She seemed to welcome such an attack. As predicted, her opponent, Bruce Braley, launched the "war on women" strategy. In speeches and TV spots he kept up a steady drumbeat about birth control, abortion, and "personhood." Despite a national climate favoring Republicans, Braley counted on mobilizing Iowa women against his pro-life opponent. Early polls showed women favoring him by 13 points. While money poured into his campaign from outside feminist political action committees such as Emily's List, Braley hoped that Iowa's poor record of not electing women to state office would hold. Iowa was only one of two states never to have elected a woman to the House, Senate, or governorship. Braley hammered Ernst on her support for an anti-abortion human life amendment. Ernst countered that the human life amendment was "simply a statement that I support life . . . I will always stand with our women on affordable access to contraception." To shrink the gender gap in the state, Ernst's supporters aired a commercial claiming that Braley paid his female congressional staff 67 cents for every dollar he paid men. Braley called the spot untrue and requested that the ad be taken down. No stations did, but by highlighting the ad, he gave it more attention.

The deeper problem Braley faced was that of any male candidate facing a female candidate. Lecturing about "women's issues" comes off as condescending. Ernst's campaign replied, "Braley's war on women is the dumbest thing that has happened in this campaign, which is really saying something."[29] Most voters decided it was pretty dumb as well. Ernst and Braley split the female vote, 49 percent to 49 percent.[30] Among male voters, Ernst won by 18 points, 58 percent to 40 percent. Given that 51 percent of the voters were female, a split vote was exactly what Ernst had hoped for. In a heavily white, conservative, and evangelical state, and with Obama having only a 39 percent approval rating, Ernst was a natural favorite and she won. Braley's attacks and bad ad-libs—deriding the popular senator Chuck Grassley as a farmer and not a lawyer and complaining that there were no fresh towels in the House gym during the government shutdown—cost Braley a Senate seat that had been held by Tom Harkin, one of the Senate's staunchest liberals.

RED-STATE LESSONS: NORTH CAROLINA, KENTUCKY, AND ARKANSAS

Democrats believed that they could keep the Senate seat in North Carolina. Obama barely lost the state in 2012, by 2 points. Democrats had mobilized women and African Americans for Obama, and only a large turnout of whites carried the state for Romney. A voter ID law in the state to be implemented in 2016 aroused progressive opponents who hoped that this might rally African Americans in the 2014 midterm. The previous year, Republicans had approved legislation that set licensing standards for abortion providers, prohibited gender-selective abortions, and mandated the physical presence of a physician during an abortion. Kay Hagan, the Democratic Senate candidate, let her base know that she was with them on social issues, but decided to spin the women's issue by feigning insult when during a debate her opponent,

Thom Tillis, said she did not understand math when it came to the budget.[31] Tillis kept his cool and remained polite during subsequent debates. While Hagan won the female vote by a full 12 points (54 percent to 42 percent), she lost the male vote by 15 points (41 percent to 56 percent).

If the "war on women" in North Carolina boiled down to umbrage, the Kentucky race was little more than a slight turned to insult, when incumbent senator Mitch McConnell described his opponent, Alison Lundergan Grimes, as an "empty dress." Democrats responded that by not using the standard cliché "empty suit," McConnell was "demeaning" his female opponent.[32] By highlighting McConnell's language, however, the Grimes campaign stirred the debate over whether she was in fact an empty suit. After McConnell won a hard-fought primary battle within his own party, Democrats thought they had a real chance of defeating him. As Senate minority leader and a Washington insider, McConnell seemed like an easy target. Any hopes that the "war on women" strategy might work failed when McConnell turned the tables on Grimes, who was herself from a prominent Kentucky Democratic family and hardly an outsider to politics. McConnell launched a negative advertising campaign that tied Grimes to the exoneration of Democratic state representative John Arnold, who escaped being reprimanded in the legislature for sexually harassing and assaulting three female statehouse staffers. The slugfest between McConnell and Grimes resulted in a Democratic slaughter at the polls, with McConnell nearly splitting the female vote (47 percent to 50 percent) and swamping his opponent with male voters (61 percent to 36 percent). McConnell turned the tables by accusing Grimes of being soft on "sexual assault"— an extraordinary feat by an embattled white, male, inside-the-Beltway Republican.

The "war on women" ploy failed in other red-state senatorial races as well. In Georgia, Democrat Michelle Nunn attempted to put her opponent, David Perdue, on the defensive when she revealed that he had been the CEO of a company involved in a class-action gender-discrimination suit.[33] In a conservative state in which Democrats needed to extend their natural base beyond Atlanta and its suburbs, Nunn downplayed abortion, contraception, and gay marriage. A liberal on social issues herself, she decided to play it safe. Perdue responded by launching "Women for Perdue," headed by his wife, Bonnie. His TV spots featured women who talked about how Perdue "helped to create and save thousands of jobs right here in America." Nunn's centrist campaign did not work in an off-year election with an unpopular president. She won the woman's vote by a sizeable 8 points (53 percent to 45 percent), but like other red-state Democrats lost the male vote by intimidating numbers, in this case by 23 points (38 percent to 61 percent). State Democrats promised that the 2016 election would be different, as Atlanta and its suburbs continue to grow with African Americans and Hispanics. They might be right, but in 2014 a centrist, tempered "war on women" campaign had not worked any better than an all-out war.

While female Democrats were singing a "war on women" refrain against their male Republican opponents in Kentucky and North Carolina, the tune proved even more off-key when incumbent senator Mark Pryor's campaign used it against his challenger, Tom Cotton, in the heavily Republican state of Arkansas. Pryor knew that a full-throated defense of reproductive rights and contraception accessibility was not the song to play in a state that had become redder and redder since Bill Clinton had been governor three decades earlier. In 2010, Pryor's colleague, Blanche Lambert Lincoln, lost her 2010 reelection bid by more than 20 points. Two years later, Republicans captured the General Assembly. When Pryor had been elected to the Senate, the state assembly had ninety-seven Democrats and thirty Republicans. By 2014, when Pryor was up for reelection, the state assembly stood at seventy-three Republicans and sixty-one Democrats. Obama lost the state heavily in 2012. Pryor was in clear trouble.

Pryor resurrected a campaign tactic that had worked for Lyndon Baines Johnson in the 1964 presidential election against Barry Goldwater: saying, in effect, "Hey, voters, I might be a liberal, but my opponent is a crazy extremist." Pryor hit heavily on Cotton's opposition to equal-pay and domestic violence legislation. The left-wing blog Kos joined the attack when it reported that Cotton's "condescending attitude toward women goes back to his college days" at Harvard University.[34]

The blog dug up an article Cotton had written for his college newspaper, the *Harvard Crimson,* in the 1990s. In the article, Cotton warned that divorced women will "slide into material indigence and emotional misery." The left-wing blogger did not note that feminist organizations at the time were criticizing "no-fault" divorce as a primary cause of female poverty. Instead, Kos reported that Cotton had led a campaign in Congress against banning federal funding for contraception and had voted against reauthorization of the Violence Against Women Act. Painting Barry Goldwater as an extremist was one thing, but it did not work on Cotton, who was Harvard University educated and an Army veteran as well!

Pryor's campaign undertook a no-holds-barred offensive, touting his cosponsorship of the Paycheck Fairness Act and reauthorization of the Violence Against Women Act. At the same time, the campaign embraced his support for the Affordable Care Act. Democrats hit the airwaves with a series of negative videos on YouTube intent on pushing a narrative of Cotton as "anti-woman." In one video, the director of a twenty-four-hour emergency center for women declared, "We've got to do something to break this cycle, and Tom Cotton is not doing anything to help." Another video had a woman asking, "What's Cotton got against women?"

In a tight race, the relatively unknown Cotton sidestepped the attacks by denouncing Obama's "war on women" talk as "demagoguery." He shifted the focus of the debate to national security and the war against Islamic extremists in the Middle East. In what all along appeared to be a tight race with two-term incumbent Senator Pryor against conservative opponent Cotton, who seemed more in line with the voters, the campaign was vicious on both sides. The race proved anything but tight in the end. Much as in the other red states, the polling results were dismal for the Democrats, maybe even worse. Pryor took the female vote by 10 points (53 percent to 43 percent), while Cotton won the male vote with a lopsided 60 percent to 36 percent margin. He won the general election, 56 percent to 39 percent.

While Republican senatorial candidates lost the overall women's vote in Iowa and Arkansas, they successfully countered the "war on women" strategy and won election.

BLUE-STATE LESSONS: MARYLAND AND TEXAS

If the "war on women" strategy failed in swing states, it failed utterly in blue states.

In 2012 black women had the highest turnout rate, 70 percent, of any voting group in America. They voted for Obama. In 2014, without Obama on the ticket, these same women stayed home. This drop-off was costly for Democrats across the board, even in solidly blue states such as Maryland, where the Democratic candidate, an African-American war hero, Lieutenant Governor Anthony Brown, was surprisingly defeated by Larry Hogan, Jr., by nearly 5 points. During the campaign, Brown bashed his Republican opponent for being anti-abortion and for being a reactionary on social issues.

Hogan won by going on the offense on the economy and jobs and by not employing fiery language on social issues. He attacked Brown as a tax-happy liberal. The central issue of the campaign became how best to improve the economy. Hogan's opponent, heavily favored at the outset to win the deeply blue state, tried to paint Hogan as an extremist out-of-touch with Maryland voters. Brown warned that, if elected, Hogan would legalize assault rifles, place new limits on women's access to contraception, and oppose gay marriage.[35] Of course, voters knew the heavily Democratic legislature would never approve any of these proposals.

Brown tried to link Hogan to another Republican candidate who belonged to a group that supported Southern secession and a sheriff accused of being anti-immigrant. As the campaign heated up, Brown and the Democratic Governors Association launched a TV ad blitz that seized on comments Hogan had made in the early 1980s in which he supported a ban on abortion, except to save the life of the mother, and a "human life amendment" that would have banned all abortions.[36]

Brown's campaign was designed to rally his base. His attacks on Hogan might have found traction in different circumstances. Although Hogan had not been elected to office, he was hardly a political outsider. He had worked for his father, Larry Hogan, Sr., a former congressman and county executive in Prince George's County. While attending Florida State University, he worked for the minority leader in the Florida House, and following graduation he served as an aide to Representative John Rousselot, who later became the western regional director of the right-wing John Birch Society. In 1992, Hogan served as secretary of appointments in Governor Bob Ehrlich's administration, where he oversaw patronage appointments. In 2011, Hogan organized Change Maryland, a grassroots anti-tax and small-government organization. Change Maryland was not officially aligned with the Tea Party, but shared an anti–big government sentiment. Democrats had systematically raised taxes in Maryland at every opportunity.

Hogan responded to the attacks with his own photo op by organizing supporters wearing pink "Women for Hogan" T-shirts at a press conference, where he declared that while he was still personally opposed to abortion, he pledged not to try to change Maryland's law protecting women's rights or to limit access to contraception. He told the *Baltimore Sun* that he opposed gay marriage but that, if elected governor, he would abide by a referendum. These moderate responses did not please the hard-core, but his moderate positions prevented his opponent from rallying his base, which he had been counting on.[37] Hogan turned the attack around by calling the ads "off-the-wall": "They're trying to make me into a right-wing, tea party Republican," he told the press, when the main issues were about creating jobs and economic opportunities in Maryland.[38] Hogan won the election, receiving 51 percent of the votes to Brown's 47 percent.

The lesson from Hogan's successful campaign against a Democratic attack aimed to demonize him was not that Republicans need to downplay their support for pro-life positions. By keeping the focus on voters' concerns about jobs, economic opportunity, healthcare, and education, while deftly redirecting attention away from social issues that can rally the Democratic base, Hogan showed how a Republican can win election even in a solidly blue state such as Maryland.

Wendy Davis's hope that she could win the governor's race in the decidedly red state of Texas provides an example of how not to run a campaign. She came into the arena having gained national attention with her filibuster as a state representative against a restrictive abortion bill that came before the Texas legislature in June 2013. She stood as a strong pro-choice candidate able to tap into the deep pockets of national feminist organizations. Her campaign plan was to put together a well-funded turnout operation.[39] She raised more than $40 million for her campaign. She promised her wealthy Democratic donors that she could turn Texas into a battleground state by bringing new voters to the polls. She failed even after an active voter registration drive.

At the heart of her campaign was her biography as a young woman who had grown up in a trailer park and experienced her own late-term abortion in 1997. She bashed her opponent, Greg Abbott, for opposing abortion even in cases of rape or incest. She also came out against the sale of guns at gun shows, usually not a winner in a gun-toting state such as Texas. This turned out to be the least of her problems. She touted her struggles as a single mother and her humble rise from a trailer park to a Harvard law degree. The story of a woman who made it on her own began to fall apart when the press found that between trailer park and Harvard she had married into wealth. Her very wealthy husband had supported her Harvard law education. When her campaign began to sag, she decided to go on the attack by airing an expensive sixty-second TV spot that criticized Abbott for siding with a vacuum cleaning company over a woman who sued it after she was raped by a door-to-door salesman. The ploy was to lure Abbott into a debate over rape. It did not work. Under a carpet-bombing attack by Abbott, Davis threw caution to the wind, airing a TV spot that opened with an empty wheelchair with a voice-over declaring, "A tree fell on Greg Abbott." Abbott, who was confined to a wheelchair following a freak accident in 1984, had been turned into a martyr by Davis. The Abbot campaign had a field day. By keeping focused on low taxes, small government, and federal healthcare overreach, Abbott received close to 60 percent of the vote, to Davis's 39 percent. Her outreach to women and Hispanics had fallen short. Forty-seven percent of women supported her, and she fared worse among Hispanics.

Texas Democrats had failed to turn back a national red tide on Election Day. As Rice University political science professor Mark Jones observed, at the end of the day Texas voters embraced the GOP "mantra of limited government."[40]

LESSONS LEARNED?

After the election, Democrats pointed to the successful reelection campaigns waged by Senator Al Franken of Minnesota and Senator Jeff Merkley of Oregon. Both Franken and Merkley employed more anti–Wall Street rhetoric rather than the "war on women" theme. Both also were elected in liberal states. These two victories allowed liberals to try to spin the election as "a good night for progressives."[41] This spin landed like a gutter ball in a beginner's bowling league. There was little consolation that two incumbent senators had maintained their seats in deeply blue states. The GOP now controls sixty-eight out of ninety-eight partisan state legislative chambers, and it holds the governorship and both houses of the legislature in twenty-four states. Democrats control only seven states. As David Wasserman, a congressional analyst for *The Cook Political Report,* observed about the election, "It was the culminating moment of a half-century of realignment. Democrats had already ceded Southern whites, but in the last few years they have lost droves of Midwestern, small-town and working class whites who feel like they have little in common with the party anymore."[42] He might have added that the gender gap had been narrowed by the failure of the "war on women" strategy.

The takeaway from the 2014 midterm elections is that Republicans found a way to counter the "war on women" attack. Each of the states won by the Republicans had its own peculiarities, and nationally it was a midterm election in the second term of an incumbent president, which was hard for Democrats to overcome. Whether these lessons are easily translated into the 2016 presidential campaign or later campaigns remains to be seen. On the sub-presidential level, it appears that the Democratic Party is in free fall, but Democrats have taken five of the last six presidential elections. Obama won reelection in 2012 by rallying his base of minority, female, and young voters. Many of these same voters did not turn out in 2014, leading to the obvious question of whether 2012 can be replicated by the Democratic presidential candidate in 2016. This is the question of the day, and it pertains specifically to women.

2

MINORITIES

REPUBLICANS NOT ONLY LOST MINORITY VOTERS IN 2008 AND 2012, they lost traditional Asian voters—Koreans and Vietnamese. Moreover, Hispanics and Asians are migrating from gateway cities along the coasts to heartland cities in the Sun Belt. They are joined by African Americans who are leaving the Northeast for jobs and lower-priced living in the Sun Belt. Red states in the Sun Belt are under threat of becoming blue states. Does the GOP have a future with minority voters? The answer is most assuredly yes.

- The face of America is changing. Interracial marriages, especially among Hispanics and Asians, and to a lesser degree blacks, are undermining the old identity politics of race.
- As minorities who have obtained educational skills for the new service- and technology-based economy replace white male baby boomers in the workplace, they will find new career opportunities and socioeconomic advancement. Their voting concerns will be less about race than about middle-class economic concerns that favor Republicans.

- Minority voters are by no means uniformly progressive on many issues. Republicans can play to these issues, as some GOP candidates have already shown in state-level races.

In the house of cards we call American politics, Democrats love to play the race card. It effectively mobilizes their base and reinforces a narrative that Republicans are racists who suppress minority votes, do not support civil rights, and are intent on maintaining "white privilege."

Massive demonstrations and violent protests across the nation against police brutality toward blacks in 2014 and 2015 allowed the Left to exploit the issue of racial justice in America. While condemning violent protesters who set cars and buildings on fire and looted stores—often minority owned—Democrats (and their media allies) took the opportunity to pursue their agenda of spending more money and lowering black incarceration rates, all the while attacking conservative opponents. In the wake of the Baltimore riot that followed the death of Freddie Gray, the twenty-five-year-old man who died after he was arrested and injured while being transported to jail, President Obama called for more funding for education, job creation, and reform of the criminal justice system. He chided Republicans for not supporting his urban policy initiatives. White House adviser Valerie Jarrett declared, "What has been frustrating has been the congressional Republicans' focus on top-down economic strategy rather than the middle-class economics the president has proposed."[1]

In a speech at Columbia University, Democratic presidential candidate Hillary Clinton called for reform of the criminal justice system. She called for the end of the "era of mass incarceration" of young black males, noting, "When we talk about one and a half million missing African American men, we're talking about missing husbands, missing fathers, missing brothers. They're not there to look after their children or bring home a paycheck." Whatever the merits of her call for reforming the criminal justice system, her argument that these incarcerated men could be home tending their children had a hollow ring when over 70 percent of black births in Baltimore are out-of-wedlock.

Cities such as Baltimore should be seen as liberal failures. The last Republican mayor in Baltimore was in the late 1960s. Does any serious person believe that more money or simply the release of black inmates is going to solve the problems of a city like Baltimore, or other Democratic-controlled cities such as Philadelphia, Cleveland, Detroit, Chicago, and Washington, D.C.?

Baltimore received over $1.8 billion from President Obama's stimulus bill, including $467.1 million to invest in education and $26.5 million for crime prevention. The city received additional millions of dollars for housing and job training. Of the nation's largest school districts, Baltimore ranked third in expenditures, at $15,287 annually per pupil. In fairness, hundreds of smaller school districts spend more per capita, but money is not the sole problem in the city. For example, of the stimulus money given to Baltimore and the state, money was wasted on dinner cruises and meals, such as one parent-teacher dinner that cost $96 a plate for fried chicken, coleslaw, biscuits, cookies, and soda. Teachers in Baltimore are poorly paid compared to teachers in wealthier suburban school districts, but school administrators are better paid. In a city of more than 600,000 people, close to 24 percent live in poverty, compared to 10 percent in the entire state. Black business ownership stands at 34 percent, but the median household income for the city is shockingly below the rest of the state: $41,386 compared to $73,538.[2]

The problems in cities such as Baltimore are multiple: high unemployment in a changing economy, a breakdown in family, bad schools, crime-ridden neighborhoods, and on and on. Liberalism needs to take some of the blame for not addressing these problems. Not totally, of course, but there needs to be some recognition that pouring in more money—through the matrix created by an unchallenged political class in one-party-controlled cities—might not do much to improve urban blight in America. Much of the federal money that cities such as Baltimore receive goes through a labyrinth of federal bureaucracies. The feds routinely siphon off a quarter to a third of the money for overhead. But would it matter if federal money passed directly to highly paid and sometimes corrupt city administrators? We have heard it takes a village to raise a child. Actually, many Democrats believe it takes a bureaucracy to raise a child: one parent, a teacher, a social worker, a health adviser, a child advocate, a disabilities expert, several coordinators, dozens of supervisors and union reps, and countless political appointees, whose main function is to counter each other's orders. And bad parenting really pays. Then we can add a sports program, anti-gang social worker, a juvenile-detention expert, several insurance claim agents, police, and judges. One bad parent funds an entire bureaucracy.

Democrats see the explosion of Hispanic and Asian voters as ensuring Democratic dominance in American politics for coming generations, as Republicans become a fragile minority party based on older white voters. In 2011, for the first time in American history, more children were born to minority parents—Hispanics, blacks, Asians, and other nonwhites—than to white parents. During the next forty years, demographers at the U.S. Census Bureau, as well as Brookings Institution scholar William Frey, project that these minorities will double because of births and immigration. At the same time, reduced white fertility and the aging white population, which grew at only a tepid 1.2 percent during the first decade of the twenty-first century, will continue to decline. In the future, America will have no racial majority, but a constellation of various minorities.[3]

There is every reason for Democrats to be optimistic based on past performance among minority voters. This appears to be particularly the case for Hispanic voters. In 2012 Barack Obama won 71 percent of the Hispanic vote, a plus-44 percent spread over Romney's paltry 27 percent. This was a 4 percent increase among Hispanic voters for Obama from 2008, when he won 67 percent of their vote, a 36 percent spread from Republican presidential nominee John McCain.

Republicans should be troubled by these numbers. Since 1980, Democrats have consistently won the Hispanic vote by double digits. The only time Republicans have cut the margins was with Ronald Reagan in 1980, when he won 35 percent of the Hispanic vote, and with George W. Bush when he won 35 percent of the vote in 2000 and increased it to 40 percent in 2004.

Furthermore, Hispanics are migrating from Gateway states in the West into traditional Republican strongholds in the Heartland and the

South. As a consequence, Sun Belt and Heartland states are becoming melting pots for Hispanics and Asians. The potential for these once-red states to become blue states will be further increased by the number of young, not-yet-of-voting-age Hispanics there. As these young voters come of age in the Heartland and the South, Republicans may find themselves overwhelmed if Hispanics vote as their parents have in previous elections. Particularly worrisome for Republicans is that among the 3,100 counties in the U.S., 53 percent showed declines in the white population. These declines were particularly severe in Heartland cities such as Detroit, Pittsburgh, and Cleveland. While white migrants are fleeing to Sun Belt states, so are Hispanics, Asians, and blacks, who are voting Democratic. Moreover, once in the Sun Belt, many of these minority voters are moving into the suburbs, once a natural habitat for Republican votes.[4]

A similar script is being written for Asian voters. Although a smaller percentage of the electorate (2.8 percent), 2.67 million Asian-American and Pacific Islander voters went overwhelmingly to Obama.[5] The Asian share of the electorate has continued to increase in the last three election cycles. These votes are concentrated in states such as California and New York, but the number of Asian-American voters is increasing in battleground states such as Nevada, Arizona, North Carolina, and Georgia. The turnout rate for Asian Americans is below the national average, but in 2012 the Democratic Party hired field organizers who used language and cultural skills to recruit hundreds of volunteers in Virginia and Nevada, where Koreans, Vietnamese, Chinese, Indians, and Filipinos were targeted. Meanwhile, the Romney campaign relied heavily on direct mail to reach Chinese and Indian voters. In Nevada, a Republican PAC called Chinese, Filipino, Korean, and Vietnamese voters. In Ohio, efforts focused on Chinese and Indian voters. In battleground states, the Obama campaign contacted close to 10 percent more Asian Americans than did the Romney campaign (63 percent to 54 percent), while in non-battleground states, Democrats contacted about 6 percent more than Republicans. Democratic efforts to win the Asian vote paid dividends, as 72 percent of the vote went to Obama and only 26 percent supported Romney. This trend is troublesome because many Asian groups traditionally identified as Republicans and many are middle class.

If these trends do not make Republicans turn to anti-anxiety drugs, the decline in the white electorate should. In 1980 whites comprised 90 percent of voters. By 2012, white voters had dropped to 74 percent of the electorate.[6] Hispanics and Asians are not turning out to vote as reliably as whites. In the 2012 presidential contest, Hispanics represented only 8 percent of the votes cast, but Republicans should not count on this figure remaining the same.[7] Once Hispanic and Asian Americans are mobilized, these voters will play pivotal roles in national and state elections. Obama showed the importance of the black vote in winning the 2008 and 2012 elections in key battleground states such as Virginia, North Carolina, and Ohio.

IS THERE ANY HOPE FOR REPUBLICANS?

Race is changing in America, but not in ways that guarantee continued Democratic victory. Why?

To begin with, old racial categories are disappearing through high rates of intermarriage.[8] Prior to 1960, multiracial marriages constituted only 0.4 percent of all marriages. By 2010, the overall rate increased to 8.4 percent. Today, multiracial marriages constitute more than one in seven of all newlywed couples. Already Asian Americans are intermarrying with whites at a rate of over 50 percent; Hispanic Americans at 35 percent; and African Americans at 15 percent. More whites are marrying people from other races. At the same time, more than four in ten marriages for Hispanics and Asians are multiracial. Blacks are marrying outside their race at a lower rate than other minorities, but among younger blacks nearly a third of marriages are multiracial. Intermarriage is taking place among higher-socioeconomic-status Hispanics and Asians, suggesting that socioeconomic mobility has allowed for greater social integration. (This is not the case for African Americans. Highly educated blacks do not demonstrate high rates of racial intermarriage. Intermarriage among blacks remains within lower socioeconomic groups.) Whatever the reasons this pattern is not occurring among African Americans, the traditional American family composed of distinct racial groups is being dramatically changed. One estimate places one in seven whites in a close-kin network that includes at least one nonwhite.[9]

These interracial marriages are distributed across blue and red states. Hawaii, a traditional Democratic state, has the highest intermarriage rate, but multiracial marriages have skyrocketed in states such as Georgia, Utah, and North Carolina, as well as Heartland states such as Minnesota and Indiana and Eastern states such as Connecticut and Pennsylvania. In Idaho and Utah, multiracial marriages among Hispanics account for over 40 percent of marriages.

The children of these intermarriages tend to identify as white and to marry whites.[10] The reconfiguring of race in America can advantage conservatives, who can win over successful Hispanic and Asian Americans as they successfully enter a workforce in which aging whites from the boomer, post–World War II generation retire.

This seismic change in the ethnic and racial composition within America is occurring with striking speed. Demographic trends show that race is being transformed in America as a new race is being born in which the categories of white, black, brown, and yellow will be replaced by completely different hues. The reconfiguring of race in America can advantage conservatives if they are able to replace the race card with new cards of their own that appeal to this new generation of Americans. Democratic appeals to race might not have the same traction as they have had in the past, when racial categories were so easily set. Racial lines are blurring, but old ideas about race in politics will remain as culture lags behind social trends.

Racial categories are going to change in the future, but Republicans should not be sanguine about it. They need to bear in mind two important caveats: one, first-time voters for a party tend to vote for the same party in later elections. Given that minority groups—Hispanics, Asians, and blacks—are voting overwhelmingly Democratic, political behavior suggests that they will continue to vote in similar patterns. Two, interracial marriages are mostly occurring among the college educated. College kids are meeting people of other races while at school, and these students are the ones mostly likely to enter interracial marriages. The bad news for Republicans is that these days college-educated voters tend to be Democrats. The key to political success for Republicans will be an intermediate strategy of cutting into the minority vote, especially among Hispanics and the diverse Asian population, while attracting the youth and college-educated vote, which has been overwhelmingly Democratic, especially beginning in the 2004 presidential election, even before Barack Obama won their vote.

THE FACE OF THE NEW HISPANIC VOTER

Nathan B., a twenty-four-year-old man with mixed ethnic parentage, became a Republican activist after having been a "big-time" Obama supporter in 2008. His conversion to the GOP presents an intriguing story of how a young progressive became an ardent conservative, with sharp libertarian leanings. He presents an example for Republicans of how young Hispanics can be won over to the party.

Nathan's mother grew up in Mexico along the Gulf Coast in a farming-fishing family. She met her future husband, Nathan's father, when he was an exchange student from the Midwest. She did not speak English, but his father's Spanish was workable. She still speaks English with a slight accent, which she has worked on overcoming. They both were in their teens. Both began dating during their first year in college while the father was attending a Midwestern university and the mother a Mexican university. Six years later, they married and moved to a small Midwestern town where his family owned a pharmacy. At the age of ten, Nathan moved with his family to the West.

Today the parents are comfortably middle class. His mother is a businesswoman and his father still works in the pharmaceutical industry. For a while the family owned a Hispanic dance club, but it failed in the 2009 crash. Nathan's parents vote Democratic. His mother, who was on the left when she was a student in Mexico, is not much interested in politics. His father is a moderate Democrat. Both are, as Nathan describes them, "strong, open-minded Catholics."

Nathan went to public schools. While in high school he became active in Obama's 2008 campaign. He said few of his classmates in the large public high school he attended were interested in politics. Nathan was different. He began supporting Obama in the primaries. He began reading on the Internet about politics and came across Ron Paul's campaign. By November, he had become a Ron Paul convert. In the end, he voted for the Constitution Party.

When asked what attracted him to Obama and later to Paul, he cited their opposition to the Iraq War, their anti-elitism, and their challenge to the political establishment. He found Paul on YouTube and began listening to him. He would not vote for Paul today, or for his son Rand, although he still tends toward libertarianism.

"Ron Paul," he said, "is a teacher. He educated me about the Constitution and explained the meaning of civil liberties, free speech, free press, and the right to bear arms." He adds that he used to favor outlawing guns, but today supports the right to bear weapons, even though he does not own a gun. He does not drink or use drugs and he is straight, but he supports the legalization of marijuana and gay marriage. He is pro-life. He remains "anti-war" but has become increasingly concerned about national security issues.

His education has been through activism. After graduating from high school, he worked for a while and began taking classes at the local community college. He decided after a couple of years to go full-time to college. At community college he sought out the Republican club and student "liberty" groups. He found about eight active students involved in the College Republican group on campus. In his first year, he became treasurer of the club and the next year he became its president. He grew the club in membership and activity. He got "hooked up" with the local Tea Party and began working for a congressional candidate. In the campaign, he was basically a "slave boy" working the phones to contact voters. When his candidate lost the primary, he went to work for a Senate campaign. He became a paid telephone-bank recruiter. He got involved in a city council race as well and took a job working at City Hall. He was just twenty-two years old, a full-time student with a full-time job.

After his associate's degree, he went to state university to study political science. After two years, he became president of the College Republicans. The club was activist oriented and consistently drew about forty students to its weekly meetings. Members range from national security hawks to moderates and quite a few libertarians. They are focused less on debating issues than on campaigns. At weekly meetings, outside speakers, usually candidates or officeholders, come to speak to the club. Most of the speakers are looking for campaign volunteers or paid workers. A few of the speakers focus on the mechanics of running campaigns.

When asked whom he favors for the 2016 presidential nomination, he replies, "Probably Jeb Bush." Why? "Well, I like his positions on immigration and education and gay marriage, but don't like much his foreign policy." He adds, "I am pro-life." His commitment to Jeb Bush is minimal. He adds that he likes Rubio "a lot." Why not Rand Paul? "Well, I am a libertarian-leaning conservative, but I don't think Rand has the temperament to be president. He is leaning too far to the left on foreign policy and civil liberty issues. It's just that I think we need to give a lot more attention to national security these days, the state of our national defense, and a more aggressive pro-American foreign policy. I believe what Ronald Reagan said, 'Peace through strength.'"

Nathan's Mexican heritage is important to him. When asked if he experienced racism or anti-Mexican bias in school, he says, "No. Most of my classmates were white, but my generation does not care about race in the way the older generation did." Most of his friends just thought he had a "dark tan." He adds, "Many people think I am from Persia and not Mexican. Some people think I am from India." He thinks race is overplayed in America these days. "Today people want us to cater to race. Kind of inverse of my views. I don't get it. Race is not important to me. My friends are of different ethnic groups and races. We need to be concerned about our national debt, education, healthcare, and jobs. We need to mobilize the lower middle class. The tax code is too burdensome."

When asked about winning Hispanics to the Republican Party, Nathan is direct. "I consider myself Mexican American. I am proud of my heritage. I am an American of Mexican ancestry. Republicans need better messaging and a better strategy in winning the Hispanic vote. Hispanics are proud of their heritage. They are family-oriented and most are religious. They are traditional about hard work, the importance of family, and community. Most want to get ahead in this country and they want a better life for their kids. The Hispanics I know are proud to be Americans. They came to this country because there is 'rule of law' and opportunity. Republicans need to appeal to this conservatism within the Hispanic community."

This is messaging, but he is concerned about strategy as well. He believes that the Republican Party, at least in his experience, tends to cultivate "established" Hispanic leaders and organizations. Republicans, he thinks, need to bring fresh Hispanic faces into the party. "Go to the churches. Tap new leaders. Go to the schools. Tap new activists. Go to the communities, not just at election time or political events. Show people that the Republican Party is involved in their communities. Then, begin to train and nominate new candidates that represent the community and that just are not coming out of 'hothouse' political cultivation."

Nathan remains optimistic about his future and the future of the Republican Party. He worries that the country is adrift, however. He wants to remain in politics, working to elect "libertarian-minded Republicans." He expects to work for a winning campaign and get a staff position or become a political campaign consultant. He believes his generation has a great future ahead of it, if the country can be put on the right path.

REPUBLICAN STRONGHOLDS UNDER THREAT

The Republican base of white voters is shrinking. The 2010 census showed that the median age for whites was 42, 28 for Hispanics, and 35 for Asians. This figure is revealing in itself, but even more striking is that only one-fifth of U.S. whites are under the age of 18, as contrasted with one-third of U.S. Hispanics who are 18 or younger. One obvious result of this trend is that minorities, especially Hispanics, will increasingly make up much of the labor force.

Hispanics are a diverse group in themselves, today numbering 50.5 million people. Those of Mexican origin constitute the largest number, with 31.8 million people, Puerto Ricans 4.6 million, Cubans 1.8 million, Salvadorans 1.6 million, Dominicans 1.4 million, and Guatemalans 1.0 million. Those from other Spanish-speaking countries in the Americas account for 8.2 million. Similarly, Asians are a diverse population, with varying socioeconomic status, educational attainments, and traditions. Those with Chinese origins make up the largest Asian population in America, but Asian populations from India, Korea, Vietnam, and other countries have grown in size. The Chinese population more than doubled, from 1.6 to 3.3 million, from 1990 to 2010, but the Asian Indian population in the United States became the second-largest Asian population, more than tripling to 2.8 million people. Asian adults are better educated than the average U.S. population, with more than half having college degrees and seven in ten having gone beyond high school.

Although most Hispanics and Asians remain clustered in what demographers call Gateway states on the West and East Coasts, ethnic minorities are increasingly moving to melting-pot cities and regions in Sun Belt states.[11] For example, the Hispanic population in Charlotte and Raleigh, North Carolina, and Nashville, Tennessee, grew over the last three decades over 1,000 percent each, with Charlotte experiencing a 1,715 percent growth rate. Cities such as Atlanta, Cape Coral, Las Vegas, Lakeland, and Orlando experienced astronomical growth rates in the triple digits. There are 90,000 Korean immigrants in Atlanta. The community and its many businesses are concentrated along a suburban highway. Asians have joined this inward migration to Sun Belt cities as well.

African Americans have begun to migrate from older industrial states to Sun Belt states, reversing in many respects the great black migration out of the South that occurred in the early and mid-twentieth century. Unlike Hispanics, who are flowing into Sun Belt cities for low-paying, low-skill jobs, many of the blacks returning to the New South or the western Sun Belt are affluent, college-educated, high-skilled knowledge workers. Blacks have contributed significantly to the tremendous growth of cities such as Las Vegas, Phoenix, Orlando, Atlanta, Raleigh, Tampa, and Dallas—among the top ten cities attracting blacks.

Whites, too, are leaving expensive, congested coastal areas, and economically depressed Great Plains, Midwest, and Northeast regions. They are migrating to the Sun Belt for the same reasons as Hispanics, Asians, and blacks: the Sun Belt is economically healthier, with lower housing costs, more job opportunities, and easier living conditions than the older coastal cities.

While the white population in the Sun Belt has grown in recent years, minority populations have grown even faster. As a consequence, Republicans will not be able to rely on their base of white voters to ensure continued electoral success in the Sun Belt. Sun Belt states will be up for grabs. Already many counties in the South and West have white population shares below 64 percent.

The Republican dilemma in winning minority voters is already apparent. Hispanics' share of voting has been increasing, albeit slightly, from 2004 through 2012.[12] An analysis of exit polls conducted by Mark Hugo Lopez for the Pew Research Center showed that the Hispanic share of the national vote increased 1 percent from 2004 to 2008, rising to a 9 percent share of the vote. In 2012 it increased to 10 percent. In both presidential elections, Hispanics voted by wide margins for Obama. This included all subgroups within the diverse Hispanic population.

In 2008, Hispanics supported Obama 67 percent to 31 percent. McCain might have taken some consolation from increasing his share of the Hispanic vote over Bob Dole's disappointing 21 percent, but McCain missed the high-water mark of 40 percent that George W. Bush received in 2004. Of particular interest is that, prior to the general election, Hispanics favored Hillary Clinton in the primaries by two to one over Obama.

On Election Day, Obama curried huge Hispanic voting margins in states with large Latino populations. For example, in Florida, a state in which Bush had won the majority of Hispanic voters in 2004, Obama garnered 57 percent of the Latino vote. This breakthrough vote in

Florida paled in comparison to other states where Obama overwhelmingly won Hispanic voters: 78 percent in New Jersey; 76 percent in Nevada; and 74 percent in California. Meanwhile, the Hispanic share of voters went up in the critical swing states of New Mexico, Colorado, and Nevada.

In 2012, Obama won an even greater share of the Hispanic vote. Obama's Republican rival, Mitt Romney, did not appeal to Hispanic voters. Republican outreach on Spanish-speaking media suffered badly in comparison to the Obama campaign's. Republicans did not have the bench to enlist an army of Spanish-speaking campaign supporters to make telephone calls, knock on doors, and go before church and community groups. The consequences were severe. The Republican share of the Hispanic vote fell to below Bob Dole's pitiful 21 percent. Romney set a new record for losing Hispanic votes, while Obama fell 1 point short of Bill Clinton's 1996 record 72 percent share.

The Asian-American vote, although much smaller, also went to Obama. What should concern Republicans is that 2012 marked a turning point when they lost the entire American Asian vote. Asian Americans are a socially and economically diverse population that includes Asian Indians, Chinese, Koreans, Japanese, Cambodians, Hmong, and Pacific Islanders. Nonetheless, Obama won every Asian-American and Pacific Island group, including the Vietnamese, who have drifted away from the GOP. More than three in four Indians voted Democratic, and among Vietnamese and Filipinos, 60 percent chose Obama over Romney.[13]

Although Obama won the Vietnamese, Filipino, and Korean vote, his support within these groups was relatively weak. His support among Asian Indians, Cambodians, and Hmong was strongest. Although Romney performed miserably among Asian Americans, he performed better among Koreans, Filipino, and Vietnamese voters (33 percent, 37 percent, and 39 percent, respectively). Romney did poorest among Asian Indian voters, winning only 16 percent of their vote. Asian Indians included a lot of struggling recent immigrants who are concentrated in Democratic states and often work in the Democratic-leaning tech industry.

In battleground states such as Florida, Nevada, North Carolina, Ohio, and Virginia, Obama's margin of victory varied. He won Florida by less than 1 percent, won Ohio by nearly 2 percent, and took Virginia by 3 percent and Nevada by 6.6 percent. He lost North Carolina by 2.2 percent. The Asian-American share of the vote in these states ranged from highs in Virginia (3.7 percent) and Nevada (3.2 percent) to lows in Florida, North Carolina, and Ohio, where the share hovered around 1 percent. The point is that Asian-American voter mobilization might prove critical in key battleground states.

The African-American vote remained Democratic, as it has since the 1960s, but Obama, the first black president, effectively mobilized black turnout in key battleground states.

A CLOSER LOOK AT BATTLEGROUND STATES

One does not need to be Karl Rove to see that the ethnic and racial face of America is changing, with profound consequences for the future of the Republican Party.

Republicans can wail—with a good deal of justification—about border control and the seeming unwillingness of Congress, including GOP representatives, to address the undocumented immigration problem in America. The fact of the matter is that minority voters are of ever-increasing importance to both parties. The high rate of intermarriage between races and ethnic groups *might* change the nature of racial politics in the future, but winning minority voters is going to be critical for both major parties in the immediate future.

In national presidential elections, Republicans have recently taken it for granted that the Pacific coastal states—California, Oregon, and Washington—would go Democratic, as would Northeastern Atlantic states. Battleground states were up for grabs, and minority voters in these states have proved critical. In key states such as Florida, Nevada, and Colorado, Hispanics make up a growing share of the electorate.[14] The non-Cuban Hispanic population in Florida, particularly the Puerto Rican population in central Florida, has been growing at an astounding pace. Exit polls taken in 2012 revealed that 34 percent of

Hispanic voters were Cuban, while 57 percent were non-Cuban. The Cuban vote went to Romney over Obama, 47 percent to 40 percent. Among the non-Cuban vote, though, Obama won 66 percent. Colorado proved to be even worse for Republicans among Hispanic voters. Here Obama won nearly 70 percent of the Hispanic vote. Given that Hispanics in Colorado made up 14 percent of the vote (up a full percentage point from the previous presidential cycle in 2008), this margin proved critical.

A similar tale unfolded in Nevada, where Obama won 70 percent of the Hispanic vote to Romney's 25 percent. This about equaled Obama's share of the vote in 2008, but the difference was that the Hispanic vote in 2012 increased its share of the total vote by 3 full percentage points, from 15 percent to 18 percent. Not only did the Hispanic vote increase; so did other minority voters. Meanwhile, the white share of the vote dropped from 73 percent in 2008 to 67 percent in 2012. The Hispanic vote increased, as did the black vote (to 9 percent), and Asians and other racial minorities rose to 9 percent as well.[15]

In other battleground states, Obama proved popular among Hispanic voters. He took 68 percent of Hispanic voters in North Carolina, 65 percent in Wisconsin, 64 percent in Virginia, and 53 percent in Ohio.

In nearly every battleground state—and soon-to-be battleground states—the Hispanic vote is increasing. Hispanics now account for over one in three voters in New Mexico; they are nearly one in five voters in Arizona, Nevada, and Florida; and their numbers are rising in Colorado. In the hotly contested battleground states of Virginia, North Carolina, Wisconsin, and Ohio, the Hispanic share of the vote is only around 5 percent, but in tight elections this can make the difference between who wins and who loses.

Even more worrisome for Republicans is that young Hispanic voters nationwide went for Obama over Romney at even higher numbers than did the youth in general. In 2012, Obama took 74 percent of the Hispanic youth vote, 14 points higher than the entire youth vote (60 percent) that pulled the Democratic lever. Most voters making below $50,000 voted for Obama.

Brookings Institution demographer William Frey estimates in his analysis of 2012 voting in battleground states that minority voters were responsible for Obama winning in Ohio, Pennsylvania, Wisconsin, Florida, Nevada, New Mexico, Virginia, and North Carolina.[16]

HOW REPUBLICANS CAN WIN MINORITY VOTERS

Republicans can win, or at least increase their share of the Hispanic and Asian vote, if they have something to offer by way of issues and candidates. The black vote is solidly Democratic and the minority bloc least likely to be turned Republican. But an attempt should be made. The Republican Party's long history of supporting civil rights legislation since its inception, the essential role it played in the passage of the Civil Rights Act of 1957, the Civil Rights Act of 1964, and the Voting Rights Act of 1965, have not paid off on Election Days. African Americans have stuck with the Democratic Party since the 1960s. Nonetheless, Republicans need to address racial divisions in America by offering reform solutions to jobs, education, urban problems, crime, and social inequality. A genuine reform agenda might not win black voters, but these are issues that concern all Americans and project an appealing image for the party. Republicans can win on the issues by projecting a new image, but most important, the party needs to continue to give minority groups and minority candidates a place at the table.

Let's consider the issues.

The issue that Hispanics found of greatest concern when they voted in these battleground states was the economy (60 percent), followed by healthcare (18 percent), the federal budget deficit (11 percent), and foreign policy (6 percent). Perhaps what is most surprising is that exit polls, as well as other polls, place immigration as a lower priority than these other issues. More Hispanics than the general electorate think that undocumented immigrants should be given a chance to apply for legal status, but one in five Hispanics (18 percent) believe illegal immigrants should be deported.[17]

The issue of illegal immigration presents a volatile issue for Republicans, but also for Democrats. A Rasmussen poll conducted in early

August 2015, when Donald Trump fever was just beginning, found that 60 percent of likely voters believed that the U.S. government was not aggressive enough in deporting those who had entered the country illegally. Only 12 percent of respondents believed that the government was too aggressive, a drop of 4 points from an earlier poll conducted in April. This concern with illegal immigration was reflected in an earlier NBC/*Wall Street Journal* poll conducted in July. Less than a majority, 47 percent, of the general public believed that the federal government should create a pathway to citizenship for those who have entered the country illegally. Seventeen percent believed that illegal/unregistered immigrants should be given legal status but not citizenship. Nearly a third of people polled believed that those who crossed the border illegally should be found and deported.[18]

These surveys suggest that there is a deep sentiment among large numbers of Americans for deportation. There were approximately 11.3 million illegal immigrants in the United States in 2015. These figures are not precise, but it appears these numbers are down from a high of 12.2 million in 2007. Of these illegal/unregistered immigrants, 38 percent have been here at least five years. Many who have been here longer than ten years own their own homes. Many of these illegals are children. Approximately 4.5 million children who are citizens because they were born here have at least one parent who is an illegal immigrant.

The immigration question remains one of the most explosive in American politics today. Calling for forced deportation or "self-deportation" makes for good campaign rhetoric and appeals to a significant number of Americans who are angry that the federal government appears unable to control the nation's borders. Yet strong anti-immigration sentiment by a candidate or party opens the door to charges of racism and xenophobic nationalism. A strong anti-immigration stance by Republicans in California contributed to its minority status in the state. However Republicans tackle the immigration issue, they will need to understand that while tapping anger within the electorate might fuel a campaign in a short term, it can backfire in the long run. Immigration is not an intractable issue for Republicans or the nation. It's complex and easily politicized. Any discussion of the issue needs to begin with how best to secure the border, compassion for those who are here illegally even though they have broken the law, and a resolve to address the problem of over 11 million illegals, many of them children, who are now here. How this is resolved will be a test not only for Republicans seeking to become a majority party, but for the nation and democracy itself.

Asian Americans could provide Republicans with an opportunity to open the door to winning minority votes, although the door is fast closing, if 2012 is any indication. Asian Americans list as their main concerns the same issues that worry most Americans: education, healthcare, national security, and old-age retirement. A survey of "very important" issues for Asian Americans ranked the economy as the leading issue (86 percent). This was followed by education (81 percent), healthcare (80 percent), national security (72 percent), and Social Security (71 percent). Ranking lower on very important issues were the environment (59 percent) and racial discrimination (54 percent). Immigration was seen as an important issue by only 43 percent of Asian Americans.[19]

These issues—the economy, healthcare, the federal budget, and foreign policy—should be natural issues for Republicans. Simply talking about tax cuts, restoring the middle class, and putting Americans back to work is not going to be enough to win minorities. Continual campaign rhetoric of cutting taxes and lowering the capital gains tax, as was seen in the Romney campaign, reinforces the stereotype that Republicans are the party of big business and Wall Street. These themes' lack of resonance nearly cost George W. Bush the election in 2000. He won, in part, because of Al Gore's debate sighs.

These are issues that should play to GOP strengths in attracting Asian Americans, just as they can in reaching the Hispanic vote. Republicans can reach minority voters by emphasizing a viable economic growth program. There is a strong entrepreneurial ethos among Hispanics and Asian Americans, especially the Chinese, Koreans, Vietnamese, and Asian Indian communities. Furthermore, an educational reform program that is integral to Republican candidates running for national and state offices can excite these voters. National security is a natural issue for Republicans, especially as terrorism, the Middle East, and relations with Russia gain increased attention from voters.

In 2008 and 2012, Democrats convinced minority voters that their party best served their interests. But Democrats should not take the minority vote for granted—neither the Hispanic nor the Asian-American vote. The key for Republicans in winning these votes begins with a simple realization that minority voters are not a single bloc. Referring to minority voters as Hispanic or Asian Americans is actually a misleading label that ignores differences of national origins, cultural and religious orientations, and socioeconomic divisions within these categories and between racial minorities.

Republicans need to pursue minority voters, without losing their base among white voters. Neither the Hispanic population nor the Asian-American population is homogenous, ethnically or politically. The Hispanic population in America is largely of Mexican origin, but it also includes Cubans, Puerto Ricans, and South Americans. There has been a major migration from Ecuador, Argentina, and Colombia. These immigrants are very different in background, culture, and socioeconomic status from many of the uneducated, unskilled workers from Central America or the wealthier immigrants who came from Cuba and Venezuela decades earlier.

Pursuing the minority vote by targeting specific political and socioeconomic and cultural interests is essential for Republican success. And these minority voters can be won over.

Some basic observations set the context for a general strategy.

Weak Party Identification

Party support among minority voters is surprisingly weak once the figures are broken down. In 2012 less than half of registered Hispanic voters (45 percent) identified themselves as Democrats. This is nearly three times as many Hispanics (16 percent) who listed themselves as Republicans.

Clearly Republicans face an uphill battle in persuading Hispanics that the Republican Party stands for them. The better news for

Republicans is that a whopping 36 percent of Hispanics declare that they are Independents. Although most of these Independents lean Democratic (60 percent), over a quarter (27 percent) tend to vote Republican.[20] Add this to those Hispanic Independent voters who say they have no party leaning, and the total of 37 percent gets a lot closer to the Democratic total. Furthermore, recent Hispanic immigrants are more likely to identify as Independents. Put another way, close to half of Hispanic Independents (49 percent) were born outside the United States. Sixty percent of recent Hispanic immigrants label themselves as Independents, as do most of the second generation (48 percent). Yet surveys show that Hispanics with longer ties to the United States are more likely to be Republican and less likely to be non-leaning Independents. Among the third generation of Hispanics, 32 percent declare themselves Republicans. Although this figure does not come close to the over 50 percent of this later generation of Hispanics who consider themselves Democrats, Republicans gain Hispanic voters the longer they remain in this country.

Party identification among Asian Americans remains equally weak. Like Hispanics, voter registration is low among Asian Americans. The Asian-American vote remains up for grabs. Surveys before the 2012 election showed that about one-third of Asian Americans were undecided on their choice until they went to the polls.[21] Nearly half of Asian Americans today identify themselves as Independents, which means that their vote could be won in the future.

Minorities Are Not Natural Liberals

Although Obama's executive order in November 2014 provided protective status to nearly four million undocumented immigrants, and deportations of undocumented immigrants have fallen recently, many within the Hispanic community continue to refer to him as "deporter in chief." While many Hispanics voted Democratic in 2008 and 2012, they are by no means uniformly liberal. Most are conservative on issues such as same-sex marriage and abortion. Moreover, Hispanics are particularly concerned about "law and order," given that they are often the victims of crime. Hispanics are not being well served by current criminal justice policies and practices.[22]

Similarly, Asian Americans are not natural liberals. For example, a Field Poll released on the eve of the vote in California in 2010 on Proposition 8, which would have amended the state constitution to ban same-sex marriages (later ruled unconstitutional by the Ninth Circuit Court), showed that Asian Americans in the state opposed same-sex marriage.[23] The poll broke out this opposition among Asian Americans to show that Korean Americans opposed gay marriage by a margin of 70 to 25 percent.

Korean Americans were overwhelmingly opposed to same-sex marriage, but they were not alone among Asian Americans, or for that matter Hispanics or African Americans. Vietnamese Americans disapproved of gay marriage by 64 percent, followed by Chinese Americans, who expressed 54 percent disapproval. Younger Asian Americans were more welcoming of gay marriage, but there was strong opposition across generational lines. The Field Poll showed opposition to same-sex marriage from Latinos by a margin of 50 to 41 percent, and from African Americans by 49 percent to 38 percent.

The point is not that Republicans should make gay marriage an issue, but they should understand that Hispanics and Asian Americans tend toward cultural conservatism when it comes to traditional family values. While Republican candidates need to cut a careful course on social issues, especially if they expect to win the youth vote in the future, they should not be afraid to talk about the importance of the family as a primary social unit necessary for maintaining and encouraging economic well-being, reducing crime, encouraging educational attainment, and addressing income and wealth disparity in America.

Educational Attainment

Hispanics and Asian Americans are entering college in numbers unprecedented in American history.[24] Educational attainment is the single most important factor in economic success in America. By 2012 there was a higher percentage of Hispanic recent high school graduates enrolled in college than the percentage of white males. The U.S. Census Bureau showed that among recent higher school graduates, a higher percentage of Hispanics (49 percent) were enrolling in college compared to non-Hispanic whites (47 percent). Of 12.5 million students in college, 7.2 million were white, 2.4 million were Hispanic, 1.7 million were black, and 915,000 were Asian. The majority of the Hispanic college students were women. From 1996 to 2012 the number of Hispanics, age 18–24, enrolled in college more than tripled (a 240 percent increase), outpacing blacks (72 percent) and whites (12 percent).

The Asian-American success story has been long-standing. Over 42 percent of all Asian-American adults have a college degree.[25] Asian Americans have the highest test scores and grade point averages (GPAs) of any racial group. Within the Asian-American population, Chinese, Koreans, and Asian Indians have done exceptionally well. For example, 52 percent of Korean immigrants had a bachelor's degree or higher, compared to 28 percent of the total U.S. immigrant population and 30 percent of the native-born population. One result is that only 11 percent of Korean immigrant families live in poverty.

As Hispanics, Asian Americans, and blacks move up the economic ladder, becoming doctors and lawyers, middle managers, and CEOs, they can be attracted to Republican issues of low taxes, reducing the national debt, as well as educational, healthcare, and Social Security reform.

Democrats have won college-educated voters in the past, but they cannot count on this in the future if Republicans construct a narrative that they are the party of reform. Can Democrats continue to proclaim themselves "progressive" as they continue to maintain the status quo on government spending, seeing every problem as a lack of spending and protecting special interests, whether it be government service or public school teachers unions or corporate interests feeding at the trough of crony capitalism?

State Minority Voting Disparities

The 2014 midterm elections highlight some important strategies for the future. Although Democrats received 64 percent of the Latino vote overall, Republicans won their votes in some key contests. For example, in Colorado, where Hispanics make up 14 percent of the state's electorate, Republican senatorial candidate Cory Gardner won the race with 23 percent of their vote. At the beginning of his race against Mark Udall, polling showed that he was supported by only 11 percent of Hispanic voters. Given that Hispanics make up 22 percent of the general population, Gardner knew he needed to increase support in this community. He began appearing at Hispanic events. He showed respect for Hispanic values and was sympathetic to difficulties facing Hispanic voters.[26] His campaign undertook extensive advertising on Spanish-language radio and television. He did not present himself as a liberal calling for more spending and welfare programs. He ran as a fiscal and social conservative who was sympathetic to the social and economic problems faced by average Hispanics.

Even better news for Republicans was received in Texas. Republican gubernatorial candidate Greg Abbott took 44 percent of the Latino vote in that election. In Georgia, incumbents for the governorship and U.S. Senate took nearly half the Latino vote, which comprised 3 percent of the voter population.[27] Texas Republicans have been more successful at Hispanic outreach and candidate development. There is evidence that Hispanics in Texas hold more conservative values than do Hispanics in other states, perhaps because they have immigrated from more conservative parts of Mexico or because they have absorbed Texas's conservative culture.

Socioeconomic Differences

Within the Hispanic, Asian-American, and black populations, there are wide social and economic disparities. Just as we see a bifurcation in voting patterns and socioeconomic status in the general American population, these divisions are apparent within minority communities as well.

There is a strong entrepreneurial ethos that prevails in the Hispanic and Asian-American communities. Hispanics and Asian Americans across the nation are small business owners of restaurants, corner grocery stores, home services, and business suppliers. Many African Americans are professionals, doctors, lawyers, dentists, and middle managers. Democrats project minorities as impoverished, uneducated, and lower class in dress, speech, and manner. This form of stereotyping can be insulting and backfire.

Left out of the discussion of race in America is any discussion of the middle class among minorities. Defining "middle class" as households that earn between $35,000 and $99,000, the Census Bureau shows that 44.3 percent of whites fall into the category. Yet Hispanics are not far behind, with close to 44 percent of their total population. Middle-class Asians stand at over 40 percent and blacks at nearly 38 percent.[28] Another measure of being middle class is homeownership. Here, too, we see a significant minority middle class. While homeownership in America continues to remain one of the highest in the world, at 64 percent, 44.5 percent of Hispanics and 42.1 percent of African Americans own their own homes. Homeownership for all racial groups has declined since 2008, but it still remains high.

Large numbers of Hispanics, Asians, and African Americans are managers, professionals, and other white-collar occupations.[29] Per capita there are more Asian managers than whites. In fact, 47 percent of employed Asians are managers and professionals, compared to 29 percent of whites and 20 percent of Hispanics. Minority women in particular are entering professional occupations. There have been significant advances in minority representation within all professions. For example, African Americans have more than tripled their representation in electronic engineering, while Hispanics have increased their representation as managers in the engineering industry. African Americans are now 7 percent of young workers in financial analysis. In nearly every professional occupation, minorities have increased their numbers. Their numbers still remain small and underrepresented across the board, but what cannot be disputed is that many members of minority groups are professionals. They see themselves as such; they live middle-class lifestyles in suburban areas and socialize with whites; and their children are dating and marrying whites. There is no reason middle-class minorities should not be Republicans.

The social distance between a black physician and an unemployed young black kid is as far as it would be for any upper-middle-class white. Differences within minority populations are all too apparent by any measure. One good instrument to use in evaluating these differences is to look at educational attainment, a good predictor of present and future socioeconomic status. A comparison of white, Hispanic, and Asian populations shows that about 9 percent of whites have less than a high school diploma, while for Hispanics that number stands at 36 percent, for Asians at 15 percent, and for blacks at 17 percent. Obviously, lower educational attainment among some Hispanics is due to recent immigration, but high school graduation rates and college attendance rates for Hispanics in general are rising.

Other measures show the problems of the minority underclass. The Centers for Disease Control (CDC) reported in 2015 that 40 percent of children are born to unwed mothers. This includes about 29 percent of white births. For African Americans, about 71 percent of children are born to unwed mothers, and nearly 53 percent of Hispanic children are born to unwed mothers.[30]

Targeting minority voters means that Republicans need to have programs and messaging that appeal to upward-rising and established Hispanics, those who are fulfilling the American Dream and those who want to attain it. A political platform designed to appeal to middle-class Hispanic business men and women, and those many Hispanics with entrepreneurial dreams, can win votes.

The desire for good jobs and a healthy economy, and for better and affordable healthcare and education, cuts across socioeconomic lines. Republicans need to do more than just tell voters that a rising economic tide raises all ships—as evident in increased employment, home ownership, and occupational status for blacks beginning in the increasingly remote Reagan years. Instead, the party needs to put forth a vision of economic reform by distancing itself from corporate capitalism and the rich. Instead of talking about lowering capital gains taxes, the party needs to project a message that it is the party of tax reform. Instead of just calling for immigration reform, the party needs to declare that it will protect undocumented immigrants from exploitation by criminal gangs and unscrupulous employers—both Hispanics and whites.

Republicans need to stand for educational reform. Take, for example, school choice. School choice programs through private and public charter schools have been taken advantage of primarily by middle-class parents. Underserved communities often remain ignorant of how to get their kids into charter schools. The GOP needs to advocate for programs—public and private—that reach out to underserved communities so that they can take advantage of better schools, better teachers, and safer playgrounds.

School choice is just one area that Republicans can focus on. Economic and educational policies designed to appeal to middle-income, entrepreneurial, professional-minded minorities, as well as the poor, cut across socioeconomic disparities within minority communities. Republicans need to tout conservative-minded programs in states such as Indiana, Ohio, and Wisconsin, where the poor and the middle class have been helped.

This underclass presents problems for all of society, but because this class does not vote in the same numbers as higher-income groups, it is easy for both political parties to ignore them, other than offering rhetoric about overcoming injustice. Republicans have allowed Democrats to present themselves as defenders of social justice. Republicans do not need to devise new government programs, but they need to be a party of reform and paint Democrats as the party of the status quo.

Republicans correctly espouse American exceptionalism. What is this exceptionalism?

It is a commitment to the rule of law, equal opportunity, and the generosity of the American people. Undocumented immigrants present a major problem for America. A sovereign nation must secure its borders. Meaningful immigration reform is required. This reform will be arrived at through a political process involving elected representatives and their constituents. Immigration reform needs to be framed in a context that shows that Republicans understand and sympathize with the motivation and plight of those crossing our borders illegally. The rule of law should be upheld, but with compassion for these undocumented (illegal) immigrants. This does not mean "open borders," nor does it mean more welfare programs once these people are here.

Millions of illegal immigrants are already living in America. Some have been here more than a generation. These illegal immigrants cannot be deported. Such a policy would be an administrative nightmare and impossible to implement. Most of these illegal immigrants are hardworking people who have sought to fulfill the American Dream. Republicans need to express a natural compassion for these people who have become Americans, in effect. This does not entail amnesty or a direct path toward citizenship, but it should compel Republicans to express an understanding that actual people's lives are involved in this debate, while respecting the nation's commitment to the rule of law and its own legal citizens. Angry campaign rhetoric against illegal immigrants might rally the base, but it does little to win other voters. The contributions of Hispanic culture and Hispanics who have lived in this country for many generations, longer than many people of European origin, should be celebrated by Republicans.

African-American voters remain steadfast in their allegiance to the Democratic Party. This is the one subgroup where identity politics still works for the Democrats. African Americans will not be won easily to the Republican Party. Nonetheless, the GOP should reach out to African Americans through their church and community leaders by showing that Republicans offer a reform agenda that addresses the problems of the inner city, poor schools, crime, and drug-infested neighborhoods.

If the Republican Party is to become a majority party, it needs to capture about 30 to 40 percent of the Hispanic vote and about 1 or 2 percent of the African-American vote on the presidential level. The African-American vote has increased to about 13 percent of the electorate. Historically it stood at around 10 percent. Whether African-American voters will continue to show such enthusiasm for Democrats without Obama on the ticket remains to be seen. A Republican Party standing for job creation, equal opportunity, and educational reform will be the first step in tempering African-American enthusiasm for a party that promotes failed policies that have left many blacks in poverty, poorly educated, and living in drug- and gang-infested neighborhoods.

Republicans can counter the race and class cards that have played so well for Democrats in previous elections by projecting themselves as intent on restoring the American Dream for all Americans, whatever their socioeconomic status or declared racial or ethnic group. A party of reform committed to fundamental beliefs about the importance of economic opportunity, safe streets, protecting our children, ensuring that rules and laws are not abused by any one class, and protecting the safety of the nation will ensure Republican dominance at the polls for years to come.

MODELS FOR SUCCESS

The key to whatever success Republicans have enjoyed comes down to a single point: giving minority groups a place at the table is critical to winning the Hispanic vote for the GOP. This was exactly how Republicans made Texas into a red state in the 1980s; elected Susana Martinez governor in New Mexico; placed the first female black Republican, Mia Love, in Congress; and critically placed Vietnamese leaders into key positions in the Arizona party. Each of these examples presents a model for what can be done in the future.

In the 1980s, Texas became a Republican state. How this happened presents a fascinating story of how conservative Republicans such as John Tower, a university professor who went on to become a U.S. senator, convinced Hispanic leaders that Democrats did not serve their interests. The Democratic Party dominated Texas politics through much of the twentieth century. Republicans were seen as the party of a wealthy and elitist establishment found in the country clubs of the Northeast. Most Texans saw Democrats as representing the values of hardworking, patriotic, Christian Americans. Democrats were a mix of strong conservatives who believed in states' rights and small government and liberals who saw the federal government and its largesse as necessary to help the urban poor, small farmers, and the struggling middle class. These perceptions unraveled in the late 1960s and 1970s with the decline in family values, a perception of an incompetent and untrustworthy federal government, a stagnant national economy, and a view that America was in decline internationally as an economic and world power.[31]

Winning Hispanic voters away from Democrats proved critical to the conservative resurgence in Texas. In 1972, John Tower won the U.S. Senate race in Texas by becoming the first Texas Republican in the state's history to win a plurality of Mexican-American and Hispanic votes. The ground for Tower's success had been laid in the 1960s, when Republicans began courting Hispanic leaders across the state, telling them that they were not benefiting from their traditional alliance with Democrats. Democrats, they said, were taking Hispanics for granted. They were being cut out of leadership positions and the benefits that come with winning elections. In his campaign, Tower cultivated Mexican Americans by supporting educational programs, vocational training, and community health centers for migrant workers. He brought Hispanics into his campaign and won the endorsement of prominent Hispanic leaders who saw the advantages of aligning themselves with the Republican Party. Tower, acting on the advice of these Hispanic leaders, deployed highly qualified staffers to work the polls and volunteer in Hispanic communities. He undertook extensive advertising on Spanish-speaking radio stations, often highlighting the corruption and abuse that the Hispanic community had endured under Democratic machine politics. He portrayed Democrats as a false friend of Hispanics. His strategy paid off. He won 45 percent of the Mexican-American and Hispanic vote.

This set the stage for Ronald Reagan's presidential campaign in Texas in 1980. In 1976, Republican Gerald Ford carried only 13 percent of the Hispanic vote in the state. The Reagan campaign knew that it needed to do better. Reagan began making numerous appearances before Hispanic crowds. He did not pander to the Hispanic vote, but appealed to them on his own terms by talking about the value of work, community, freedom, and independence. In his campaign appearances he avoided terms such as "illegals" and praised the Hispanic community for the importance they placed on family, dignity, and self-respect. He carried a message of hope for a better future. His efforts paid off. He won twice as many Hispanic votes as Ford did and made Republicans into an acceptable party for Hispanics.

One more subtle point should be made about the Reagan campaign's appeal to Hispanics: Reagan's support for the military. Since the Vietnam War, Hispanics have been a large part of the U.S. military. This is partly about national pride in the United States, which Reagan understood, but it is also about job training and upward mobility through military service. Tower was a major force in the Senate, supporting the military and advocating educational benefits for veterans. Liberals called for military cuts, a direct attack against upwardly mobile Hispanics. Strong patriotic feelings on the part of Hispanics should encourage Republicans to recruit candidates from Hispanic veterans.

There are more recent examples of how Republicans can win minority votes and elect minority candidates. In 2010, Susana Martinez became the first female governor of New Mexico and the first Hispanic female governor in the United States. She won election because she was principled and pragmatic. She came into office facing the largest budget deficit in state history and turned it into a surplus. Working with Democrats, her administration promoted a friendly business environment, enacting tax reform that reduced the tax rate on businesses from 7.6 to 5.9 percent. She emphasized educational reform by working with parents, teachers, and professionals to improve schools. With her background as a prosecutor, she made it a top priority to require DNA samples for all felony cases.[32] In 2014 she easily won reelection over her challenger, with 57 percent of the vote.

Martinez appealed as a Republican to voters in a purple state with strong Democratic leanings by projecting herself as a reformer. She offered competence in government, an ability to work with the other side, and pride in being Hispanic. A large part of her campaign focused on her background growing up in a hardworking middle-class family. Her parents started a security guard business from scratch. Her mother did the office paperwork in her family's kitchen, while Susana worked as a security guard at night and went to college at the University of Texas, El Paso, which prepared her to earn a law degree from the University of

Oklahoma School of Law and later to be elected as a district attorney in southern New Mexico, a position that she held for fourteen years.

If Susana Martinez represents the future of the Republican Party, so does Mia Love, who won the race for Utah's 4th Congressional District, and became the first black Republican woman in Congress. She joined three other elected black Republicans in Congress, including Will Hurd from Texas and Senator Tim Scott from South Carolina.[33] Love defeated an incumbent moderate Democrat narrowly. She ran as a conservative in a state with only a 1.2 percent black population. A former mayor of Saratoga Springs, Utah, she presented a different image. Haitian-born, she often wears her hair in urban-style braids more common in Brooklyn, where she grew up with her parents after they fled Haiti in the early 1970s with $10 in their pockets. A former Roman Catholic and flight attendant, she converted to Mormonism and moved to Utah, where she met her husband, Jason Love. Her story inspired voters. On the stump she spoke often about her immigrant parents' faith in the American Dream. She frequently quoted her father telling her, "Mia, your mother and I never took a handout. You will not be a burden to society. You will give back." She spoke of a united America, one not divided by income level, gender, or social status. Upon her victory, Love told the crowd, "Regardless of whom you voted for today, I hope you know that I am going to Washington to represent everyone in the district and invite you to engage with me in finding real solutions to the challenges we face as a country."

Having lost the minority vote in 2008 and 2012, Republicans are now building a base of leadership. Following the 2014 midterm elections, there were nine Hispanic Republicans in the House. In the Senate, there were three Hispanic Republicans and only one Hispanic Democrat. Moreover, Republicans are building a strong bench for the future. As of 2015, Republicans controlled thirty-one state legislatures. This translates into 4,115 state senators and state representatives affiliated with the Republican Party, close to a thousand more than the Democratic Party. State legislatures are the training ground for future national leadership. Critical to this leadership training will be the recruitment of Hispanic candidates.

The Republican Party can win the battle for minority voters by presenting itself as a party of reform and inclusion. The Democratic strategy of dividing Americans through identity politics and class war can be countered by a Republican Party that is willing to tap into an American electorate tired of politics as usual and frustrated with a spendthrift government and crony capitalism. The American electorate stands center-right in its politics and distrusts radical social and policy experimentation, but it seeks meaningful, well-considered reform. Ultimately, a politics based on division confronts a strongly rooted sentiment that America is a country founded on individual opportunity, equal protection under the law, and an optimistic faith in its noble experiment in democracy.

3

MILLENNIALS

IN THE 2008 AND 2012 PRESIDENTIAL ELECTIONS, YOUNG VOTERS
went overwhelmingly for Obama. If these voters continue to vote Democratic, the possibility for the GOP to become a majority party is nil.
Does the Republican Party have a future?

- Contrary to media and Democratic Party hype, the youth
  turnout was not high.
- In the new economy, educated youth will have more
  opportunities than ever before. As they mature and enter the
  middle class, these voters can be won by the Republican Party.
- Youth are not uniformly liberal in their political views. Many
  favor small business and the privatization of Social Security.
  Many younger millennials are trending conservative already.

Republicans appeared to be in trouble with the youth vote as early as
2004. In his reelection campaign, George W. Bush won every age cohort
except the 18- to 25-year-old vote. Unconcerned about this warning,
four years later the Republican Party nominated as its presidential candidate a seventy-two-year-old Vietnam War veteran, John McCain, who

sought to make the Iraq War the principal issue of the campaign. Given widespread opposition to the war, especially among the youth, this issue was not going to reclaim the youth vote for the Republican Party. Faced by a youthful Barack Obama, an unpopular war, and an economic meltdown, McCain lost decisively in 2008. Republicans lost the youth vote again in 2012. If Mitt Romney, the Republican candidate, had won the same percentage of the youth vote that George Bush had won against John Kerry in 2004 in the swing states of Ohio, Pennsylvania, and Virginia (45 percent), he would have won the White House in 2012.

The problem faced by the GOP is that today's young voters will constitute tomorrow's majority. A classic rule in American political behavior is that first-time voters for a party tend to continue voting for that same party in later elections. Although the turnout among young voters remained low in 2008 and 2012, young voters who are going to the polls are identifying themselves as Democratic or leaning Democratic. Obama appealed to the youth in 2008 with his anti-war stance, and with his promise for a post-partisan new world. Four years later, many of Obama's young supporters had become disillusioned by his failure to end partisan politics, but any disappointment on their part did not translate into a switch in party affiliation.

For many young Americans, the GOP represents the party of old rich white men concerned about protecting corporate and elite power, maintaining themselves in office, and offering little that is new for the future. The problem for Republicans, however, is not just the messaging, but a failure to utilize new technologies that reach the young. Democratic strategists tapped into social media—Facebook, Twitter, and blogs—that generated enthusiasm and presented Democrats as the party of the future. John McCain did not even use email. Republicans appeared old and tired because of the candidates they were nominating, the issues they were concerned with, and the way they campaigned for office.

Any discussion of the "youth" vote can be misleading, for two reasons. Obviously, the youth vote is transitory. Young voters become older voters within a few years. What concerns young people changes as they get older—culturally, socially, financially, and politically. Second, talk of a particular generation can be misleading. Not everyone in any particular generation shares the same concerns. Within any generation, there are sharp differences of socioeconomic status, educational attainment, race and gender, and life goals. This is especially the case in the millennial generation, those born after 1985. Four in ten members of this generation are nonwhite.

Republicans can win this generation. For all the talk about youthful enthusiasm for Obama, many of the young are not wildly enthusiastic about Obama eight years later. Obama's main contribution to young America was to increase student loan debt. Younger voters who have come of voting age after 2008 and 2012 find Obama disappointing. While the millennial generation expresses support for social issues such as gay marriage and legalization of drugs, like most Americans their primary concerns are about jobs and the economy, healthcare, and opportunity.

Youth allegiance to the Democratic Party is soft, as indicated in both the 2012 presidential election and the 2014 midterm elections. Most millennials remain independent, and the vote is segmented. Divisions within this generation will become more apparent in the future, as many take advantage of the new knowledge economy. Others will be left behind. Republicans can win large sections of this generation—the new middle class—while cutting into those struggling to enter it. Republicans can win the millennial generation with a message that the GOP stands for serious reform, job creation, and challenging politics-as-usual. While seemingly more liberal on economic and some social issues and more secular in their worldview, young Americans are distrustful of big government and divided in their support of capitalist free markets.

At the moment, millennial voters tend to view the Democratic Party more favorably than the Republican Party. It is the only generation in which liberals are not significantly outnumbered by conservatives. Younger generations often hold more idealistic views, but time and experience tend to temper idealism. Millennials are more accepting than older Americans of homosexuality and abortion, but believe that single parenting is not the best way to raise children. They tend to align with the Democratic Party, but in 2012 the GOP made significant gains among younger (as well as older) voters. For example, in 2008, young voters under 30 overwhelmingly identified or leaned Democratic (60 percent). By 2012, this support had shrunk to 52 percent. There is evidence that eighteen-year-old voters in 2012 across the spectrum were more conservative than eighteen-year-olds in 2008. There was still a significant gap in party alignment, but the once-28-point advantage among the under-30 age cohort had shrunk to only a 14-point advantage for Democrats. Among voters over 30, this gap stood at only 2 points in favor of Democrats. Furthermore, young voters, as revealed in a survey conducted by John Volpe at the Harvard Institute of Politics, are growing more disillusioned with and disconnected from Washington.[1] This negative attitude toward politics-as-usual in Washington found expression in the 2014 elections, when young conservatives expressed greater enthusiasm in voting, while the turnout declined among younger voters on the whole, and young liberals in particular.

The media narrative that young people are infatuated with Obama and his party is a manufactured romance at best and a fragmented perception at the very least. In 2012, Obama won young nonwhite voters handily. Nonwhites comprise 42 percent of voters aged 18–29. He won these young voters 60 to 37 percent. What the media left out of the story, however, was that, in contrast to 2008, Obama lost young white voters in this same age group by 10 points, 54 percent to 44 percent.[2]

This narrative, constructed in 2008, began to fall apart by 2013. Indeed, David Leonhardt, writing in the *New York Times* before the midterm elections, warned that younger millennials are "coming of age with a Democratic president who often seems unable to fix the world's problems." By 2015, Leonhardt's observation seemed like a severe understatement. The world's problems had gotten worse.[3]

The number of youth aligned with the Democratic Party began to shrink by 2012, and today's young Democrats are decidedly less enthusiastic about their party.

More recently, a Harvard University Institute of Politics survey of young Americans' attitudes toward politics showed that only 41 percent of 18- to 29-year-olds approved of Obama's performance, while 53 percent disapproved. This drop has occurred among young male and female voters and young white, black, and Hispanic voters. Less than 14 percent of young Americans believe that the country is headed in the right direction.

The erosion of Democratic support among youth can be tied directly to waning enthusiasm for Obama. Second-term presidents usually experience declines in popularity. More worrisome for Democrats, though, has been a rejection by the youth of some of his key programs, particularly the Affordable Care Act. The news gets worse for Democrats in this study: of those young voters who cast ballots for Obama in 2012, 17 percent said they would not support him if they could re-cast their votes today.[4] On specific issues, things don't look any better for the Democrats. When young Americans aged 18–29 were asked if they approved or disapproved of the comprehensive health reform package signed by Obama in 2010, a solid majority disapproved. Only 20 percent said they planned to enroll in the program, and an over-whelming majority (5 to 1) believed that healthcare costs would go up with Obamacare and that the quality of care would decline. Obama has left many young voters disappointed and demoralized. The majority of young voters still lean Democratic, but the youth vote is increasingly up for grabs. Remember that Ronald Reagan won the youth vote in 1980. It can be done again.

THE FACE OF THE NEW PARTY

Tyler B. won election as county chairman of the Republican Party at the age of twenty-six. In winning election he challenged longtime party leaders who were well connected in the metropolitan area. His campaign for election to this important party post rested on a single theme: the party needed fresh faces and youthful leadership, one that could respect different factions and cut across generations. He is articulate, energetic, and especially adroit politically given his relative youth.[5]

Like many of his generation, he was not politically involved as a teenager in the early 2000s. In college, he met a few libertarian students and was invited to discussion groups. There they discussed principles of liberty, the free market, and the Constitution. He described the meetings as "interesting but a little abstract." He decided to become more politically active by joining the College Republicans chapter. Its membership was not much larger than the libertarian discussion group, although there was little crossover between members. The College Republicans drew fewer than a dozen students to their meetings. By pushing the club toward greater campus activism and campaign involvement, he grew the club's membership. He was elected president of the club and got to know party leaders in the state.

When asked why he became interested in Republican Party politics in the first place, he said it was a general concern for where the country was headed. He added that it might be "genetic." His parents were typical yuppies of the 1980s. They were not terribly interested in politics, although they voted Republican. Their main concerns were their jobs and raising a family. When he became involved in politics, however, they told him about his great-grandmother, who had been active in Republican politics in the 1950s. Tyler had never met her, so he was surprised by her story, and it inspired him. When his great-grandmother's husband died in a mining accident, leaving her three children to raise, she went to work in a local five-and-dime store. She worked there her entire life. Even while raising three kids and working full-time, she found time to get involved in politics. She became the district chairperson of the party and was also a grassroots activist. Learning about his great-grandmother encouraged him to pursue his interest in politics.

After college, Tyler used the money he had saved while working in college to go to Europe. He said that while in Europe he found an even deeper appreciation of "American exceptionalism" and the "blessing of the Constitution and the Bill of Rights." He decided to commit himself to political change, not to advance his career but to "advance the country." When he returned home, he began attending Republican legislative district meetings.

Most people attending were older conservatives. Many, he said, were "lazy," enjoying status as party leaders but not doing the "gut" work that makes a party active. A few urged him to run for legislative district chair, even though he was young. He said he did not know much about party structure, but with support from a few older members, he ran and won. As legislative chair, he learned about political donors, and making sure people did what they said they were going to do. Instead of just having speakers at district meetings, he organized workshops on how to do things. The district party became involved in a suburban city council race, and when Republicans swept the election, turning the city Republican for the first time in its history, respect for Tyler grew. The best way to be a political leader is to get votes.

At this point, some people suggested that Tyler run for Republican county chair. In a three-way race, he won. The position does not pay well, and trying to resolve personal differences among precinct chairs, Tea Party activists, and the establishment takes up an immense amount of time. Most of the activists, he points out, are "older people." His message is that the party needs to unify and go out and win elections. He respects what party leaders and local activists have given to the party, but they are "sixty-five and older and not the future of the party."

The key, he believes, is the youth, especially college youth. The party needs to have websites, blogs, and Facebook pages. The Left, he maintains, has outorganized conservatives. The Left has organized for action with groups such as MoveOn.org. Republicans need to organize for action as well, sharing events and talking about leadership opportunities, organizing nuclei groups, and reaching out to other organizations.

He is involved in a national project, Turning Point, to recruit the young. When he was running for president, Ron Paul began organizing the youth, but he stopped doing this. The goal of Turning Point is to change the face of the Republican Party. Tyler is traveling across the country meeting other county chairs and "lots of state chairs" to talk about grassroots activism. "Too many state chairs," he observes, "only look at the bigwigs in the party. Less attention is given to the grassroots and to winning the youth. At the same time, the party has too many 'haywire' groups that are easily portrayed by the media as nutty extremists."

Tyler is convinced that the party today thinks too much about "messaging." The message is important, he thinks, but mechanics are even more important. Focusing on activism brings together different alignments in the party. Better relations can be developed between libertarians and conservatives, religious and nonreligious. But the future rests, he emphasizes, on winning the youth with a broad message about civil liberties, the national debt, and governmental intrusions restraining job creation and opportunities for all Americans. Most millennials lean libertarian, whether they see themselves as on the right or on the left. These libertarian sentiments need to be translated into deeper political beliefs.

He adds, "This does not mean that Republicans need to come up with better slogans or just better messaging. The goal should be to take issues of concern, get students and the young involved in grassroots movements, and then bring them to the party. Republicans don't need to organize these organizations, but they should support them and get involved in them." This is what his involvement with Turning Point is really about. Its slogan is "Government Sucks." Through this slogan, Turning Point activists are involved in education and campaigns about regulations and civil liberties. The goal, he says, is to organize the activists, and then the activists will change the party. The older generation of the party needs to move over and stop occupying chairs. "This new party is going to be about serious reform, not just the politics for winning office, a party of the people, and not just crony capitalists."

Whether Tyler and others will be successful remains to be seen. His generation faces real opportunities, but also some serious obstacles.

THE MILLENNIAL FUTURE

Young Americans ages 20–44 make up a greater proportion of the population than they did in 1972. In 1972 the young made up 32.7 percent of the population, compared to 36.5 percent today. This generation will replace the boomer generation.

The economy that millennials will inherit is going to be a knowledge-based economy. Even during the doldrums of the Great Recession, knowledge workers saw their incomes increase. Goods-producing workers have not seen an increase in their incomes. As a result, knowledge workers—those with technical skills in the sciences, mathematics, computer sciences, and quantitative analysis—are finding jobs in a tight labor market in which employers are competing for employees. Today, a new auto factory can produce 300,000 vehicles per year with just 1,300 workers. Twenty years ago, there would have been 5,000 workers. These knowledge workers have skills that most of the American workforce lack. American economic productivity relies heavily on creative workers with skills gained through education and experience. While the percentage of GDP resulting from manufacturing has not declined, the manufacturing sector is producing more with fewer employees. As a result, demand for unskilled workers has decreased.

What does this entail for millennials entering the new economy in the twenty-first century? The answer is obvious: those with high educational attainment will find jobs with higher incomes, live more comfortably, and lead healthier and longer lives. They will replace the white, mostly male, boomer generation as leaders in business and public affairs. Among those lacking education and the knowledge skills that come with it, many will be left struggling in a world of sharp income and wealth inequalities. These disparities will manifest themselves socially and politically.

Labor participation in the United States stands at a pitiful 62 percent in 2015, the lowest in forty years. Many Americans have dropped out of the workforce and rely on an array of social services to get by. In 2013, the Census Bureau reported that 109 million Americans were receiving benefits from means-tested federal programs. This figure included traditional types of welfare such as Temporary Assistance for Needy Families (TANF), as well as food stamps and a food program called Women, Infants, and Children (WIC). These 109 million Americans included children and older Americans, who cannot work. Furthermore, many receiving means-tested benefits are working. For example, of the 47 million Americans who receive food stamps, over 61 percent work.[6] The point is that those on welfare are working, and Republican candidates should not dredge up "welfare queen" myths to inflame voters.

The soaring costs of maintaining large numbers of Americans on government dependence will have two major social and political consequences for future American voters. As older Americans enroll in Medicare and begin receiving Social Security old-age benefits, tensions between the boomer and millennial generations will increase. Second, as disparities increase within the millennial generation between those with high educational attainment and those without, political differences within this generation will sharpen. It is easy to identify oneself as liberal when one is young, supported by a part-time job, parents, and student loans. Once one is working in a full-time job, paying taxes, and making political decisions that actually affect one's life in readily apparent ways, being a liberal takes on a different meaning. One is reminded of the extremely liberal medical student who started voting conservative as soon as he paid his first income tax bill as a high-paid surgeon.

America spends more on primary, secondary, and higher education, as a percentage of GDP, than any European nation. Proportionately, more Americans have graduated from secondary school than in any European country, although younger Europeans are catching up.[7] The view that we are not spending enough on education should be compared to what Europeans spend. The fact is that we spend a lot on education. Two caveats are in order, however: while many Americans are going to college, fewer than 60 percent who enter college will finish in six years. And those who do will be heavily in debt, on average more than $30,000 per student.

The question is whether this expenditure is paying off. The answer has profound consequences for the future of the American economy and politics. While educational disparities are already apparent within the millennial generation, there are even greater educational disparities between millennials in America and their counterparts in nineteen other nations. These disparities have deep implications, not only for the ability of members of this young generation to get jobs in a globally competitive workforce, but also because the nation needs revenues from their taxes to pay its bills on the national debt run up during the Great Recession, to pay for the soaring costs of health care, and to prevent creating an insolvent dependency state.

American youth are not being prepared for a globally competitive economy. A 2015 study by the Educational Testing Service (ETS) reveals the failure of our educational system to train future workers for an increasingly knowledge-based economy.[8] Competency in literacy, numeracy, and problem solving is essential for a successful, increasingly complex economy. Those economies without a workforce skilled in these areas will not be able to compete, and individuals without these skills will have the odds stacked against them.

The ETS study shows just how woefully handicapped our youth are in developing these skills. The figures are startling:

- Literacy: American millennials rank near the bottom of the twenty-two participating countries, above only Spain and Italy.
- Numeracy: American millennials rank lowest, above only Spain and Italy.
- Problem solving: American millennials ranked last, along with the Slovak Republic, Ireland, and Poland.

The details of this report are even more dismaying. Most American millennials fail to reach minimum standards in reading literacy and numeracy. One half of America's millennials failed to reach the minimum level in literacy and 64 percent failed to reach the minimum level in numeracy. Also disturbing is the poor showing among top students. American millennials in the top 90th percentile scored lower than the other top-scoring millennials in every other country except their peers in Spain. Worse yet, the scores of U.S. millennials with the highest levels of educational attainment were less than high school counterparts in almost every other participating country. These numbers should be a wake-up call, and things are not getting better. The youngest age cohort of U.S. millennials (16- to 24-year-olds), who could be in the workforce until 2065, ranked dead last among their peers in numeracy and were at the bottom in problem solving.

Educational attainment is going to be critical for those millennials who will succeed in the future. The United States is graduating more students with college degrees, especially young white and minority women. As the boomer generation retires, these graduates will replace them. Labor scarcity for highly skilled workers will drive up the demand, salaries, and opportunities for those with high educational attainment. The question raised by the ETS study is whether these graduates will have the skills necessary for a competitive economy, or whether American businesses will have to import better-trained, foreign-educated workers. The high-tech industry already recruits from abroad. While immigrant techies thrive, poorly educated native-born Americans will tend their yards, care for their children, and flip their burgers. If this proves to be the case, the immigration issue might take on a different slant. In the meantime, the millennial generation faces its own internal disparities.

Along with educational disparities evident in high school and college graduation rates, other socioeconomic and cultural differences reveal that the "youth" vote is not monolithic. While pollsters look at age cohorts, Republican strategists looking at winning the youth vote should understand that the millennial generation is segmented in terms of marriage, single parenting, cultural values, and political engagement. These differences will become more pronounced as this generation matures. Republican strategists need to mobilize these segments and convince them that their interests rest with the Republican Party.

★　★　★　★　★

Marriage: American youth are marrying later and having fewer children. About 25 percent of the millennial generation will never marry. This trend has economic, social, and cultural consequences, all of which frame current and future politics. While a fierce debate has occurred among social scientists and media pundits over the importance of marriage for maintaining social stability and raising children, marital status influences political behavior.

Being married in one's twenties or thirties is typical. Furthermore, the proportion of never-married people has risen from 16 percent to 35 percent. Fewer marriages mean fewer children. In 1976, approximately 10 percent of women ended their childbearing years with no children. By 2000 that proportion had risen to 19 percent, while those having four or more children declined from 36 percent to 11 percent from the mid-1970s to 2000.[9] Does this mean that obligations to children and general social commitments in the future will decline? Perhaps, but changing attitudes toward marriage and family among the youth challenge Republicans campaigning on "pro-family" values.

Large numbers of voters, especially in red states, support this agenda, so Republicans should not run from core party values. On the other hand, this agenda won't attract large numbers of young voters.

At this point in their lives, large numbers of the young do not believe marriage is important. Two-thirds of those between the ages of 18 and 29 (67 percent) believe that society is better off if people have priorities other than marriage and children. This response is perhaps not surprising coming from a young person who has other priorities. While such a negative attitude toward marriage might dismay a member of the older generation, there is a good deal of inconsistency among the young (not surprisingly, since the young often do not have well-conceived worldviews). Most Americans (68 percent), including the young, believe that if couples plan to stay together, they should marry. This is especially the case if they plan to have children. Never-married blacks place an even higher importance on marriage if couples plan to stay together. Most young Americans believe that raising children is best within a traditional marriage.

Furthermore, most of the young expect to get married eventually. For all the talk about changing cultural mores, what young males and young females look for in a spouse remains pretty traditional. Young, never-married females (78 percent) say that what is most important to them in looking for a spouse or partner is finding someone who has a steady job. They want a provider for their family. Never-married men look for someone who shares their ideas about raising children. They look for good mothers for their children. Some things don't change.

★　★　★　★　★

Single parenting: One of the greatest causes of disparities among the younger generation is single parenting. Over the last decade, out-of-wedlock births have declined for teenagers, including minorities, by about 20 percent. So why do we have more single parents and out-of-wedlock births than ever before? While teenage out-of-wedlock births have fallen, the number of unwed mothers aged 25–34 has soared by 70 percent. These unwed mothers are getting pregnant unintentionally or "semi-intentionally" even if contraceptive resources are available.

Out-of-wedlock births have soared for all racial and ethnic groups; they cut across socioeconomic lines, and cement continued social inequality. The issue of out-of-wedlock births is both race- and class-based. The groups with the highest rate of out-of-wedlock births are those struggling economically. The out-of-wedlock birthrate for non-Hispanic whites stands at about 29 percent, for blacks at 72 percent, and for Hispanics at 54 percent.[10]

Nonmarital births to college-educated women are less than 10 percent. This rate has not risen much since the 1970s. Nonmarital births to black college graduates are about 25 percent and have fallen by a third over the last twenty years. Nonmarital birthrates have soared among the economically disadvantaged, especially among less-educated women.

The problem for many children born to unwed mothers, whether white or black, is that they are more likely to live in dysfunctional communities. In these communities, kids have fewer adults supervising them, providing support networks, watching out for them, or advising them how to advance themselves socially or economically. They are more likely to suffer abuse and less likely to develop what the sociologist Robert Putnam describes as "noncognitive skills"—self-control, emotional stability, and optimism in the face of challenges.

Out-of-wedlock births and their destructive consequences for children raised in single-parent households are cultural issues that cannot be solved solely by politicians.

Public expenditures caused by out-of-wedlock births, however, are a political issue. The burden of paying for welfare, drug programs, and law enforcement falls on taxpayers now and in the future. Republicans need to convince voters that they are a party of opportunity and meaningful reform, including welfare reform.

In the 1990s, conservatives and neoliberals convinced Americans that welfare needed reform to bring the poor out of a state of dependency. A Republican-controlled House pushed President Bill Clinton to undertake meaningful federal welfare reform. Many progressives squawked and warned of the cataclysmic effects of reform. Nonetheless, reform and a prospering economy led to a drop in welfare rolls. In New York City, the work-based approach of Mayors Rudy Giuliani and Michael Bloomberg to welfare reform shrank welfare rolls from more than 1 million recipients to fewer than 350,000 by 2013, even in the midst of the Great Recession.[11]

★ ★ ★ ★ ★

Cultural Values: Today's youth are more secular and more progressive than their elders on many social issues. The majority of young voters support gay marriage and legalization of marijuana. Yet to paint the youth vote as monolithic can be misleading. Not all young voters are secular; many remain deeply religious. Many don't support gay marriage or legalization of marijuana. Moreover, young voters are not stereotypically progressive on social issues.

Abortion, though, is another matter altogether. Support for making abortion broadly illegal is growing fastest among young adults. Democrats know this, so they want to make the "war on women" about contraception, not abortion. Gallup surveys of public opinion trends on abortion conducted in 2010 and again in 2015 show that young adults (aged 18–49) and middle-aged adults (aged 50–64) have converged in their opposition to unrestricted legal abortion. For both age groups, support for abortion-on-demand stands at around 25 percent. The sharpest decline in support for unrestricted abortion has come in the 18- to 29-year-old group, dropping from a high of 36 percent in 1994 to 24 percent in 2009. Moreover, the support for "illegal under all circumstances" has risen in this age cohort from 14 percent to 23 percent. Those supporting legal abortion only under certain circumstances represent a majority (51 percent) of young Americans.[12]

Even more disconcerting for Democrats are surveys of teenagers. As early as 2003, a Gallup poll showed that over 87 percent of teens aged 13–17 thought abortion was morally wrong. Among teens who attended church, 91 percent believed abortion should be legal only under certain circumstances (51 percent) or illegal in all circumstances (40 percent).

These surveys show that the American electorate, including the young, remains divided on the abortion issue. For this reason, abortion can be a no-winner issue for both parties. Young voters who vote are not uniformly liberal. Republican candidates should not flee from principled positions in order to placate a stereotypical view of the young voter.

Nor should Republican candidates assume that every young voter is nonreligious.[13] Support for traditional religion, church attendance, and the religious basis for a good society has declined significantly among today's youth. Yet many millennials remain deeply religious. In particular, those who are marrying and having children, albeit a decreasing number, are returning to church. These young Roman Catholics and evangelical Christians tend to be conservatives.

The number of self-identified "conservatives" has increased among those going to church, especially the young.

Surveys show that Americans have become less religious over the last four decades. Yet numbers showing this general decline can be misleading. Evangelical Protestant church membership remains relatively steady. Although there has been a slight decline in the growth rate in recent years, these churches are still attractive to many American youth. Religious attendance of younger Americans in numbers and percentages is not that much lower than it was in the 1970s, although this was a low point in church attendance in the post–World War II period. Many young Americans have turned to evangelical Protestantism and traditional Catholicism as a way to bring order and belief to their lives. Although religious affiliation and church attendance have declined significantly among Roman Catholics, Catholics have a higher proportion of young adults than do any of the Protestant traditions—around 55 percent. A new generation of St. John Paul II Catholics has emerged, playing important leadership and lay roles in the Church. Moreover, many of these young people are much more conservative on social issues such as homosexuality, homosexual marriage, and abortion than the older generation of evangelicals.

Critical to this religious revival among today's youth is marriage. Married men and women are more likely to attend religious services than their unmarried peers. Young never-married men and never-married women are less likely to attend service regularly. Women—Catholic and Protestant—attend church services more regularly than do men. Women who attend religious services tend to be married (60 percent). Most have children (73 percent). Put more directly, those who go to church regularly are likely to be married and have children. They also tend to be younger. Adults aged 21–45 make up 40 percent of adherents of every major faith.

Young people who go to church regularly tend to be more involved in their communities and give social and national issues a higher value than money. While secularized youth worry about social justice, they tend not to act on their beliefs. Princeton University sociologist Robert Wuthnow, in looking at social survey data, finds that among secularized youth, concerns for social justice (war, economic inequality, climate change) remain abstract. Few of the secularized youth are involved in political or social causes. They voice concerns about these abstract concepts, but they do not act on them. It is a lot easier to text righteous indignation about injustice than to get involved.

As Wuthnow discovered, young married evangelical Christians place a higher priority on helping the poor than do young non-churchgoers. These young married evangelicals are involved in their communities through food kitchens, clothing drives, tutoring the disadvantaged, and so forth. Young married evangelical Protestants and young traditional Catholics also tend to vote.

Yet whether secular or religious, the young are looking for leadership, and many are dissatisfied with the current social and political culture. Most are not voting, however.

★　★　★　★　★

Political Engagement: For all the media hoopla about the youth rallying to Obama in 2008 and 2012, most eligible young voters did not vote. The media were misled by the large number of young people who attended Obama rallies. Turnout remains low among young voters for both Democrats and Republicans. In 2008, 48.5 percent of eligible Americans aged 18–24 voted. In 2012, this dropped to 41.2 percent. While young voters went Democratic by large numbers in both 2008 and 2012 and might have played a critical role in some key states in both elections, the fact remains that young voters are less engaged in the political process than older voters. In fact, voter turnout among those 65 and older rose in 2012 to 71.9 percent from 70.3 percent in 2008.[14]

The youth vote would be larger if all the eligible adults born after 1985 voted. As a proportion of the eligible voting population, the youth make up about 26 percent of the age-eligible electorate. By 2020, they could make up over 36 percent of the age-eligible population. If the standard rule in political science holds, people as they grow older tend to get more involved in elections. Being married, having children, and owning a home all predict greater voter participation.

Given the number of millennials who consider themselves aligned with the Democrats and view themselves as progressive on social issues and government involvement, this bodes ill for Republicans. Republican strategists should not count on the continued apathy of eligible millennial voters. They are voting at about the same rate as did boomers when they were young. In 1976, the vote among 18- to 30-year-olds was 50 percent, 2 points less than the 52 percent of millennials who voted in 2008. Worth noting is that in 2008, boomers (44- to 62-year-olds) who did not vote when they were young turned out at a rate of 60 percent.

Yet there are some signs of light for Republicans as they look at this generation's future political participation. While college students went overwhelmingly for Obama, it would be a mistake to view this bloc as overwhelmingly liberal.[15] On the contrary, self-identified liberal college students entering college in 2012 decreased by 4 points for men, down to 20 percent, and 5 points for women, to 32 percent, from 2008. Those identifying themselves as conservative stayed steady from 2008, with about 20 percent of women and 26 percent of men. The political position that has increased among first-year college students is identification as "middle-of-the-road," an increase of 4 points since 2008. This shift to "middle-of-the road" reflects, in part, Obama's decline in the share of the youth vote (30-and-under) in 2012, from 64 percent to 60 percent, a drop of 4 points.

What all this suggests is that the young adults who will take the place of the boomer generation will vote as they get older, but large numbers might well be as apathetic as the electorate has been throughout the twentieth century. With rare exceptions, voter turnout has declined throughout the twentieth century. Those who do vote will be divided politically. Confronted with the high costs of maintaining social programs for the poor and the elderly, middle-aged voters of tomorrow will be less concerned about the younger generation or the older generation. Every indication is that these future voters will be just as polarized as the current electorate. They will be ideologically divided, just as current voters are, between those who are educated and those who are not; those who are married with children and those who have remained single; and those who depend on government and those who do not.

The millennial generation manifests an even deeper distrust of government and politicians than the general American public. Their distrust of government conflicts, however, with their specific view that government should be doing more. This confusion is perhaps a sign of youth, and is also found in the general public, which often wants the government to do more but generally distrusts American political institutions and politicians. Trust in government, politicians, and especially Barack Obama declined significantly from 2008 to 2014. By the 2014 midterm elections, more than three in five Americans aged 18–30 believed that political involvement rarely has tangible results. Furthermore, close to 58 percent of young voters, a rise by 7 points from 2008, believed that "elected officials don't seem to have the same priorities I have."[16] Less than a third have confidence in the president, Congress, the Supreme Court, the federal government, the United Nations, state or local government, Wall Street, and the media.

Yet even this acknowledgment of the deep distrust of governmental institutions can be misleading. While millennials distrust Wall Street, they agree that the country's strength rests largely in the success of American business.[17] They are less critical of American business than are members of the boomer generation. While they are less skeptical of the effectiveness of government to solve social problems, they are not wild about the welfare state and the expansion of the safety net over the last fifty years. There has been a steady decline among this generation since 2007 in support for federal assistance for the poor. In this respect, they are not different from other age cohorts. Furthermore, most millennials (56 percent) call for Social Security reform through the privatization of accounts. They want a complete overhaul of the system.[18] They are divided on cutting benefits, but most believe that Social Security will be bankrupt by the time they reach retirement age (which shows how insecure many are about Social Security). Moreover, statistics on millennials favoring larger government can be misleading in other ways. As a whole, more than half (52 percent) favor bigger government with more services. Yet only 44 percent of white millennials do.[19]

Not that many millennials are working yet. Only 66 percent of adults aged 18–29 are employed or seeking employment. Many, in fact, are not working and are underemployed and in debt. The average debt for college students stands at about $30,000, nearly triple what it was in 1989. While income for households headed by adults over 65 grew 109 percent from 1967 to 2012, income for households headed by adults younger than 35 grew in the same period only 29 percent. Millennials are being left behind in the new economy.[20]

Republicans will need to convince eligible voters that politics does matter. They need to excite the apathetic and win over young Americans who once voted for Obama and convince them that the GOP is the party of the future. Millennials do not trust government, are leery of the runaway-welfare state, think Social Security needs reforming, and are basically supportive of American business. These are Republican messages that can attract young voters in the future. Learning some lessons from the last two presidential elections and the 2014 midterms is the place to start.

HOW THE REPUBLICANS LOST THE
YOUTH VOTE IN 2008 AND 2012

Obama slam-dunked the youth vote in 2008 and 2012. His message of inclusion and multiculturalism was appealing. He was also new and exciting. He was youthful enough to shoot hoops. Obama was a perfect example of what young voters thought a president should be like. Young voters went for similar types of candidates with Kennedy in 1960 and Clinton in 1992. The Republican loss of the youth vote reflected its nominating of candidates, John McCain and Mitt Romney, who lacked much youth appeal. This, though, proved to be the least of their problems. Obama's campaign carried an attractive message for youth, and it outmaneuvered Republicans in organizational mechanics. Obama's appeal to youth was natural: he not only offered generalized "hope and change" with his promise to bring in a post-partisan era, he was anti-war, youthful, glib, and charismatic, and he reached the youth through social media. Republicans prided themselves that, in 2012, the youth vote for Obama declined by 2 points and tried to reassure themselves that voter turnout among the youth had not increased much from previous presidential elections and had declined slightly from 2008.

Obama's campaign understood the importance of voter registration among the youth. The goal was not simply to register more young voters across the country, but to target youth registration in key swing states or vulnerable red states that could go blue. The campaign took aim at college towns to tap into a reserve of potential voters who could be decisive in critical states. The Obama campaign first deployed this strategy in the 2008 primaries. Boulder, Colorado; Bloomington, Indiana; Gainesville, Florida; Madison, Wisconsin; and Athens, Ohio, provided low-hanging fruit for increasing the youth vote.

Obama understood the importance of registering new voters. As a community organizer he had worked with grassroots activist groups, some of them quite radical, in voter registration drives. In 1992, he had run a major voter registration campaign in Chicago to attract new black and Hispanic voters. Obama's Project Vote registered 150,000 new voters. The success of this campaign brought Obama to the attention of powerful Illinois Democrats and helped launch his political career, first in the Illinois Senate and then in the U.S. Senate in 2004.

When he decided to seek the presidential nomination in 2007, he understood that if he was going to defeat his main rivals for the nomination, Hillary Clinton and John Edwards, new voters had to be enlisted in the primaries. The message was important (although most of his speeches were vague on specifics), but this alone could not win him the nomination. His campaign pioneered online and social-media campaign techniques. One of the campaign's most important innovations was a website that allowed small donors to contribute to the campaign.[21] Once a donor gives, they vote for a candidate. Obama developed a major Facebook presence, and later developed powerful email and text-messaging services. In developing this new media capacity, he hired young developers from Howard Dean's 2004 campaign and a developer of the Orbitz travel site. These tech-savvy twentysomethings brought ability and agility to politics in an age of new technology.

Rivals, first in the primary battle against Clinton and then in the general election against John McCain, were outmatched. While Obama's young techs utilized new technology, his rivals employed robocalls and direct mail. If the election was a boxing contest based on technical skill, the referee would have ended the fight in the first round.

Obama's election marked a triumph for progressives. Too much was made of this triumph at the time, however. The electorate, though bigger, remained surprisingly similar to the ones that had twice elected Bill Clinton and George W. Bush, neither of whom was a progressive. There was neither a dramatic swing to the left nor any other sign that a progressive era had begun. Obama inspired many young voters to action, but voters under the age of 30 accounted for about 18 percent of the electorate in 2008—barely up from the 17 percent they represented in 2004. To be sure, he performed well among these voters, receiving 66 percent of their vote. By contrast, the previous Democratic presidential nominee, John Kerry, won only 54 percent of young voters in 2004.

★　★　★　★　★

Youth rallies for Obama and their volunteer efforts on his behalf were important. The enthusiasm generated by the young for Obama projected an aura that this was not "politics-as-usual." Carefully orchestrated youth rallies appeared to give substance to Obama's message of "hope and change." Young voters, looking for something new, reinforced an image that Obama was a Washington outsider. As a result, thousands of college students became involved in his campaign as volunteers, knocking on doors, making telephone calls, tweeting to their friends, and using social media. The Obama campaign did not use blanket bombing in advertising and outreach. Having developed sophisticated databases that provided every sort of information—party preferences, previous voting records, age, occupation, race, ethnicity, consumer patterns down to books read—the Obama campaign employed young volunteers to target voters. The campaign also hired a young talented artist to design a postmodern poster that was sold at campaign events and online.

Jonathan Kopp, a partner with SS+K, managed the communication agency that directed Obama's youth communications.[22] He began working to set the campaign's brand among youth before Obama's announcement in 2007. For twenty-one months, he pushed the Obama brand as young, charismatic, and personifying change. The message was based on deep research that young people were frustrated and wanted change. The young are leaning toward Obama but they needed to be convinced to vote for him. The key, he said, was not to "over-market." The young are savvy to marketing. They can embrace a brand, but only as long as they can trust it. The social media campaign pushed frustration over the Iraq War, gas prices, and healthcare. They linked these issues to voter registration with the tagline "Don't get mad. Get registered."

In 2012, the Obama reelection campaign utilized the skills and techniques developed four years earlier. Running as an incumbent president gave Obama an immediate advantage over his rival in 2012.

Throughout his first term, he continued to campaign, often looking more like a candidate running for office than the president of the United States. He spent one out of every nine days of his first term on college campuses. Obama supporters organized year-round registration drives and sponsored events with celebrities such as Scarlett Johansson and Pitbull. Once the official reelection campaign was launched, college offices were set up in swing states.[23] The one problem he faced in keeping the youth vote was that he could not claim that he was running against Washington, D.C. He was Washington, D.C. He ran against Romney and the rich—ignoring the fact that Wall Street fat cats supported him in 2008 and 2012. Most Wall Street money went to the Democrats in both elections.

In 2014, young voters were less enthusiastic about Obama and the Democratic Party. They had been mobilized for change in Washington, but Obama now was in the White House. Obama needed to convince young voters that change had happened and with their support would continue. He heated up his social media campaign, placing even greater emphasis on Facebook, the favored medium among many youth.[24] Nonetheless, much of the enthusiasm of the youth was gone, after having placed extraordinary faith in Obama's message in 2008. Many now saw him as just another politician.

Obama's campaign returned to social media to promote his reelection. College students became a major focus of the campaign. The Obama campaign understood that young people in college or with college experience were almost twice as likely to vote as those without college experience.[25] College students were also easier to reach because they were concentrated around schools. The Obama team hosted events around colleges in key states and then bused people to early voting polls in swing states such as Ohio. Romney's campaign put minimal specific efforts into winning the youth vote. When a *Boston Globe* reporter asked the Romney campaign if it was doing anything similar, a Romney spokesman replied, "The juice on that is not worth the squeeze."[26]

Young voters did not turn out in the numbers they had in 2008. Most voted for Obama when they did vote. Their vote proved critical in the swing states of Ohio, Florida, Pennsylvania, and Virginia, where

61 percent to 66 percent of youth voted for Obama.[27] If Romney had been able to split the youth vote 50–50, he would have won the election.

Romney's loss of the youth vote, combined with the loss of the minority and women's vote, proved decisive. But there were glimmers of hope and change for Republicans. Romney won white 18- to 29-year-olds, taking 51 percent of their vote. In 2008 this cohort went for Obama, 54 percent to 44 percent. Moreover, Romney did well in polling among non-college students, but many did not turn up at the polls on Election Day. The Romney campaign might have benefited from reaching out to these hard-to-reach voters more.

A TURNING POINT FOR REPUBLICANS?

By 2014, Republican candidates knew that they could not neglect any segment of the vote. Voter turnout among young voters in midterms is considerably lower than in presidential elections, which we know is not high in the first place. Republicans swept the midterm elections in 2014, and picked up 1 point from the 2010 midterm among the 18- to 29-year-old vote, even though it still broke for Democrats, 54 percent to 43 percent. This was a daunting 11 percent margin, but the good sign was that the Democratic margins among the youth were lower than in 2008 or 2012.[28] In key swing state U.S. Senate and governor contests, the youth vote ranged between 9 and 15 percent of total voters. In most key races, the youth vote favored Democrats by slight margins. In the Arkansas U.S. Senate race, Republican nominee Tom Cotton had the widest loss among youth, with a 14-point margin (53 percent to 39 percent), while Mitch McConnell in his heady reelection victory won the youth vote by a full 6 points (51 percent to 45 percent) and Tom Tillis, the Republican candidate, lost the under-25 vote by only 3 points.

As Republicans look forward to 2016 and afterward, the youth vote cannot be ignored, any more than Hispanic and minority or women voters. Young Republicans in particular offered a searing indictment that the party had failed to win young voters. In 2013 the College Republican National Committee issued a report, "Grand Old Party for a Brand New Generation." The sixty-page report criticized the party on its branding, the propensity of party candidates to use polarizing language, and its singular focus on downsizing big government and cutting taxes.[29] The report noted that Republicans' primary focus on cutting taxes and reducing the size of government failed to resonate with young voters. It concluded that this kind of agenda fails (and will fail) to attract new blood to the party. The report also noted that bashing "big government" did not play well with focus groups.

On a more positive note, the report found that on many economic issues the young, who might not have voted for Republicans, were on the same page. Surveys and focus groups showed that there was deep support for entrepreneurship, encouraging small business, and slashing government funding. The central point of the report is that the GOP needs to translate its pro-business, economic opportunity, and individual rights policies into the language readily understood by young voters. Republicans need to develop new rhetoric and language that will appeal to young voters.

Two policy areas might prove difficult for the GOP to address with young voters, while keeping their base: gay rights and foreign policy. Most young people support gay marriage; and most young voters oppose an expanded military. Terrorism did not rank high on their concerns at the moment. Of course, opinions changed in late 2015. On the issue of gay marriage, young voters probably won't change their minds. Foreign policy and terrorism will prove different, depending on the circumstances.

The message that the Republican Party conveys is important, but messaging and branding are only part of a general strategy of invigorating the party. Grassroots mobilization is critical. Organizations such as Turning Point USA are equally important.[30] Formed by a young activist, Charlie Kirk, Turning Point USA is a national student movement to mobilize the young behind the principles of "fiscal responsibility, free markets, and limited government." It is working outside the party. This nonpartisan organization is now found in various capacities on more than eight hundred high school and college campuses. The organization is modeled on left-wing activist groups such as MoveOn .org and Organizing for Action. Led by seventeen full-time staffers, it seeks to mobilize young students who don't necessarily identify them-selves as conservative. Door-to-door organizing, events, and discussion groups aim to spark conversations about free markets, organize protests against Obamacare, and register voters. As Kirk says of the campaign, "This is 'activism of substance.'" Field activists are required to make at least 1,500 student contacts per semester. Major registration drives have been launched in key swing states. While Turning Point USA does not match the muscle of leftist activist groups, it shows how conservatives (Republicans) can rally young voters to an agenda of reform.

THE CASE FOR REFORM

Millennials are going to face a future of debt, both personal and na-tional. Young college students are now saddled with more than $1 tril-lion in college debt. A college student today has to borrow six times more per year than the average student did in the 1970s. This personal debt precludes most students from buying a home after leaving school or having much in the way of discretionary income, even if they do find a good-paying job. As if this were not enough weight to carry, the mil-lennial generation and their children, who won't be many, are going to be left with a huge national debt and runaway entitlement budget defi-cits from paying Social Security and Medicare costs for their parents and grandparents. The International Monetary Fund (IMF) estimated last year that in order to pay for these entitlement obligations, all taxes would have to rise by 35 percent "immediately and permanently," while all federal entitlement benefits would have to be cut by another 35 per-cent. Economists estimate that within thirty years, government obliga-tions will exceed 100 percent of everyone's earnings.

Looming debts incurred by boomers, with expectations that they will be paid by millennials and their children, create a generational conflict as to how to pay these costs. Boomers expect to live comfortably in retirement and have their healthcare costs paid by the government. Tax burdens will fall mostly on working millennials. The political ramifications of this divide remain unclear; what is clear is that mil-lennials will pay the high costs through increased taxes. What cuts across generational lines is a simple fact of political life: people don't like paying higher taxes, once they have to start paying them. Young millennials might tell pollsters now that they want more government involvement in their lives and do not mind paying higher taxes for the common good. Once reality strikes, however, and they discover that there is more government intrusion and they are paying taxes, their opinions will change. If there was ever a reason for Republicans to stand as a party of reform willing to tackle the national debt, budget deficits, and job creation, this should be the time to do so. Greater efficiency in government is a necessity. Reform is demanded. It is in the national interest, and in the political interest of the Republican Party.

4

BOOMERS

THE GOP WON OLDER VOTERS IN THE 2012 AND 2014 ELECTIONS, after having lost them in 2008. This is good news, but building a sustainable majority party based on older voters has its obvious limitations. Older voters provide both advantages and disadvantages to the Republican Party.

- Older voters have swung heavily back to the Republican Party. These voters are informed and turn out more for elections.
- This base of older voters can win state elections, but it is not large enough to win presidential elections.
- Older voters are not uniformly conservative, but younger baby boomers and those 46–61 years of age are generally conservative.
- Older voters tend to support downsizing government and fiscal responsibility, but are hesitant to reform Social Security and Medicare, the two drivers of budget deficits.

Boomers bring good news and bad news for the Republican Party: the good news is that this generation is increasingly leaning Republican;

the bad news is that many boomers won't be around to vote in twenty years, so this generation does not offer a long-term solution to the Republican Party's woes with younger minority and female voters. While boomers will one day leave the scene, the elderly are not going away soon. In 2030, when all the baby boomers (those born between 1945 and 1964) will be 65 or older, more than 20 percent of the total population will be elderly. And while the number of boomers declines through mortality, this shift to an increasingly older population will continue. Projections are that by 2056, the population over 65 will be larger than the population under 18. Republicans cannot ignore older voters now or in the future. They have clout from their sheer numbers and because they turn out for elections.

Winning the boomer generation offers a test case for how well the Republican Party is going to do in the future. The one positive sign is that many boomers—combined with the "Silent Generation," those born shortly before or during World War II—are leaning conservative, and they turn out to vote at higher rates than any other age cohort. Joining boomers and the Silent Generation are Generation Xers, born between 1966 and 1980, who also lean Republican. These older voters tend to favor smaller government and fiscal responsibility—with two big exceptions: Social Security and Medicare, the two entitlement programs that threaten to bankrupt the nation. Social Security and Medicare are flies in the ointment for the Republican prescription of downsizing government and enforcing fiscal responsibility. Older voters might agree that balanced budgets, smaller government, and lower taxes are desirable, but without serious and thorough entitlement reform, budgets are not going to get smaller. Federal programs will continue to grow, and lower taxes will be a dream unfulfilled.

Republican proposals to reform Social Security have always left them open to negative attacks. Who can forget the TV spot depicting a Republican throwing a grandmother in a wheelchair off a cliff? Social Security and Medicare programs need reform. They are headed toward bankruptcy. A few Democrats are entitlement reform deniers, in the face of a mountain of government and economic reports projecting an impending crisis. Nancy Pelosi, the leader of the Democratic Party in

Congress, has cynically said that taxes will just have to be raised. But it is not just that these programs are headed toward bankruptcy; the costs of maintaining these programs will blow up the national debt. Reform is in the national interest. The question is, is it in the Republican Party's political interest to stand for reform?

Even small steps in this direction allowed Democrats to paint Republicans as a party of the uncaring corporate rich. Democrats presented voters with a portrait of their opponents as a heartless, ruthless party of the elite who sought ungainly wealth at the expense of minorities in the inner city; undocumented immigrants fulfilling their dreams; debt-ridden, underemployed, and war-weary millennials struggling to get a foothold in a bad job market; and anxious elderly people worried about how they were going to afford the costs of old age.

Standing for meaningful and responsible reform, trying to convey complex issues to a generally uninformed electorate, and not alienating one bloc of voters to win another, are no mean feats. But unless Republicans can accomplish these feats, they might as well get in a cart and roll off a cliff.

The first step for Republicans in determining their future is to understand that winning older voters is just as important as winning Hispanic and female voters. A presidential election cannot be won with just older voters, but they are essential to midterm elections. Older voters—overwhelmingly white males and females—have been critical in midterm elections for Republicans. The principal reason is that they turn out in larger numbers than do minority and young voters. This particularly benefited the GOP in 2014. Older voters proved especially critical in key swing states, and this will continue to be the case. Everyone knows that without Florida, the GOP's chances of winning the White House are absolutely nil. Without Florida, Republicans forfeit any chance of breaking the Democratic lock on the Electoral College. Older voters are important in other states as well. New Mexico might become an especially important state if Virginia is lost. New Mexico has a large Hispanic population, so Republicans need to cut into this chunk of the Democratic electorate. New Mexico also has a large boomer population. Santa Fe County has close to a third of its population aged 45–64.

The importance of winning older voters is apparent when turnout is broken down by age in the 2012 elections. In 2012, 18- to 24-year-olds constituted 18 percent of voters, while those 45 and above totaled 54 percent of the electorate! If this age cohort is broken down further, 45- to 64-year-old voters constitute 38 percent, and those over 65 contributed 16 percent of the vote. In the midterm elections, 18- to 29-year-olds made up only 13 percent of the turnout, while voters 45–64 made up 43 percent and those over 65 made up 22 percent. More precisely, voters 45 and older contributed an extraordinary 65 percent of the turnout. In low-turnout Seattle city elections, half of the votes are cast by those over 65. Overall, 75 percent of voters in 2014 were white. What this means is that Republicans are relying on white male and female voters over 45 years old.[1]

Today more than half of the nation's voting-age population is over 45. This population boom has given boomers immense political clout at every level—national, state, and county. Given this political clout, and their high turnout in elections, both parties are paying close attention to this age cohort. Party strategists dissecting these older voters have found a complicated picture. Boomers tended to vote Democratic until the 1980s, but then began to shift Republican, as they prospered with Reagan's low-tax boom. In the 1990s, many returned to the Democratic column. More recently, they have been returning to the Republican fold. Yet, just like the millennial generation, stereotypes do not capture the subtle nuances found in the boomer generation. For example, older boomers born before 1948 and younger boomers born in 1962–64 tend to be more Republican.[2] Furthermore, as might be expected, the boomer generation breaks apart by education, ethnicity, and family structure.

Those who received good educations have prospered. Many have not, and will have to rely on Social Security and government assistance not to fall into poverty. There might be flashpoints that bring the generation together—preserving Social Security, protecting long-term care—but this generation will not stand united when it comes to raising taxes, investing in schools, funding public transportation, and reforming public pension programs. They are all over the map, but they share a moral passion that makes compromise difficult. Nonetheless, the potential for intergenerational warfare over Social Security, Medicare, and pensions underlies the thinking of strategists in both parties.

A look at where social trends are headed for the boomer generation, and those that will follow, reveals four salient points that Republicans need to understand for crafting a short- and long-term strategy: (1) Most boomers have done pretty well in their careers, but some are going to be caught short in their retirement by having to rely heavily on Social Security benefits; (2) Social Security and Medicare entitlements cannot be sustained at this pace; (3) without reform, the nation is headed off a financial cliff; and (4) boomers might have age in common, but they are divided politically and economically.

A BOOMER VOICE

Tall, distinguished looking, with a full head of slightly graying hair, Bill B. speaks in the well-modulated voice of a mid-level insurance executive now in his mid-sixties. His story typifies much of the story of his generation.

He grew up in a two-parent family. His father was a second-generation Italian immigrant. After fighting in the Pacific in World War II, where he was wounded, Bill's father bought a home with his wife in the expanding Sun Belt. Bill's father took a job in the post office. His mother occasionally worked part-time to make ends meet, but her primary responsibilities were at home. Neither parent was college-educated, but they had many books in the house. Bill's father liked going to used bookstores to buy books for himself and his kids. They raised Bill and his sibling in the home that they lived in until they were unable to care for themselves. The neighborhood was mostly white working-class.

Bill went to neighborhood public schools. In the large public high school, Bill was an outstanding student. He was a bit of a radical, and he got into some trouble when he distributed anonymous leaflets protesting the school's dress code. His guidance counselor wrote a bad letter of recommendation that cost him a scholarship at the state university. Bill enrolled in the local community college, where he majored in philosophy, winning the outstanding major award. He worked full-time. Like most of his peers, he was anti–Vietnam War. When Martin Luther King, Jr., was assassinated, he believed the world was coming apart. He declared himself a socialist and a pacifist, although he recalls, "I probably was not much of either, but I was clearly on the left." He began attending anti-war meetings and drove with a group of activists to San Francisco to march in a massive anti-war demonstration. He began experimenting with LSD and other "hard" drugs. "For about four months," he recalled, "I felt like I was leading a double life."

In high school, he had become a Christian. Neither of his parents was especially religious or attended church regularly. His father had been raised Roman Catholic and his mother Swedish Lutheran. When he was thirteen years old, a neighbor invited him to a local Christian youth group meeting. "I went probably so I could meet girls," he declares. He recalls that he liked the kids, started attending church, and declared himself a Christian. His conversion was likely aided by a girl he met in the club whom he began dating. His high school sweetheart later became his wife.

This double life of a student radical and drug-taking hippie conflicted with his religion and his other life. Shortly before graduating from the community college, he decided to settle down and get married. He took a job in the mailroom at a large corporate insurance company. He planned on working and then going back to college. He never did. Within nine years, he had worked himself up to a managerial position, the head of a department of about thirty employees. He was putting away money for his retirement, but his salary was not enough to support a growing family. To move up in the corporate ranks, he would need to relocate to San Francisco as the company wanted him to do, but he and his wife did not want to move away from their family.

He and his wife had bought a home not far from his parents' home. The neighborhood was deteriorating, though. Crime was going up and much of the housing was being turned into rental properties. The high school that Bill had graduated from now had metal detectors to stop kids from carrying guns into the classroom. When their son began having problems in third grade with a teacher who could not control the students, Bill and his wife decided that they needed to move to the rapidly growing suburbs.

Bill decided to cut out on his own. A former employee had started an insurance agency selling everything from life insurance to business insurance, mostly to local farmers. Within two years, Bill had bought out his partner and was running a business with about twenty employees. Being responsible for twenty people, making payroll, and trying to get good employees kept him up at night. When a larger publicly held company offered to buy his agency, he sold out and went to work for the larger corporation. He stayed there nine years, and then decided to strike out on his own again.

This time around, he kept his expenses low, working out of his house. He did well for six years, but then decided to sell the business and go work for another company. He has now been with the company for ten years as an account executive. His salary is based on the premiums paid by his clients. He works largely in risk management with large corporate clients and loves his job. "I like learning about people's businesses. I learn a lot each day and I like my clients. The key is listening to what they need and having the technical knowledge to help them." He is not planning on retiring. "There are two reasons, as I see it to retire: either you don't like your job or you have something more interesting to do with your life," he says. "Well, I like my job, and although I have other interests, I don't have a great enough interest in them to devote full-time. I am not interested in rebuilding an engine of a classic car."

Bill and his wife are devoted to their community, their two daughters and son, and their grandkids. His wife babysits a couple of the grandchildren after school while their mothers are at work. "Usually we have about four to six grandkids in our house at any one time. We love it, although it has its problems sometimes. Sometimes my wife is accused of feeding the grandchildren too much junk food. Trying to feed kids after school carrots and vegetables is a little difficult."

Bill and his wife attend church with their kids and grandchildren. Bill says he goes to be with the family. He has some "doctrinal" problems with the church they attend, but the family experience is more important. He and his wife used to belong to a church downtown. "It was great," he said. The congregation was racially diverse and did a lot of charity work in the community. After moving to the suburbs, they continued to attend this church even though it was an hour's drive each Sunday. After a year, though, they joined a community church closer to where they lived.

Both Bill and his wife became increasingly involved in their community. They began attending city council meetings after their utility rates shot up. They began looking at the city budget and helped organize a local taxpayers' association. His wife had become active in the local parent-teachers association, eventually becoming president. After friends urged her to run for the city council, she won a seat on the board and later became president of the council. She also was elected president of the local chamber of commerce. "Her strength," Bill says with pride, "is knowing how to run a meeting. She lets people talk, but keeps the agenda moving forward."

Bill, too, became involved in politics. He won election and served two terms on the district health board. He lost the seat, he said, because a large hospital conglomerate opposed him and threw money into his opponent's campaign. While on the board, he had opposed a large hospital expansion plan. He thought it was foolish. Most hospital care these days is outpatient. Medical providers have built huge hospital complexes that are redundant and unnecessary, he believes.

Both he and his wife are Republicans. "I have been accused of being a 'Republican In Name Only [RINO],'" he declares, "but I am conservative on fiscal and social issues." His biggest concern is how government spends money, but he adds, "I am pro-life. I believe that life begins at conception. However, I don't believe in overturning *Roe*." He knows from personal experience about abortion; he advised a daughter's friend against having one. When she did, Bill got angry with her. "When I confronted her, and at the time we were helping her financially, she began crying." He is still regretful about this. "What right do I have as a white male making a young girl cry about a decision she made? It was a terrible situation. The decision had been made. I should have been more consoling." He believes that people who oppose abortion, as he does, should support counseling and adoption centers.

Both he and his wife do in fact support these centers. Both are also actively involved in a community anti-gang program that picks kids up from school and takes them to an after-school program where they can play and get educational mentoring. "These programs are expensive," he notes. "We have to pay for the vans to pick them up and then the after-school mentoring. We bought our own building. We did this as a community group."

"I am anything but a RINO," he says emphatically. "When I was running for office, I would get these questions on how I stood on nuclear proliferation or gay marriage. The office I was running for did not have anything to do with nuclear weapons and our health district did not perform marriages. I am personally opposed to gay marriage, but if people want to get married, that's their business. It's more of a culture issue, and we have wasted a bunch of time on this when we are confronting major problems in this country."

So what does he think are the major problems in the country? He answers quickly, showing he has given some thought to these issues. "I would list these major issues: race relations, immigration, and healthcare costs." He considers racial relations the most important. We have a serious problem with poverty in this country, he believes. Poverty among African Americans, he feels, is directly related to the breakdown of the family in the African-American community. This is related, in part, to the breakdown of the black church. Government should be helping those in poverty, especially when they need it, but he is convinced that maintaining a dependent class of people on government welfare only backfires in the long run. "As Christians," he affirms, "we have a responsibility to care for our brothers and sisters. This means being directly involved in the community."

He is also worried about immigration. "Both of my parents were immigrants," he says. "We are a nation of immigrants." Republicans need to address the immigration problem. Too often their rhetoric comes across as racist. "Sure, we have to control our borders," he says, "but we also need to reach solutions to make sure that illegal immigrants find a place in our society as workers and, for some, as citizens."

He is worried about the financial state of America, especially rising healthcare costs. "I work in the industry, and I know how healthcare costs are going through the roof. My clients are employers. They are going broke trying to keep up with healthcare. I cannot go to my clients and tell them that costs are going up sixty-four percent and expect them to eat these costs. Republicans need to have a plan. Just attacking Obamacare should not be enough." He adds that he knows that there are plenty of plans proposed by different Republicans, but they need to agree on one plan and present it to the American people.

He remains concerned about national security. "America is weaker in the world today than it was six years ago." He is quick to point out that he is not a "big defense hawk. I don't like politicians who like to rattle the saber." Nonetheless, he believes that America, as the most powerful nation in the world, needs to exert leadership, and he wants a strong president.

In general, Bill remains suspicious of most politicians. He is tired of gridlock in Washington. "I want politicians in office who can get results." In business, he declares, "if you don't get results you get fired. I cannot tell my company that their deal did not get done because of this or that. I cannot make excuses: Everyone in politics makes excuses. There is always some external fact. My advice to these politicians is simply: Get the job done. Get results. Stop making excuses. Fix the problems." He is tired of all the infighting in the Republican Party. He is tired of rhetoric and wants solutions and fixes. He does not believe the problems will be easy to fix, but it is clear that he is tired of "politics-as-usual." He is solidly Republican and will continue to vote Republican, since he does not like liberals and their "anti-market" agenda, but he demands a "principled pragmatism" at the core of the party.

BOOMERS AND THE ECONOMY THAT WENT BOOM

While many Americans lost their shirts, their jobs, their homes, and their 401(k)s during the Great Recession in 2008 and the years that followed, boomers on the whole prospered. Many kept working, putting off retirement. Corporations needed their talents and knowledge to keep going during these tough times. Boomers who lost their jobs found work as consultants or took their talents to other companies. As a result, boomers not only weathered the recession, they prospered.[3]

Boomers continue to be a large part of the workforce. About eight in ten boomers in their early fifties are in the workforce. While 50 percent of those in their sixties are working, and a third of those in their late sixties are working. Most of those postponing retirement are males, and they are projecting that they will work at least part-time after they retire. Their voices in business are going to be present for quite a while.

Boomers and the generation born during World War II, the Silents, are more well-off financially than any previous generation entering retirement. Given their wealth, involvement in elections, and numbers (75 million), this generation is already exerting and will continue to have huge political clout. In 2029, when all boomers will be 65 and older, more than 20 percent of the total U.S. population will be over 65. Their numbers are projected to drop to 59.8 million by 2030, and only 2.4 million are projected to survive to 2060. Republicans should note that most of those surviving from 2030 to 2060 will be women. Nonetheless, the sheer numbers of boomers and their proportion of the total population for the next thirty years are going to give this generation power in American politics and the American economy. Plus, they will have wealth and time to be engaged. Most boomers are native born, American educated, and English speaking. They are the last generation to have a common culture, much of it shaped by early network TV. Millennials might think the future is theirs, but baby boomers know better, as they always have.

Most members of this generation consider themselves to be in excellent financial shape. Of course, not every senior is wealthy, but on the whole this older generation has fewer poor members than previous elderly populations. In the past, the elderly were usually poorer than other age cohorts. Today they are wealthier. And they know it. Close to half of the boomer and Silent generations believe that they are in good or excellent shape financially. The self-perception is accurate. More seniors fall into the middle class, i.e., the 40th and 80th percentiles of income, than ever before. Median assets of people aged 65–74 doubled between 1989 and 2013, a greater increase than in any other group in America. Their share of income has risen markedly in the percentile of upper-income groups. It shows in their spending habits. The average household expenditures for those 65 and older has increased a solid 15 percent from 1989 to 2013. Seniors in America have money to spend.

This wealth has come through continued earnings from work, rising housing prices, family inheritance, and the growth of 401(k) funds, even in this age of near-zero interest rates. In the late 1990s, only one in five older Americans had a job. This is in sharp contrast to today's workforce, in which nearly one in three people in their late sixties work. One reason to work is better health. An American aged 64 today has the same health profile as a 60-year-old in the 1950s. Work has allowed seniors to build their retirement income. An added benefit of continuing to work is that senior workers have increased the value of future Social Security payments. For each year they postpone drawing Social Security, monthly payments rise about 8 percent until 70 years of age, when Social Security benefits stop rising.

Many boomers within the workforce plan to continue working. Nearly half of the boomers still working, especially those in their late forties or fifties, say they don't expect to retire until they are 66 or older. One in ten declare they will never retire.[4] This refusal to take retirement increased after the 2008 recession, and as a result, boomers still constitute about one-third of the workforce, about the same as millennials (33 percent) and Generation X (32 percent). Two things are certain in this life, however: taxes and aging. Boomers will eventually retire or follow Jim Morrison by breaking on through to the other side. This will create opportunities for millennials, but the transition is going to be gradual.

Talking in generalizations about any one generation can lead to facile overgeneralizations. Within the boomer generation, there are elite boomers with good degrees, who prospered in a global economy and adjusted during the ups and downs of the economy. Others in this generation have not prospered. This socioeconomic divide breaks down by educational attainment, race and ethnicity, and family structure.

On the whole, boomers have prospered in the new economy. Those who have not tend to be those who, either through circumstances or choice, failed to attain good educations or refused to keep up their skills. About 10 percent of people over 65 are living in poverty. Many of the poor among the boomers are single women, blacks, and Hispanics. These differences can only become more pronounced as the working poor retire. Increased poverty among these segments should be anticipated.

Yet one single fact that every study shows is telling about this generation: boomers have the lowest rate of poverty among all age groups in America today. Whatever their differences, this generation is a sleeping giant that is going to have immense power at the polls for the next twenty years.

Many boomers are going to lead extremely comfortable lives in retirement. Already they account for nearly half of all consumer spending. They are not counting on Social Security benefits as their sole source of income. For many, it will be a ready source of disposable income, much like they might have experienced as a teenager with an after-school job or an added allowance from their parents. Some, however, are expecting to rely totally on Social Security as a primary source of income. Prior to the stagnant years just before the Great Recession, only 27 percent of workers expected Social Security to be their major funding source. After the Great Recession, nearly a third of those in the workforce today believe that they will have to rely on Social Security.[5] Close to half of workers, however, are not counting much on Social Security. They are looking to their 401(k) retirement plans as the fundamental source of retirement. Social Security is going to be a volatile issue in the future. It is going to need additional funding, as well as benefit cuts to survive. Support for reform will break not only along generational lines, but also according to how reliant people are on the system.

BOOMER POLITICS

When boomers eventually retire completely, many will move to no-income-tax or low-income-tax states such as Florida, Arizona, and other Sun Belt states. When they arrive, they will find sizeable boomer populations already living there. The soon-to-be-senior population, those aged 55–69, the leading half of the boomer generation, has changed the political dynamics in many Sun Belt states. This age cohort grew from 2000 to 2015 in Colorado by 76 percent, faster than any other state except Alaska. This pattern is found in other western states as well. It grew 69 percent in Utah, 65 percent in Idaho, and 66 percent in Nevada and Washington. Boomers began moving to these states in their thirties and forties, and they are staying.[6]

The boomer generation is a difficult one to pigeonhole. Their political divisions are telling. Some started coming of age before Kennedy's assassination, while the politics of younger boomers were influenced by Reagan's inauguration. These formative life experiences shaped their politics. Most boomers did not want much to do with the Republican Party until the Age of Reagan. Then things began to change, beginning in the 1980s. Older boomers who first voted Democratic in 1968 and 1972 continued to maintain their faith in the Democratic Party. But younger boomers who came of age under Ford, Carter, and Reagan began to align with Republicans. How boomers vote today reflects this partisan division. Older boomers, those born in 1946–1948, tend to be less significantly Democratic and are leaning Republican, while middle-year boomers, especially those born between 1950 and 1953, have the highest Democratic leanings. They came of age politically during the Watergate scandal, which hurt the Republican base. Younger boomers, those born in 1963–64, have joined the Silent Generation, their parents and grandparents, in voting Republican.[7] The younger boomers came of age during the Reagan boom and were more likely to have careers in business. Many founded their own small businesses. In 2008, Democrats held an over 11 percent advantage among boomers. The failures of the Obama presidency turned boomers Republican. By 2013, the Democratic advantage in the age cohort had dropped about 3 points and was falling. Younger boomers who came of age during stagflation and the Iranian hostage crisis remember the consequences of a bad economy and a weak U.S. foreign policy. Their major concerns remain economic growth and national security. By 2021, this more conservative bloc of young boomers will enter the ranks of seniors and clearly shift them in a stronger Republican direction.

Here is the only age cohort in which Republicans have a clear majority of voters. The proportion of older voters will continue to grow in the coming decades. If the voting trend for boomers and the next generation, the Y generation, holds, Republicans should have a strong base in the future. They cannot rely on this vote to win the White House, but the GOP will have strength in midterm elections for the foreseeable future. Obviously, in the long run, boomers will pass from the scene, but Republicans can be optimistic in the short term. If they are going to win the White House and create a new majority, though, minority and younger women and male voters are going to have to be persuaded that the GOP is not just the party of old white folks.

Boomers tend toward activism. This generation witnessed great social change, perhaps equal only to the Civil War generation. This was the time of the civil rights movement and the women's movement. The boomers came of age during the rise of mass education and the expansion of public universities. Female boomers saw the first cracks in the glass ceiling and the prospect of equal opportunity in the workplace. They saw the stagflation in the 1970s, the boom years of the 1980s and 1990s, and the growing impact of an increasingly globalized economy. They witnessed and contributed to a revolution in computers, medicine, and technology. Millennials like to talk about computer and technological know-how, but boomers, both in the workplace and in retirement communities, make ready use of the Internet, Facebook, and Twitter. They are technologically savvy.

In their youth, many boomers were activists. Historians tend to distort the 1960s as an age of radical protest. Most of the young in the 1960s were not New Left radicals or hippies. More young people belonged to the conservative Young Americans for Freedom than ever joined the leftist Students for a Democratic Society. Young Americans for Freedom once filled Madison Square Garden with conservatives drawn mostly from New York City. At the time, Students for a Democratic Society could not even attract five hundred people to a national meeting. There were conservative activists as well who went to work for Goldwater in 1964 as teenagers and others who supported Ronald Reagan in the 1960s. There were as many young people who proclaimed "Victory to the Viet Cong" as those who called for "Bombing Hanoi Back to the Stone Age." These were small percentages on both sides. What joined the generation together, though, was a generalized support for change. It came with Eugene McCarthy in 1968 and Ronald Reagan in 1980. Now, as this generation looks toward retirement, they are planning on becoming volunteers in their communities. Nearly 60 percent of boomer women and 58 percent of boomer men already volunteer their time to cultural, educational, and political causes.[8]

While most boomers will live comfortably in retirement, they are going to face two major issues: rising medical costs and the financing of Social Security. These issues are not going to go away. The costs of these programs drive heavily rising budget deficits and the national debt.

Boomers pride themselves on their fitness. If taxes and aging are constants in life, so is deteriorating health. Boomers might live longer than previous senior generations, but many are not necessarily living healthier lives. The U.S. Centers for Disease Control and Prevention (CDC) reports that chronic conditions among boomers have increased significantly over the last ten years.[9] In a survey of chronic diseases during the period 2002–2012 among 55- to 64-year-olds, the CDC found that diabetes rose from 16.7 percent of the population to 18.9 percent. Similarly, obesity rose about 2 percent over this period, so by 2012, 40.6 percent of the boomers were considered obese. High cholesterol went up 11 percent to include over half the population of 55- to 64-year-olds, and hypertension rose by about the same amount to include over half the population. To a degree, this diagnosis reflects medicine's tougher standards of what counts as chronic, but chronic diseases are endemic to the elderly, and it is clear there will be higher medical costs.

The primary reason for longer lives is the increased use of prescription drugs. Boomers were known as the drug generation. Now drugs are prescribed by doctors. Adults aged 55–64 are taking more drugs than ever before. For example, there has been a 30 percent increase over the last ten years in anti-diabetic pills and a 54 percent increase in cholesterol-lowering drugs.

This will be the largest age cohort to enroll in Medicare over the next ten years. The Medicare system will collapse under the weight of boomers receiving federal healthcare. Medicare will join the rubble along with Social Security, if reform is not undertaken. Those opponents of reform—Democrats and lobby groups—who deny there is a crisis and deride those who call for reform are playing rocking chair politics: It's motion without moving forward. All the while the floor beneath the rocking chair is collapsing.

Trustees of the Social Security and Medicare Board offered a dire warning in 2012. Both programs, the trustees warned, are experiencing "cost growth substantially in excess of GDP growth in the coming decades."[10] Social Security and Medicare constitute the two largest federal entitlement programs, accounting for 36 percent of federal expenditures. The largest single factor contributing to this crisis is the large size of the baby-boomer generation entering retirement and the lower numbers of later generations entering the workforce. The trustees urged lawmakers not to delay addressing the long-run financial challenges of these two programs. The sooner the better; otherwise, options for addressing the funding crisis become narrower and beneficiaries will have less time to make adjustments. Congress must act, but the politics of Social Security and Medicare makes it difficult for politicians or any political candidate to stick their necks out for reform.

In the early 1980s, Social Security found itself in a similar crisis. With benefit checks months away from insufficient funds, President Ronald Reagan adroitly addressed the situation by appointing a commission to study the problem and make recommendations. The commission's report proposed raising Social Security taxes, and extending the retirement age before recipients could draw full benefits provided the political cover for reform. In 1983, legislation was enacted, which gradually increased the retirement age by two years, increased scheduled taxes, raised taxes for the self-employed, and taxed a portion of benefits for higher-income individuals. These reforms worked. For the next three decades, the system took in far more revenue than it paid out in benefits. The surplus was invested in special non-tradable Treasury bonds, with interest paid to the system's trust funds. By 2013, these trust funds held more than $2.8 trillion in Treasury bonds.

This fix worked until 2008; then demographics and economic circumstances caught up. Mortality rates had been falling for decades. But then the Great Recession kicked in. Negative economic growth and fewer average hours worked caused tax receipts to fall; lower interest rates generated less income from the trust fund's assets, while disability claims soared. All this occurred when the first boomers began to collect benefits. Deficits began to increase in 2010 and 2011, around $49 billion in 2010 and $45 billion in 2011. The trustees projected an average annual deficit of $66 billion through about 2019, and then projected that deficits would rise even more sharply and dangerously. The trust funds that covered the deficits are expected to be exhausted by 2033. Perhaps that is when the political system will be forced to act.

Similarly, the Medicare program is facing a crash. Even if projected cost savings for healthcare under the Affordable Care Act are realized, the trustees warn that medical costs at the current rate of growth will crash the system. Trustees project that Medicare costs will grow from approximately 3.7 percent of the GDP to 5.7 percent by 2035, and will increase gradually to about 6.7 percent of the GDP by 2086. Efficiency-enhancing innovation in healthcare pay and delivery, as projected by the proponents of Obamacare, even if they are realized, are not going to solve the problem of too many people drawing benefits and too few people paying into the system. Starting in 2026, the Medicare trust fund simply will be unable to cover fully promised benefits.[11] The United States currently spends 17.6 percent of the GDP on all healthcare. Other countries spend 9 to 12 percent. Costs seem certain to rise. Medicare and Medicaid are the fastest-growing entitlement programs. There are monsters eating their own children.

The numbers are clear enough, although it is a little mind-numbing to read them and downright scary to realize their full implications.[12] In 2010, the population of those 65 and older numbered 40.4 million. They represented about 13 percent of the population. About one out of every eight Americans was elderly. This over-65 population had increased about 15 percent since 2000, compared to an increase of 8.7 million for the under-65 population. But here's the problem from an actuarial point of view: projections are that these boomers drawing on Social Security and Medicare are going to grow, and grow, and grow over the next two decades. The 65-and-over population of 40 million will reach 55 million in 2020 and 72.1 million by 2030. They will account for over 19 percent of the population in 2030. This population will be mostly white, although percentages of Hispanics, African Americans, and Native Americans will grow. Perhaps even more foreboding is that old-age dependency is projected to nearly double from 19.5 percent in 2030 to 35.5 percent in 2050.[13]

Cuts in Social Security benefits and shortfalls in Medicare produce a social nightmare of epic proportions.[14] Reform is necessary. Some solutions seem obvious: benefit eligibility based on life expectancy, i.e., extending the retirement age for eligibility, is the first step. Increasing taxes on higher-income groups for both Social Security and Medicare is a second step. Reviewing the Social Security and Medicare programs as part of the discretionary budget, such as education or defense, could help plan a long-term future for the program, even though it might mean budget caps. Incentives to increase private retirement savings and health savings accounts could help moderate the insolvency cliff the nation is headed toward. Without reform, Social Security, Medicare, and Medicaid will consume all federal tax revenue.

The problem of reform is a political dilemma for both parties. George W. Bush in his second term urged that Congress explore privatization of Social Security by allowing a small proportion of funds to be invested by individuals in government-specified private funds. Bush did not offer a specific plan for how this was to be done. Even a suggestion of partial privatization of Social Security backfired. He came under attack by Democrats, who played on the fear that beneficiaries would lose their checks. This became a theme of the 2006 midterm elections, in which Democrats regained the House.

The politics of Social Security is not just the lack of political courage on the part of leaders in both parties. The underlying problem is the American public's unwillingness to understand the complex issues involved in tackling the problem. Social Security and Medicare touch individuals more directly than just about any other federal program. By 2012, some 57 million Americans received retirement, disability, or survivor benefits from the system. The cost was $786 billion, with 161 million people paying taxes into the system from which they expected to receive benefits.

Across party lines, Americans support Social Security and Medicare. Few Americans want benefits to be cut or delayed. In fact, 41 percent of Americans in a Pew poll in 2012 said that Social Security should be increased. Only 10 percent said it should be cut.[15] Not surprisingly, in the 2012 Pew survey, Democrats are more disposed to raising benefits, but 35 percent of Republicans in the survey felt that Social Security funding should be increased. Only 17 percent of Republicans said it should be decreased.

Further evidence of general support for Social Security came in a huge survey conducted by the National Academy of Social Insurance in 2013.[16] Across the board, Democrats, Republicans, and Independents declared they would be willing to pay more Social Security taxes. The numbers of those saying they would pay more taxes is remarkable: 91 percent of Democrats, 86 percent of Independents, and 74 percent of Republicans. They agreed that paying higher taxes is critical to preserving the system. If the choice is between increasing taxes on working Americans or increasing taxes paid by wealthier Americans, most Americans overall (87 percent to 82 percent) favor taxing the wealthy. This encourages a Democratic strategy in political campaigns of using class rhetoric to rally voters to tax the rich.

The elephant in the room in any debate on entitlement reform is that there is a looming debt crisis in America. Social Security trustees, the Congressional Budget Office, and the U.S. Treasury, as well as many others, keep warning of the coming crisis. One of the most serious warnings came in an IMF study in 2011.[17] In a working paper, IMF economists warned that American entitlement programs threatened the entire financial health of the nation. Neither low interest rates nor the passage of the Affordable Care Act have addressed the rapidly rising costs of Social Security or healthcare. They warned that the size of the financial gap was 50 percent larger than what had been projected in 1999, reaffirming the continued massive fiscal deficits over the past decade. Furthermore, they project that healthcare costs will continue to rise because of technology, even with federally mandated cost controls. Their report concluded that in order to fully eliminate fiscal imbalances, all taxes would have to go up and all benefits would be cut. This was not new. What caught many by surprise was the degree of tax hikes and transfer cuts that were necessary: 35 percent on both sides—hikes and reductions. They said these tax increases and benefit cuts needed to be done "immediately and permanently."

In 2011, they projected that without action being taken, spending on entitlement programs would outdistance revenue by 2030. After this, the revenue-expenditure gap would only widen. They presented a "Menu of Pain" of how these expenditure reductions and revenue increases could be made under different economic scenarios. "Menu of Pain" was an apt phrase to describe the necessary reforms. Despite increased revenue with a better economy or constrained healthcare costs through projected cost containments embodied in the Affordable Care Act, fiscal imbalances will worsen. One of the major consequences of these imbalances is exacerbated generational inequities, in which wealth is transferred to an older generation.

These grim projections were reaffirmed a year later in a complex study released by the National Bureau of Economic Research in March 2012.[18] The title of this paper captured it all: "Game Over: Simulating Unsustainable Fiscal Policy." Conducted by three university economists, the study found that U.S. federal liabilities (official debt plus the present project expenditures) exceed federal assets (the present value of taxes) already by $211 trillion, or fourteen times the GDP. To close this gap requires an immediate and permanent 64 percent hike in all federal taxes. They were not recommending a tax increase policy, but simply stating a fact.

Their main concern, however, was projecting fiscal sustainability over the next thirty years. On its current course, the United States will likely find itself in a "game over" situation in about thirty years. The United States is unlikely to default. The American economy is too large and the tax base is too broad. Nonetheless, paying for the huge national debt will have profound consequences for the nation and international capital markets.

The political consequences of a public's unwillingness to undertake meaningful entitlement reform places Republicans in a swampland of bad choices. How can Republicans stand as a party of reform if they avoid tackling Social Security and Medicare? How can the party insist that federal deficits and the national debt be reduced without attacking the largest driving forces of deficits and debt, Social Security and Medicare? How can Republicans keep their necessary support among boomers while proposing meaningful entitlement reform? And can Republicans continue to maintain their pledge for "no new taxes" without raising taxes at least to some extent on Social Security and Medicare?

Republicans, looking to leave the swamp, have some things in their favor. Since 2014, the general public has more confidence in Republicans on Social Security than they have in Democrats. The once-massive advantage Democrats had on this issue evaporated by 2014, and today Republicans have a slight advantage.[19] In the 2014 midterms, Republicans touted their "senior bill of rights," a rather vague platform of preserving Social Security and extending its future. Republicans understand that their Democratic opponents also face a dilemma on how to address the issue. While Democratic activists, aligned interest groups, and a few media pundits deny that there is a funding crisis, most experts understand that entitlement reform is necessary to maintain these programs and for the health of the nation.

Hillary Clinton, running for the Democratic nomination in 2008, opposed taxing millionaires and billionaires by lifting the payroll tax cap to strengthen Social Security finances. She called for reining in the Social Security budget and a "pay as you go" system. She called for a commission to recommend Social Security reforms. President Obama created such a commission, but he was silent on the commission's subsequent recommendation to cut benefits. After all, Social Security was a signature program for Democrats, extending back to Franklin Roosevelt's New Deal. Republicans for the most part have stuck by their guns in calling for Social Security reform through tax hikes and benefit cuts. Mike Huckabee, when seeking the Republican presidential nomination in 2016, was the exception. Reversing his previous position on reform, he came out in favor of preserving Social Security as it is.

BOOMER POLITICS

Republicans have won boomers and their elders. Now the party needs to keep and extend this age cohort, while parsing the interests of older voters with younger and minority voters. This will be tricky given the massive transfer of wealth from younger voters, who must pay the costs of Social Security and Medicare benefits that go to older voters. However Republicans (or Democrats) finesse generational issues, winning older voters is essential to political success. It's worth repeating: older voters make up a disproportionate share of the electorate. They are numerous and will grow more numerous. They turn out to vote and their votes are especially potent in midterm elections, when younger and minority voters tend to stay home.

The first signs that boomers might be turning Republican came in the 2004 presidential election. In 2004, the boomer vote went by a slight margin to President Bush. In 2008, boomers divided nearly equally between John McCain and Barack Obama, who won every age cohort except those 65 and older. The economy was the major issue for most voters in 2008, with the collapse of the financial markets, but boomers viewed the economy differently than did millennials. For boomers, the economy was *the* major issue, with healthcare coming in a distant second. Boomers worried about their 401(k)s and the drop in home prices. The shift of boomers to Obama began with the 2008 meltdown. At the same time, many boomers (35 percent)—more than any other age cohort or minority group—believed that it would be a bad thing if someone over 70 was elected president. This view was not shared by African Americans (11 percent) or women (9 percent). Boomers became especially concerned about McCain's age after he selected Sarah Palin as his running mate. To say the least, boomers were not wild about Palin. Finally, in the end, many boomers picked up the enthusiasm of their children toward Obama.[20]

In 2008, boomers composed 27 percent of the electorate. They broke for Obama by 1 percentage point (50 percent to 49 percent). The over-65 vote went to McCain. The importance of the 45–54 vote was important because of their high registration rate.[21] Obama won the 45–54 vote in the key swing states of Wisconsin, Virginia, Ohio, Florida, and Ohio.[22]

In 2012, after a fierce primary, Republicans nominated Mitt Romney. After four years of Obama, older voters began to shift back to the Republican Party, although not uniformly. The Silent Generation, born before the baby boom of the postwar years, and Generation X, those born after the boomers, went Republican. Old boomers, those born in 1946–1948, tended to remain Democratic. Yet overall, the boomer generation climbed on the Romney bandwagon. They were already trending toward more conservative positions as the election approached, expressing support of smaller government, less support for legalization of marijuana (having children had changed their views on this subject), and less support for gun control.[23] This shift to more conservative positions was in line with the views of the Silent Generation (ages 66–83). The Silent Generation held the most consistently conservative views about limited government and social issues. The overwhelming majority of Silents had become the most strongly disapproving of Obama. They had not voted for him in 2008, and as the 2012 election approached, they had become downright angry. They were the most politically energized of any generation, the whitest, and the strongest believers in American exceptionalism.

Boomers followed in their anger toward government, followed by Gen Xers. The only thing Silents and boomers shared with Democrats was the importance of preserving Social Security. The Silent Generation was only lukewarm toward allowing younger workers to invest their Social Security taxes into private accounts and using their Medicare benefits to purchase private insurance. This stood in sharp contrast to millennials, who enthusiastically embraced these proposals. On the other hand, the Silent Generation was the strongest of any age cohort in raising the retirement age. They did not need to worry about raising the age for benefits since they were already in the benefit pool.

As the 2012 election approached, the Silents and the boomers showed disillusionment with Obama. Obama's four years in office confirmed for the Silents that they had been right in not voting for him. Many boomers had begun to rethink the favorable views of Obama that they had held four years earlier. The majority of boomers, like the Silents, had begun to identify themselves as conservatives. This generation was not monochromatic, though. Those who had come of age during the Nixon presidency tended to be Democrats; younger boomers and Generation Xers, who had come of age in the Reagan, Bush, and Clinton years, were a little more Republican and Independent. In 2012, Romney won every age group over 45 years of age.[24]

The Romney campaign and its supporters targeted the boomer vote in ways they did not target the youth vote. Both campaigns used social media as well as direct mail to reach voters, but Romney relied especially on direct mail to reach older voters. Many younger voters pay bills online and never look at mail. If they live with their parents, they may literally never see any mail. Romney and the Republican National Committee spent more than twice as much as the Obama campaign did on direct mail.[25] In Florida, the Republican campaign relied on mailings to seniors pledging to "preserve and strengthen Medicare" and promising "no change in benefits for those in or near retirement." Mailings declared, "Florida seniors CAN'T TRUST President Obama. BARACK OBAMA HAS FAILED OUR SENIORS." The Romney campaign believed that direct mail was especially important in reaching boomers, who they believed were less influenced by social media. While direct mail is useful for explaining complex issues, the Romney campaign might have underestimated the power of social media with senior voters. The fact is that many seniors, especially boomers still working, use Twitter and Facebook extensively.

Romney won older voters in key swing states.[26] The result was an apparent generational divide: older voters went Republican; younger voters went Democratic. For some on the left, this loss of older voters was explained away as a racial divide. Democratic pundit Ronald

Brownstein, who had suggested the demise of the Republican Party, declared that the election results showed a generational conflict between boomers and millennials.[27] Although not noted by Brownstein, the irony in this generational divide was that boomers, who had been characterized in their youth for not trusting anyone over thirty, had become less infatuated with youth. Age does change views.

Brownstein explained the generational divide not as an issue of age, but rather as one of race. Boomers were mostly white, and many millennials were ethnic or racial minorities. The election, he declared, revealed a "sustained competition and conflict between the brown and the gray." The Democratic Left often boils every issue down to race. Any suggestion that this generational divide might be over principled issues of the role of government, budget deficits, and well-ordered and efficient government was ignored by Brownstein's analysis. Brownstein noted himself that many younger nonwhites—blacks and Hispanics—were not so socially liberal on questions such as gay marriage. On this issue, they stood closer to white seniors. Brownstein implicitly argued that the election was not really about boomer concerns on taxes and public spending. Older voters are whiter than younger millennials, but what divided them fundamentally was their view of government. Millennials were not uniform in their support of big government (after all, they supported privatization of Social Security), nor were older voters uniform in their dislike of big government. Yet when all was said and done, older voters simply were not persuaded that more spending, a larger government, and additional federal programs were going to do much to solve the financial problems facing the nation. Perhaps older voters were jaded about big government and political promises because they had lived with failed promises and bad government for longer.

Boomers and seniors bristled at the Affordable Care Act's use of Medicare funds for coverage for the working uninsured. Brownstein suggested this attitude was latent racism, but seniors worried about the rising costs of medical care, and it is doubtful that boomers were especially irritated that funds were being transferred from Medicare to young minorities. Brownstein warned of "endemic racial polarization" unless the common interests of these generations were recognized. Of course, boomers who had seen and supported the black civil rights revolution in the 1960s had not become racists, and Brownstein's surmise was not based on empirical evidence. Surveys at the time showed that what most concerned 45-and-over voters was long-term stability for Social Security and Medicare. Survey findings showed that they were concerned about the way politics in Washington was working, or more accurately how it was not working. By double digits, senior voters expressed a greater concern with corruption in the federal government than with political gridlock in Washington. They supported reducing the federal deficit and had more negative views on raising taxes to solve this problem.[28]

The 2012 campaign set the stage for Republican victory in the 2014 midterm elections, where boomer turnout counted more because of the lower turnout of minority and young voters. In each of the key states won by Republican candidates, elder voters swung heavily conservative. Republican candidates crushed their opponents with older voters in numbers that were extraordinary. Republican candidates swept the 50- to 64-year-old vote and the over-65-year-old vote that buried Democratic rivals. The gaps in contested Senate races ranged from 5 points among the 50- to 64-year-old vote to as high as 29 points in the 65-and-older vote.

The numbers are worth knowing: In the U.S. Senate race in Georgia, which many pundits thought was going to be a toss-up state, Republican candidate David Perdue, facing Democratic Michelle Nunn, won the 50- to 64-year-old vote 54 percent to 44 percent (a 10-point spread), while winning the 65-and-over vote by a 39-point spread. A similar story unfolded in the North Carolina U.S. Senate race. Here, Republican candidate Tom Tillis beat Kay Hagan, winning the older voters in every age cohort from 45 and up. This was repeated in Iowa, where Republican senatorial candidate Joni Ernst beat Bruce Braley, taking the 50-and-older age cohorts by wide margins. Arkansas and Colorado Senate races proved much the same. In Arkansas, with Tom Cotton running against the incumbent senator Mark Pryor, Republicans won older voters by large spreads. Colorado's Republican Senate candidate, Cory Gardner, won older voters. Indeed, his opponent, Mark Udall, took only 33 percent of the 65-and-older vote.[29]

Overall, in congressional midterm elections, senior voters favored Republicans by a 16-point margin: 57 percent voted for the GOP and 41 percent for the Democrats. Older voters came out in large numbers to vote Republican. A full 22 percent of voters were 65 and older. The contrast of the proportions of the youth and older voters in the electorate was evident. In 2014, voters younger than 30 comprised about 13 percent of those who showed up at the polls. Voters 30–44 years old made up 22 percent of the 2014 electorate, down 5 points from the 27 percent of the electorate in the presidential election held two years previously in 2012.[30]

LESSONS LEARNED

The reality of the 2014 election offered dismay to the Democrats and hope for the Republicans. In 2014, about 13 percent of the vote was cast by millennials, and over 35 percent was cast by boomers. Republicans are not assured of either of these percentages in 2016 or future elections. Trends suggest that the boomer vote, although not monolithic, is going to remain Republican in the future. If Republicans can deepen this vote, maintain the white vote, and cut into the minority and youth vote, the future should be theirs.

To do this, however, Republicans need to realize that they will not always have Obama to kick around, as they did in 2014. They need to present fresh faces and new ideas that provide real solutions to the problems facing the nation. The entitlement problem hangs over the nation like the sword of Damocles, and unless Social Security, Medicare, and other entitlement problems are addressed, the nation is going to find itself in bankruptcy. Addressing these problems will take political courage and policy acumen. Real reform will involve compromise and a willingness by political leaders in both parties to place the national interest above short-term political gain.

Whether democratic governance within a highly polarized electorate can address issues of reform is a test for American democracy. At present, most voters support maintaining the current system through higher taxes. However, only so much wealth can be transferred from the young to the older generation. Those boomers receiving benefits or about to receive benefits through Social Security and Medicare are insistent that they paid into the system and therefore deserve to receive their due. Young voters are not confident that either Social Security or Medicare will be around when they reach retirement age. The clash of generations appears inevitable. Some basic education might help. Everyone needs to know that most Social Security recipients receive far more benefits than they ever paid in taxes. The fact that today's taxes pay today's retirees is not well understood, but it could be taught.

Republicans hoping to maintain and extend their support among boomers while bringing younger voters into the party face a political quandary. But this quandary is not as problematic if the party stands for genuine policy reform. Young and old voters want politicians who are practical, realistic compromisers, inclined toward principled pragmatism. Those who argue that boomers do not see shades of gray other than their own hair and have a propensity to say "My way or the highway" are wrong.[31] Boomers, however uncompromising and idealistic they were in their youth (which is often overstated), have learned the importance of working within the system. Similarly, whatever the idealism of younger millennials (which, too, is often overstated), they will confront serious economic and national issues that call for solutions. In the end, Americans across generations are by nature practical and not given to extreme ideological division. The American political party that strikes the right note in appealing to the idealism of voters and their demands for realistic reform will win elections and achieve an enduring majority. Republicans have the opportunity to be this party.

5

MIDDLE CLASS

IN THE 2008 PRESIDENTIAL CAMPAIGN, BARACK OBAMA CONTINUED to blast Republican rival John McCain for "not getting" the financial anxiety of the American middle class. Obama continued this theme that Republicans just do not connect with the middle class in his reelection campaign in 2012. His rhetoric, however, proved less appealing in 2012 as middle-class incomes overall continued to decline. Both Democrats and Republicans understand that they need to win middle-class voters. Republicans are primed to win this vote.

- The white middle-class vote has been in the Republican column since the 2012 election and increased in the midterm 2014 elections.
- If Republicans have a problem with Hispanic and minority voters, Democrats have a greater problem with the white population.
- The issue for Republicans is sustaining the white middle-class vote, while extending it to minority voters and aspiring blue-collar voters by emphasizing job creation, economic growth, educational reform, and national security.

- This means distancing itself from its image (and policies) as a party of big business and the country-club set. Instead, the party needs to stand for serious entitlement and education reform, equal opportunity, and national unity.

Boomers grew up in an age of an expanding middle class, a growing economy, and intact nuclear families. This world has changed. Today political, social, and religious institutions are weaker and the middle class is under duress, culturally and economically. Both political parties relied on the white middle-class vote to win elections. The last two presidential elections, which were won by Democrats, reveal that winning a majority white vote is not necessary for Democrats. The white vote has become the base of the Republican Party. The white vote, male and female, went overwhelmingly for Romney in 2012. It was not enough to carry him to the White House. This places Republicans in a dilemma: can the white vote be expanded to win the White House for Republicans in the future, or should they shift toward a strategy of winning minority voters? Of course, the two strategies are not mutually exclusive. But campaigns win or lose on these kinds of questions.

George H. W. Bush swept into office in 1988 with the white vote. To put into perspective just how different today's political configuration is from the late 1980s and early 1990s, Republican presidential candidate Mitt Romney carried the white vote by about 20 percent in 2012—the same percentage that led to a George H. W. Bush presidency twenty-four years earlier. As Pew demographer Paul Taylor observes, if the 2012 election had been held only among white voters, Romney would have won by 18 million votes, instead of losing by 5 million votes.[1] The elder Bush won 426 Electoral College votes; Romney took just 206. Within this twenty-four-year period, whites lost some of their electoral clout.

In 2012, some 26 percent of voters were nonwhite. Romney won just 17 percent of this vote. And trends show that this nonwhite vote will increase, as younger voters come of age. Projections are that by 2043 the majority of the population will be nonwhite. Both parties, Democratic and Republican, need white voters to win elections, and neither party can expect to win the White House totally relying on the white vote.

While ethnic and racial blocs today are voting along color lines, economic interests cannot be dismissed as an important factor in voting. Hispanics, Asians, and blacks have voted Democratic because they believe that the Democratic Party best represents their economic interests. Barack Obama, as the first black presidential nominee and elected president, obviously appealed to minority voters, and these voters did not believe that the two Republican candidates, John McCain in 2008 and Mitt Romney in 2012, represented their interests.

The middle class has been under duress for the last two decades, but the struggle to maintain a middle-class lifestyle intensified in the last decade. Since the housing bubble of 2006, the median household wealth—assets minus debt—has fallen by more than a third.[2] This has been accompanied by a sharp rise in income inequality. But the middle class is not just under pressure to maintain its living standards; the middle-class lifestyle is becoming a thing of the past. Older children are not leaving home, and two-parent households are becoming something of a flashback to the 1950s. Nearly 40 percent of all millennial men aged 18–31 and 30 percent of women this age were still living with their parents in 2012. So much for the dream and the dread of becoming an "empty nester."

All Americans, no matter their race, aspire to be middle class. Many blacks, Hispanics, and Asian Americans are already in the middle class. The middle class, however, is majority white. As a result, any political strategy aimed at winning the middle-class vote is largely about winning the white vote, while projecting the American Dream to all voters. A successful political strategy for Republicans must understand the current state of the middle class, the problems faced by middle-class Americans, and their value in winning elections.

THE TRAVAILS OF A MIDDLE-CLASS AMERICAN WOMAN

Roxane H.'s youthful looks do not convey her struggle to enter the middle class and maintain her status there. A middle manager of a large publicly supported agency, she is a twice-divorced, single white woman with two children, a teen girl and a twenty-nine-year-old son. She lives mostly paycheck to paycheck, with little savings to spare. She finds herself with a home mortgage and sizeable credit card debt that was accrued when her husband, whom she divorced recently, lost his job, and she was placed on furlough in the 2009 downturn. Any unforeseen medical, house, or car expense places her in a near crisis, financially and emotionally.

The American Dream of being middle class has been her aspiration. She grew up in small towns in Utah with her younger sister and stay-at-home mother. Her father was usually absent, working in larger towns and only occasionally visiting the family. They were Mormons and did not believe in divorce. She attended public schools, often moving town to town with her mother, whom she describes as "flighty." When her father unexpectedly died when she was seventeen and in her last year of high school, her mother told her that she should take her sister and they would have to be on their own. She had been working since she was fifteen, so she was told she could support herself and her sister. All this came as a shock. Because her parents were converts to Mormonism, she did not have an extended family to turn to. She and her sister lived in Roxane's car for a couple of weeks and then began living with friends. She was able to graduate from high school, but eventually her sister dropped out.

Roxane got by as a manager of a fast-food restaurant. She was working full-time and taking classes at the local community college, when she got pregnant. She was not the run-around type, so she was not using birth control. The boy was younger than she was, but he offered to marry her. After the baby was born, the couple moved in with the boy's parents, who were fairly well-to-do. The marriage lasted less than a year. When it broke up, she moved with her baby to Salt Lake City. She went to work for a fast-food franchise that paid full benefits. She managed ten restaurants. In Salt Lake, she met her future husband. They lived together for about six years while she managed her restaurants and began doing contract work for a California-based record company. She did advance work and made sure that everything was set up backstage for such bands as Guns N' Roses, Live, and White Zombies.

Her live-in boyfriend and his family helped with child care. Her sister had moved to Las Vegas, but for the first time in her life she felt she had a real family. She was working ten hours a day, often on the night shift at the restaurant and working club venues on weekends. Her boyfriend worked various jobs as a manager of a car wash and a truck rental company. Things were not bad, but her former husband insisted that she and her son move closer to him and his new wife. Threatened with a custody battle, she and her son moved closer to him in another state.

She took a job with corporate at the fast-food restaurant. She was making pretty good money, although the hours were long, often sixty hours a week. Three years later, when her former boyfriend, who had gone back to technical school, wanted to get back together, she agreed. They married three years later. Shortly after the marriage, she was pregnant with her second child. By then, he had taken a pretty good job as an electronic technician. They lived in apartments, but when her son reached middle school they decided to buy a house in a developing suburb. She felt like she had finally made it. She had a home, two kids, and a husband with a job.

Her husband was now making enough money to support the family, so she took the opportunity to return to school at the local community college and later the state university. She was an honor student with a double major in literature and religious studies. Because she had a career before entering college, she felt that she could major in things she was interested in. She liked literature, and her own background in the Mormon church, which she had left long before, made her interested in religion. Her intention in returning to school was not to get a higher-paying job, but to receive an education. She thought about going to graduate school after she graduated.

Everything looked good. She had returned to school, was attending her son's baseball games, and was volunteering at his school. Life revolved around school and her kids. Her husband had started a small electronic service company, which she helped develop. The company failed after two years, largely, she says, because of her husband's mismanagement, but he found another well-paying job. After college graduation, she took a full-time job with a state-funded institution. The job did not pay as much as when she was working corporate, but it was a good job with regular hours.

Then disaster struck in 2009. Her husband lost his job in the Great Recession. Because of state budget cuts, she had to go on furlough. Their income fell by half. While out of work, her husband began to run up a huge credit card debt, unbeknownst to her. They had taken out a house mortgage credit. Much of her college had been paid for with scholarships, but she had taken out student loans as well. They had no equity in their house, and they fell behind in their IRS payments. They found themselves barely keeping themselves above water.

The financial situation put a strain on the marriage. Her husband did not want to hear about finances. He seemed lackadaisical about finding work. After a year's unemployment, he finally landed a job as a computer technician, but the marriage bond had been broken. In 2014, she filed for divorce. She was on her own again. She had a teenage daughter, a house payment, credit card debts, IRS payments, and student debts looming.

Throughout her life's struggles, she always voted. She took her kids to the polling station so they could see what voting meant. She usually voted Republican, based on the candidate and not the party. She voted for George H. W. Bush in 1988 and Bill Clinton in 1992, and then returned to the Republican column in 2000 and 2004. In 2008, she decided to vote for Obama after McCain put Sarah Palin on the ticket as his running mate. She thought McCain's selection of Palin was "ridiculous." She did not think Palin seemed bright or well informed. Given McCain's age, she did not see Palin stepping into the White House if something happened to McCain.

She stuck with Obama in 2012. It did not bother her that Romney was a Mormon, although given her experiences in Utah she did not much abide Mormons. What bothered her about Romney was that he seemed out of touch. "I don't expect politicians to understand people like me or my problems, but Romney seemed like he never would get it." She was not enthusiastic about Obama at this point, but at least he seemed able to relate better. She said that during the campaign she followed Ron Paul a little. He seemed interesting. Her decision to vote for Obama came only a couple of weeks before Election Day.

She calls herself a Republican, but her final vote is determined by the candidate. She looks for a track record in public service. "I want somebody who understands the issues and the problems that concern regular Americans." Usually this means voting Republican. She sees Hillary Clinton as offering more of "the same old thing." She does not plan to vote for her, but her final decision will be based on whom the Republicans nominate in 2016.

When asked what issues concern her most, she says, "This crazy wealth inequality. I don't understand the mentality of some of these people having to make millions and millions of dollars." Along with wealth inequality, she thinks more should be done about education. We are spending huge amounts of money on education, she thinks, without much in the way of outcomes. "Our educational outcomes in this country compared to other developed nations [are] absurd. We need to be able to compete." She is also worried about the aging population. Our entitlement programs, she feels, cannot be sustained. She says, "We need to take care of the poor," but adds, "we are headed off a cliff financially."

She is not much concerned about national security. She is more worried about some of the "crazy" people in this country than about being invaded by ISIS. "I don't like the idea of Iran getting a nuclear bomb," she adds. "This could be a real problem, but for right now we need to focus on creating more jobs in this country." Her apathy toward foreign policy is similar to her views on social and cultural issues. "For me, these issues are nonstarters." She is opposed to abortion, but she is not going to vote on that issue. As for gay marriage, her view is "get government out of the bedroom. I don't like government making moral decisions or involved in morality." She adds that she basically believes in small government and prides herself on having never been on welfare, even though she could have.

She thinks the Republican Party is not inclusive enough. It seems too much like "an old boys club that knows what's best for the rest of us." She does not care much for Democrats either, though: "It's a bit too left for me." She sees Democrats as always looking to government for the solutions to problems. She wants a "middle path between two extremes, right-wing Republicans and left-wing Democrats."

She is quite optimistic about the future of America. "Ten years ago I was not very optimistic, but today I am, mostly because of young people." She declares that she has "great faith in young people today. They are more than just consumers and are thinking differently about the world." Her optimism about the nation's future is more tempered when it comes to her own future. She is working her way out of debt and her life is gradually getting back on course. On the other hand, she is worried about retirement. "I have not put much away and I don't have enough money for retirement." In fact, she wonders whether she will ever retire. "I don't want to be dependent on my children. That's why I am working as hard as I do. I like my job, but I plan on moving up and getting a higher-paid job. My job skills in the private sector are more valuable, but right now I am working hard at the job I have and showing people my talents." She believes it will pay off in the end; at least she hopes this is the case. She wants to remain in the middle class and is working to ensure that her and her teenage daughter's life gets better. She does not count much on politicians for help, but she understands that having good leaders in office is important for her to realize her dreams.

THE SAD, INDEBTED STATE OF MIDDLE-CLASS AMERICA

Roxane's personal story is unique, but it represents the struggle many middle-class Americans are facing today. Both political parties, Republicans and Democrats, proclaim themselves defenders of the middle class. But aside from the rhetoric, what exactly is the middle class? The middle class can be measured in four ways: income, wealth, consumption, and self-identification. The narrowest definition is income. A general agreement is that the middle class includes everyone between the top 20 percent and the bottom 20 percent of income earners, those earning between $40,000 and $140,000. Of course, income is not a terribly good measure, because it excludes savings and investments. If wealth is taken as a broad spectrum, the middle class can be defined as the middle three-fifths of the wealth spectrum, those not in debt (excluding mortgages). Some economists believe that consumption is a better measure because spending on food, housing, entertainment, and other items better shows wealth. If measured in terms of self-identification, then most Americans, excluding the very poorest and the very wealthiest, define themselves as middle class. In 2014, 44 percent of Americans identified themselves as middle class. This was a drop from 2008, when 53 percent said they were middle class, before the Great Recession.

Voters' perceptions of themselves as middle class can vary widely given a particular time and view of the economy. In a Pew poll in 2012, the majority of whites (51 percent) and close to a majority of blacks (48 percent) and Hispanics (47 percent) said they were middle class.[3] The average white middle-class person has a higher income and wealth than the average black and Hispanic member of the middle class. The view, though, that all African Americans or Hispanics are poor is belied by facts. Of a total of 14.7 million black households in America, in 2010 approximately 38 percent were in the middle class, with earnings between $35,000 and $100,000 annually.[4] Well-established black middle-class neighborhoods can be found in Atlanta, Washington, D.C., Los Angeles, and other major metropolitan areas. Middle-class blacks work with whites; they shop with whites; and their children go to school and play with whites.

The only thing that the black middle class does not do with whites is vote for the same candidates or parties. Blacks—rich, poor, and middle class, young and old—vote Democratic. The last time they voted in any significant way for a white Republican presidential candidate was Gerald Ford in 1976, when 17 percent of black voters went Republican. Winning over 15 percent of the black vote should be recorded in the annals of modern Republican victories. In 2008, Republicans won a paltry 4 percent of the black vote, and they won 6 percent in 2012. If Romney had won just 10 percent of the black vote in Florida, as opposed to the 4 percent he actually won, he could have edged Obama and won the state. In Ohio, he lost by 1 percentage point. If he had 10 percent of the black vote in this critical swing state, instead of the 3 percent he received, Republicans would have carried Ohio. Republicans can count on Obama not being on the ticket again, but unless they cut into the black middle-class vote, history might repeat itself.[5]

If the middle class is defined as the middle 60 percent of households, the average income stood at $53,042 in 2011. This was down from $58,009 in 2000.[6] One major result of this decline is that the middle-class share of the country's income, which once stood at 51 percent, had fallen drastically by 2011. The share of national income of the top fifth of households grew to 51.1 percent from 44.1 percent in the last decade and a half. The rich have become richer, while the middle class clings to a decreasing share of wealth.

Much of this problem is due to stagnant wages, which have come from an economy in the doldrums. At the same time, the middle class has become a class of debtors and poor savers. In the two decades from 1991 to 2010, debt for the middle third of families increased 161 percent! The median level of debt stood at about $32,000 in 1991. By 2010 it had swelled to $84,000. With high debt, the middle class is understandably saving less. In 2001, two-thirds of middle-class families said they had been able to save money. By 2010 this had fallen to below 55 percent.[7]

Being middle class just is not falling into a certain salary range or wealth level, however; it's also a relative concept and an aspirational ideal. Depending on where you live, a middle-class lifestyle can differ. Living in many cities is more expensive than living in a small town. For example, a "middle class" couple making $250,000 a year (five times the U.S. median income of $52,000) in New York City would have a different sense of what being middle class is than a couple making the same amount in Bloomington, Indiana. In Maryland, the median income per household to be considered middle class is about $75,500, while in Oklahoma it takes far less—about $45,690. Being middle class is relative to what one can buy for the money. Household spending on food, housing, utilities, and so forth has fallen from 53 percent of disposable income in 1950 to 32 percent in 2014. In other words, the middle class has far more disposable income available to spend on luxuries than it did sixty-five years ago.[8] It takes fewer hours worked to pay for a television, a refrigerator, a car, clothing, and most food. Today, a typical middle-class household will have iPhones, iPads, and laptop computers. The cars they drive would have been luxury cars sixty-five years ago. The middle class is living in larger homes, dresses better, eats better (in terms of what they can buy at the supermarket), and spends more on entertainment, eating out, and travel than did their middle-class parents or grandparents. In 1973, the average home size was 1,525 square feet; in 2010, it was 2,169 square feet. Only 120,000 households (12.5 percent) had TVs in 1950. By 2006, 98 percent of households had television sets, 2.7 per home.[9]

But being middle class projects an aspiration about owning a house, living in a safe neighborhood, and educating one's children. Americans like to consider themselves middle class and aspire to be middle class. It is this aspiration that encourages most politicians to proclaim themselves guardians of the middle class, even if they rant against the rich.

Middle-class Americans are feeling pinched today. If the Republican Party can convince them that it actually does represent them by offering real solutions to their problems, the GOP will become the new majority party. The simple lesson learned in the last two elections is that the GOP cannot come across as just a party of big business. Most Americans know that growing the economy matters. A growing economy means more jobs, higher incomes, and greater opportunity. Across the board, whether it be minorities, women, youth, seniors, rich, poor, or the middle class, American voters rank the economy and jobs as their major concerns. Middle-class Americans know from their pocketbooks that healthcare and education costs are skyrocketing. They know that their children are failing to get the jobs they thought they would if they finished high school and college. What they are not convinced of is that the American economy can rebound dramatically because of its inherent strength, and they are not convinced that either party is capable of addressing the problems of an entitlement state that is headed toward financial collapse.

America is expending over 17 percent of the total GDP on healthcare, which seems to absorb and will keep absorbing increasing amounts of the GDP.[10] The rise in healthcare expenditures has been dramatic and alarming. In 2001, total healthcare expenditures (including public and private spending) accounted for about 13.5 percent. The largest factor in this growth has been in public healthcare, rising from about 40 percent of total expenditures to over 53.1 percent. The public funding in healthcare in the United States is almost as great a percentage of the GDP as the *entire* percentage in Japan or Britain, where there is almost no private healthcare spending. Medicare and Medicaid are driving up public health expenditures. As boomers flood the system and as Medicaid enrollments expand, more money is going to have to be spent. Once the Affordable Care Act subsidies for Medicare and Medicaid return to a 50–50 state-federal contribution, state budgets will find themselves spending more on healthcare, leaving less and less money for education, infrastructure, or any other government service. Constraining costs on patient care, physician services, inpatient hospital stays, and exams makes for good rhetoric, but the demographics of an aging population and the dynamics of healthcare costs belie easy talk that healthcare will be affordable. If costs cannot be contained, state governments will have to raise taxes. There is no other way around this in the current system. At the same time, premiums for public and private health insurance will skyrocket. The burden will fall on the middle class. The poor have Medicaid, although finding general practitioners or specialists will become increasingly difficult; the wealthy are taking care of themselves through "concierge" programs that allow them, for an annual fee, to get access to better doctors, frequent exams, and cutting-edge medicine.

Medical care is not the only thing the middle class has to worry about these days. There is also college tuition for their children. This is the largest financial worry of American parents today.[11] Seventy-three percent of parents of children younger than 18 say that funding college for their kids is their major concern. And the middle class should be worried about college tuition. Going to college has become extraordinarily expensive. College costs have risen faster than food, gas, and the general cost of living.

Today the average annual cost for undergraduate tuition, room, and board is over $15,000 at public colleges and about $39,000 at a private college. Since 2002, prices for undergraduate education rose 38 percent at public schools and 27 percent at private schools.[12] Financially pressed states are cost-shifting public higher education from taxes to tuition. Parents are paying for this largely through federal student aid, including tax credits, grants-in-aid, and student borrowing. Experiencing their own fiscal crisis, many states have scaled back funding to public higher education.

An average student graduating today from a four-year college will carry a debt of $30,000. The total student debt for the nation stands currently at $1.2 trillion.[13] Student debt prevents recent graduates from buying vehicles or homes. Not only has a burden for paying for college been placed on the middle class today, but a future generation of aspiring middle-class Americans is going to be stuck paying for the student debt bubble.

University budgets have soared since the 1960s. A much higher percentage of high school graduates are attending college. In 1970 there were 4 million full-time college students; today there are 19 million. The demands of students, professors, and administrators have all contributed to the cost of higher education. Today's students demand more than a small dorm room with twin beds. They expect to live in campus apartments. No longer will a cup of regular coffee at the local diner do; instead, café lattes at the campus Starbucks are required. They demand fancy recreational facilities with workout equipment, treadmills, and cycling machines. Classrooms with a lectern and a blackboard aren't good enough. Classrooms need to be "smart," with equipment allowing professors to put on PowerPoint presentations so students can learn visually, even while they look at their computers or iPhones instead of taking notes. All this costs money.

Professors' salaries have risen faster than those of any other professional group except doctors. A full professor today at a public four-year doctoral institution makes on average $126,981.[14] Of course, there are wide disparities within universities and between universities. Nonetheless, higher salaries for professors contribute to the cost of education. Professors demand more pay for teaching fewer classes. Meanwhile, some university administrators are making out like bandits. There are many more of them, and they are being paid corporate salaries. Administrative expenses have risen a whopping 60 percent, while instruction costs rose about 40 percent, from the mid-1990s through 2008, before the crash. Still, the federal government also played a role in driving up administrative costs. The expansion of university administration is increased by federal mandates and reporting imposed by the Environmental Agency (EPA), Occupational Safety and Health Administration, (OSHA), and an array of other regulatory agencies.

The rising costs of university and college education have been subsidized by the federal government through student loans and research grants. These federal subsidies have allowed colleges and universities to increase student tuition. It's a pyramid scheme. Students go into debt to pay for a college education in hopes of finding a well-paying job to pay off their debt. Meanwhile, billions of dollars of unpaid student debt build up the wobbly pyramid. Resting at the very bottom of this pyramid is the middle class, looking for political leadership to address this mess. Promises of free university education sound good in a political campaign, but they are another example of "kicking the can down the road."

Most middle-class Americans cannot send their kids to college because they are not saving enough and they are in debt. Many middle-class Americans are just scraping by. One sobering poll conducted in 2014 found that 41 percent of Americans say their top financial goal is "staying current on living expenses or getting caught up on the bills." This survey confirmed other reports that more than half of U.S. workers are not saving anything for retirement.[15] Americans on average are putting about 5 percent of their disposable income into personal savings. This contrasts with a nearly 13 percent savings rate in 1976. The vast majority of Americans are saving through 401(k)s, but many are in debt up to their necks as they look forward to retirement.[16] Americans have one of the lowest savings rates in the Western world. Even Spain, with a 13.5 percent savings rate, ranks higher than the United States.[17]

Just keeping up on the costs of day-to-day living, middle-class Americans cannot save for the future. Only a little over a third of Americans have more than $1,000 in savings and investments, other than employer-defined IRA benefits. Only 60 percent have up to $25,000 in savings or investments.[18] This has created anxiety within middle-class America. Less than a quarter feel "very confident" that they will have enough money to support themselves in retirement. The vast majority of Americans have "some confidence," a "little confidence," or "no confidence" that they will have enough money for retirement.[19] Thirty-something Americans are especially anxious about retirement.

Scraping by, Americans are debt ridden. Many are living off their credit cards, the third-largest source of household debt, next to home mortgage and student loan debt. The average American household owes $15,609 in credit card debt. The average mortgage debt per household stands at $156,706, and student loan debt stands at $32,956: bad for the people in debt, but not so good for the nation, either. This translates into $11 trillion of personal debt owed by Americans ($8 trillion in mortgages, $1.2 trillion in student loans, and $884 billion in credit card debt). In a single year, 2014–2015, personal debt increased 7.5 percent.[20]

The problem of middle-class indebtedness goes way beyond personal debt. American cities and states face a pension crisis. Somebody is going to have to pay for the costs of promises made to public service retirees. Only one state in the nation, Wisconsin, has a pension system surplus. The other state pension obligations are underfunded, which means that there are not enough funds to fulfill the promises made by public officials to their employees. These state and local systems are already crashing down, and it is going to get worse. Detroit has already restructured, and more jurisdictions will follow. Investors in state and local government are going to take a shellacking, but so is the middle class, who will experience the tax hikes necessary to cover the costs of these pyramid pension schemes concocted by myopic public officials anxious to placate unions and their voters. The pensions themselves are likely to be restructured.

They were abetted in this scheme by corporate America, which told them not to worry about paying the costs of golden retirement packages offered to public service unions because it could all be paid for by issuing municipal bonds. To get people to buy the city and state bonds,

Wall Street offered high interest rates. It was a good merry-go-round ride for a while. Anxious to win election and placate public employee unions, politicians agreed to labor contracts that promised retirement dream packages. And what dreams there were: an Oakland, California, hospital administrator with a $400,000 annual pension; a casual employee in San Bernardino, California, who qualified for a pension by working for one day. For some people, the American Dream had a new rip-off twist. Chicago and New York financial houses convinced city officials not to worry, because selling bonds—that is, a little debt—could fund the whole thing. "Don't worry about hiking taxes," city and state governments were told. Once good economic times rolled around, tax revenues would increase and these bonds could be paid off.

Unfortunately, eventually the debt has to be paid. Running up one credit card to pay the interest on another credit card can work only so long. In 2009, the pyramid began to crack. The middle class is going to take the fall. Municipalities and states facing default are faced with three stark choices: default on the bonds by declaring bankruptcy; cut public services; or raise taxes. Declaring bankruptcy sends investments of bondholders up in smoke. Once burned, they are not likely to play the game again. Cutting public services or raising taxes leaves the middle class with less. Either way, the middle class is left carrying the bag.

This pension crisis should not be underestimated. Already, Detroit and three cities in California have been forced to declare bankruptcy. The losses for investors have been chilling. In Stockton, California, mutual fund giant Franklin Templeton suffered losses up to 59 percent of its investment. In San Bernardino, bondholders and insurers faced losses up to 99 percent. The investment and legal mechanics of these losses are complex, but the single lesson to take away is that things are not going to get better. The Center for Retirement Research reports that 150 state and local pension plans are already underfunded, and as more retirees enter the system, problems are only going to get worse. The survey found that the average ratio of assets to liabilities was 74 percent. For every dollar owed, the fund held on average only 74 cents in assets. Chicago's six pension plans are 40 percent underfunded. New Jersey's are 51.5 percent underfunded. Overall, the per capita debt across states averages amounts to over $16,000. Pension funds do not have to be totally funded. Fund assets can grow, tax revenues can be increased, and interest rates on investments can rise—all of which can lessen the pension debt problem. Nonetheless, nobody should be a Pollyanna about this looming problem.[21]

There is no lack of bad statistics to show the depth of the problem. Politicians and the public were living in a dream world, playing high-stakes roulette. The wheel kept spinning and spinning and then stopped. Bad bets had to be paid. Even in a casino, reality eventually spoils the game. The United States is not going to become another Greece, defaulting on the national debt. Uncle Sam, after all, can print money. But state and municipal defaults are another animal altogether.

WINNING THE MIDDLE CLASS

No wonder the middle class is anxious. They are in debt, saving little, and the cities and states and country are in the same condition. The party that demonstrates an understanding of this anxiety and that has ways of alleviating it will have a golden future. The American electorate, the middle class, is looking for leadership. Americans are by nature optimists, but behind this optimism lurk deep resentments that have a history of being captured by adroit, often opportunistic politicians. In 2008 and 2012, Obama Democrats proved especially skillful in tapping into the Jekyll-and-Hyde personality of the American voter.

Progressives, in general, like to present a gloomy future because it fits their agenda for expanding the entitlement state and the redistribution of wealth. Class warfare plays upon the resentments of those who feel left behind in achieving the American Dream. Progressive calls for "social justice" for the poor play on the natural goodwill of Americans to be thy brothers' and sisters' keepers.

The gloomy picture painted by progressives and some conservatives revolves around four key points: (1) new technology is displacing workers; (2) manufacturing is no longer the driving force in the economy; (3) high-paying jobs, which once supported a vibrant American middle class, have been replaced by low-paying jobs in the retail and service sectors; and (4) American jobs are being shipped overseas. There is some truth in these claims, and they make for good political rhetoric that callous and self-serving corporations and Wall Street are attaining wealth at the expense of average American workers. But the economic argument is questionable. It is true that the number of American manufacturing jobs outside the computer and electronics industry has declined.[22] But most of this decline is because of automation, not outsourcing. The manufacturing payrolls fell by 5.7 million jobs between 2000 and 2010. At the same time, the American manufacturing sector runs an enormous trade deficit. Trade with China explains an estimated 40 percent of the decline in manufacturing employment. In the service industry, though, America runs a surplus, but this sector is being challenged as well in the global economy.

So is there any hope economically for the nation and politically for Republicans? Does the decline in American manufacturing mean that Republicans need to become a party of protectionism, redistribution of wealth, and anti–global capitalism? First, while automation and robots are displacing workers, these advances directly produce economic advantages by reducing labor costs. Currently, cheap Asian labor has the advantage, but lower manufacturing costs in the United States will encourage production to return to the United States. While old-time assembly jobs are going to be fewer, new technology will create new opportunities for skilled workers.

More importantly, America has gained real advantages in the energy sector, especially natural gas. Low energy invites energy-intensive sectors such as chemicals and plastics back to the United States. This return would result in about one million new jobs in manufacturing. In addition, as natural gas energy develops, low fuel costs mean cheaper transportation costs. Technological advances in the biomedical, pharmaceutical, chemical, and electronic sectors will enable America to remain globally competitive.

On the political front, Republicans need to frame arguments to persuade American middle-class voters that they stand for economic growth. America has the highest marginal rate of corporate taxation (39 percent) of any other competing economy. This rate is 14 points higher than that of any other nation and induces firms to locate overseas. The United States lags in workplace skills. Effective high-quality vocational education is one way of reversing the deterioration of U.S. workforce skills. Modernization of the nation's physical infrastructure is also essential for lowering transportation costs and fostering the export sector. Any traveler who passes through foreign airports notices how dated America's airports are.

Republicans need to learn the lessons of the 1970s, when many leading pundits and liberal politicians talked about economic stagnation and the end of the American Dream. For these pundits, as well as for Jimmy Carter, this was the age of malaise. Dozens of articles and books appeared, looking to Japan as the model to revive the economy. Ronald Reagan, however, projected an optimistic faith that America was not on an irredeemable path of decline. Reagan tapped into the natural optimism of the American people, while assuring voters that Republicans believed in helping the truly needy, supporting good education, protecting the environment, and undertaking serious entitlement reform. He asked voters, "Are you better off than you were four years ago? Is America as respected throughout the world as it was? Are we safer today than we were four years ago?" These questions have as much resonance today as they did in 1980.

Reagan won the White House by winning the white middle-class vote. If Republicans are going to have a political future, they will have to maintain their base among white voters and either cut into the minority vote that has gone Democratic in recent midterm and presidential elections or extend the turnout of middle-class and lower-income whites. A fierce debate among Republican strategists is occurring over whether Republicans can win just by carrying the white vote or whether they need minority voters to win. Obviously, the two strategies are not necessarily mutually exclusive, but these approaches have profound implications for where to put party resources.

The white middle class forms the base of the Republican Party. This base was not large enough to win the White House for Republicans in 2012, contrary to the hopes of Republican strategists. The middle-class white vote won Congress for Republicans in the 2014 midterms.

Whites have trended Republican in recent elections. Sean Trende, an astute political analyst, argues that this trend began in 1952.[23] The question is, will an increase in the number of white voters be enough to win elections, or will this increase be offset by a growing Hispanic vote and the solid African-American vote for the Democrats that was seen in 2008 and 2012? In attempting to answer this question, strategists such as Trende have become embroiled in a number-crunching argument, the kind of stuff that fascinates people who like regression analysis and modeling.

At the root of the debate is a fundamental argument: will voters—white, Hispanic, and black—vote along ideological (and class lines), or will they vote along racial lines? Political historians have long accepted that Americans from the earliest days of democracy voted along ethnocultural lines. In short, the ethnic group and religion of a voter determined how they voted. Socioeconomic class and ideology were less important. Trende does not dispute that partisan politics of the future might come down to identity politics, but he argues that Republicans can become a majority party in midterms and presidential elections with a base of Republican voters. In making this case, he does not dismiss Hispanic and black outreach efforts. His main point is that Democrats and many Republicans have assumed too easily that the key to victory is the Hispanic vote, because this population is growing and the proportion of whites in the country is declining.

Trende's argument is sophisticated and based on modeling, but it is central to the question of whether Republicans can become a majority party based just on white voters. Based on projected population growth, he finds 6.5 million fewer white voters in 2012 than should have been expected from the 2008 vote. This drop-off in white voting primarily occurred across upstate New York, Michigan, and New Mexico. Whites who turned out broke 60–40 for Romney. If these "missing" white voters had shown up and voted in the same percentages for Romney, he still would have lost the election. In the next presidential election, however, if Republicans can expand the white vote, and the African-American vote drops to its traditional average of 11 percent instead of 13 percent, Trende argues that Republicans could win narrowly, even without moving the Hispanic, black, or Asian vote.

He maintains that these "missing" white voters are largely lower-income and rural. They are the same kind of voters who turned out for Ross Perot. These voters, he argues, could be attracted to a Republican candidate who is more populist in tone, less pro–Wall Street and big business. Such a candidate would have to thread the needle of talking about conservative economic policies and downsizing government without scaring off these downscale voters.

In his analysis, Trende observes that 75 percent of Americans eligible to vote are white. Although the proportion of white voters has declined with the rise of minority voters, more whites are voting Republican, while there is a significant decline among whites going Democratic. This trend suggests that Republicans will continue to pick up the white vote and Democrats will continue to lose this vote. Trende shows as well that Romney won among whites who identified as Independents. Democrats have reaped the benefits of a more diverse electorate—i.e., winning minority voters—but as Trende shows, it has cost them white votes. This share of the voting population will decrease, although not by much and surely not enough that Democrats can afford shedding them at the current rate. He challenges the argument that Republicans face an "existential" crisis caused by the larger demographic shift in America. Democrats are bleeding white voters, and the prediction that Hispanics will continue to vote Democratic in the same percentages is highly arguable. Furthermore, Trende notes that Republicans in 2012 increased their vote across whites of all ages. The percentages are striking. Among white voters 18–29, the Republican vote rose 7 points to 51 percent; 30–44, by 2 points to 55 percent; 45–59, by 6 points to 62 percent; and over 60, by 2 points to 59 percent. In this shift, young white voters trended more heavily Republican than any other racial group in 2012. Romney received 51 percent of the young white vote.[24]

Trende does not dismiss the importance of winning minority voters. Republicans can win without them, but he maintains there are good reasons to believe that minority voters can be won to the Republican

Party. He notes that until 2008, Republican presidential candidates usually won about 10 percent of the African-American vote. Furthermore, he predicts that African-American participation probably won't stay at the 2008 or 2012 levels, although Democrats such as Hillary Clinton enjoy strong support among black voters. He observes also that the Democratic black-brown-yellow coalition is fragile. Most African Americans are in favor of immigration reform.

Although Democrats have made much of Census Bureau projections that show whites becoming a minority by 2040, Trende predicts that Republicans will have enough electoral votes to win every election from 2016 through 2040. Only in 2044 does the tide turn. This prediction assumes that Democrats will receive 90 percent of the black vote, 75–90 percent of the Hispanic vote, and 64–88 percent of the Asian vote, based on past voting behavior. Republicans do well in his projected scenarios until 2048, when he predicts that Texas will go blue.

If Trende's predictions seem overly optimistic, he makes some fascinating observations about previous voting patterns and voter opinion. In looking at exit surveys, he finds that the majority of Hispanics did not place a high value on immigration. What motivates Hispanics are primarily the same issues that motivate white voters: jobs and the economy. The reason they have voted Democratic, he finds, is that they tend to be poorer than whites. This suggests that there is great opportunity for Republicans to win middle-class Hispanics by the same margins as they do middle-class whites. Trende challenges the notion that Hispanics are naturally liberal. The more appropriate question is, how much of the Hispanic vote can be won with a "Bush-like" candidate who could take 40 percent of the Hispanic vote? To accomplish this, Republicans would need to nominate a near-perfect candidate who appeals to Hispanics.

Of particular interest is Trende's counterintuitive finding that Hispanics have been gradually trending Republican over time. Hispanics are about 5 percent more Republican than they were in the 1970s. This reflects a socioeconomic trend. As Hispanic voters rise socioeconomically, they tend to vote Republican. Trende believes that socioeconomic status matters more than previous ideology. Furthermore, he confirms that ethnic attrition among Hispanics is high. Surveys show that just

over half of Hispanics with only one Mexican-born grandparent identify as Hispanic; more than 40 percent do not.

Trende knows that predicting voting patterns is scientific tea-leaf
reading. Candidates and environments matter. Although he believes
that increased white voter turnout should serve Republicans well, he
understands that there is a dispiriting possibility that the diverse electorate might tend toward "racial cleavages" in which "polarization be-
comes inevitable."[25]

He concludes, "Republicans should pay attention to the concerns
of the millions of alienated working-class voters who sat out the 2012
election because the GOP needs them—not at the exclusion of many
minority voters, many of whom are also working class, but in addition
to them—to forming a winning coalition in the future."[26]

There are quite a few "ifs" in Trende's analysis: white voters who
sat out could be won by Republicans; African-American turnout will
return to "normal"; Democrats will continue to face erosion among
whites; and voters will vote along socioeconomic and not racial lines.
He has come under criticism from other political analysts, Democrats
and Republicans alike.

Ronald Brownstein, writing in *The Atlantic,* offered the most extended counteranalysis.[27] Brownstein accepted Trende's point that Obama
lost ground in 2012 with nearly every segment of the white electorate.
Obama won the Catholic vote by a smaller share than any other Democrat since Jimmy Carter in 1980, largely because the white Catholic vote
went heavily against Carter. This small victory could not compensate
for losses among white women, white seniors, blue-collar men, and even
Democratic-leaning college-educated women. The issue, he counters, is
whether this structural loss will deepen even further for the Democrats.

In the end, though, Obama won 51 percent of the popular vote,
garnering 332 electoral votes. He amassed, as Brownstein notes, a solid
60 percent majority among voters under 30. Brownstein directly criti-
cizes Trende's assumption that the white voting share could reach as
high as 70 percent. He counters that this kind of turnout would require
a "heroic turnout effort." There is no reason to predict that this is going to occur, he concludes. On the other side of the coin, if Democrats

attract support from roughly 80 percent of minority voters, they would need only 37 percent of the white vote to win the popular vote. In the 1984 landslide, Ronald Reagan was the only modern Republican to reach over 60 percent of the white vote. Furthermore, Brownstein finds, even if Republicans could mobilize white working-class voters, this share of the electorate has been steadily declining, reaching a low of 36 percent in 2012. Moreover, across the spectrum, the share of whites in the electorate is declining, including married white women, white religious voters, white noncollege voters, and white Southern voters. At the same time, Obama increased his share of college-educated minorities, as well as noncollege whites, in twenty-two of the thirty-one states in which exit polls were conducted. Finally, a woman on the Democratic presidential ticket has the strong potential to win back single white women. Nearly 90 percent of Romney's total support came from whites. He lost. To double down on extending the white vote, Brownstein concludes, is to walk further down the path to oblivion.

Trende's argument that Republicans could rely solely on white voters to win future presidential elections came under attack from other quarters as well, including Republican candidate Marco Rubio's pollster Whit Ayres and Republican strategist Karl Rove. Political columnist Alan Abramowitz and demographer Ruy Teixeira offered a particularly pointed critique. Accusing Trende of reinforcing conservatives opposed to immigration reform, they argued that the "missing white voter" theory was unrealistic on a number of counts. First, they pointed out, a substantial number of nonwhites dropped out of the electorate in 2012. It was a fallacy to project that the number of missing white voters could not be countered by Democrats mobilizing disenchanted nonwhite voters. Turnout in 2012 was lower for whites and nonwhites than in 2008. According to the American National Election Study, a highly respected academic survey, dropouts, those who failed to vote, favored Barack Obama over Mitt Romney by a somewhat larger margin than returning voters. If these "missing voters" had voted, the survey showed, it would have added to Obama's margin in 2012. Furthermore, nonwhite Obama-leaning dropouts tend to be more interested in politics and better informed about politics than white dropouts. Abramowitz and

Teixeira's strongest argument, however, was that demographics favored Democrats. Given the "near inevitability" of nonwhite voters becoming an increasing share of the voting population, a Republican strategy of relying just on white voters ignores this "fundamental and irreversible trend."[28]

Many Republican strategists agree. Whit Ayres, whose clients include Senator Marco Rubio, echoed this view: "The fundamental challenge for my side is the seemingly inexorable change in the composition of presidential electorates." He added, "And there's no reason to believe that that's going to stop magically."[29] Ayres's comment could be dismissed because he was advising Marco Rubio, whose appeal to many Republicans is that he is an articulate and well-informed Hispanic. Karl Rove, who engineered George W. Bush's successful reelection campaign in 2004, which won 40 percent of the Hispanic vote, was no less adamant in criticizing Trende. He took particular aim at conservatives such as longtime grassroots activist Phyllis Schlafly and former presidential candidate Pat Buchanan, calling their view that Republicans needed to focus only on white voters in order to win back the White House totally misguided.[30] Rove, a man who loves numbers, pointed out that in order for Romney to have prevailed over Obama in the electoral count, he would have had to carry 62.54 percent of white voters, a tall order given that Ronald Reagan in his landslide 1984 victory received 63 percent of the white vote. White voter share of the electorate is declining because the nonwhite share of the vote has doubled from 1984 to 2012, from 13 percent to 28 percent.

The rising minority vote has important consequences in looking at Electoral College outcomes. In 1988, George H. W. Bush received 60 percent of the white vote, winning 426 Electoral College votes; in 2004, his son George W. Bush won 58 percent of the white vote but won only 286 electoral votes. Similarly, if Romney had won 35 percent of the Latino vote instead of the 27 percent that he did, Obama still would have won the election. Rove concluded that Republicans need a smaller increase in the share of the white vote (about 1 percent) and an increase of the Hispanic vote to about 35 percent. Increasing the white vote, Rove shows, won't be easy given that the nonwhite vote has increased in every presidential election since 1996 by 2 percent, while the share of the white vote has dropped each election.

LESSONS FROM 2008 AND 2012

In this debate, one thing stands out: Republicans lost the 2008 and 2012 presidential elections because there were not enough white voters to counterbalance the minority voters who went Democratic. Longtime Washington insider Senator John McCain in 2008 and financier Mitt Romney in 2012 were hardly the kinds of candidates to carry a populist banner to attract those "missing" lower-income working-class voters whom Ronald Reagan carried in 1980. Romney increased the share of the white vote in 2012, but he came across as distant. Most voters saw President Obama as somebody who understood their concerns. Likability is not the only quality that wins elections. Richard Nixon might not have been likable in the same way that Bill Clinton or Barack Obama proved to be, but he came across as a candidate who understood what he called "the silent majority," average middle-class voters.

McCain carried into the 2008 election the baggage of a two-term Republican president who had become increasingly unpopular. A financial meltdown in 2008 sealed McCain's fate. Romney challenged an incumbent president who entered the campaign with a huge war chest, a well-organized political machine, and enough personal popularity among voters to keep him in office.

McCain tried to project an image as a "maverick." After he had spent twenty-six years in Washington, the "maverick" label seemed a little contrived. For the reserved, buttoned-down Mitt Romney to have presented himself as a populist would have been as absurd as King George III declaring himself a "man of the people." Romney had other qualities as a candidate, and he increased the youth vote, the white vote, and the female vote for Republicans, but it was not enough to win the White House.

McCain entered the 2008 election facing an uphill battle. The American electorate overall was disenchanted with prolonged wars in Afghanistan and Iraq. George W. Bush, having won reelection in 2004 after squeaking into the White House in 2000, had lost favor among voters, and Democrats retook the House of Representatives in 2006. McCain's credentials as a Vietnam War hero and his expertise in foreign affairs appeared irrelevant when a banking crisis erupted in the midst of the presidential campaign.

On election night, McCain kept the white vote by a 13-point margin, 55 percent to Obama's 42 percent.[31] McCain's support among middle-class and upper-income voters, which included all racial groups, revealed his weakness as a candidate. His showing among lower-income voters earning less than $15,000 a year was dismal. He won only 25 percent of this vote, compared to Obama's 73 percent. Given that this group constituted only 6 percent of the electorate, this was not fatal. But he was hurt among middle-class and upper-income voters. He lost the lower-income tier of those earning $15,000 to $29,000, 12 percent of the electorate, by over 20 points, Obama's 60 percent to his 37 percent. He lost the next tier, $30,000–$49,000, and he split the $50,000–$74,000 income group. These two groups accounted for 40 percent of the electorate. Even worse for Republicans and McCain were the next two income tiers, the upper middle class and the high-income earners. Among voters earning between $75,000 and $100,000, 15 percent of the turnout, Obama won a surprising 51 percent to McCain's 48 percent. Among those making over $100,000 a year, the vote split evenly between Obama and McCain. If anyone believed that Republicans were a party of rich folks, that belief was belied by the vote.

Topping off reasons for the Republican defeat was the desertion of moderate, conservative, and Independent voters. Moderates and conservatives made up 78 percent of those voting in 2008. Obama crushed McCain (the "maverick") among Independents (29 percent of the vote), taking 52 percent to McCain's 44 percent. Even more discouraging were those voters who declared themselves conservative (34 percent of the electorate, compared to liberals, who accounted for 22 percent). Obama won a surprising 20 percent of self-identified conservatives. Many of these conservatives were African Americans who were expressing racial pride.

After the 2008 elections, Republicans had only one way to go—up. The 2008 election showed that Republicans were in real trouble with middle America. The Romney campaign believed that the election hinged on middle-class white voters. Romney's entire strategy was based on winning this vote. It worked pretty well, in that Republicans regained the confidence of middle-America white voters. What the Romney campaign failed to see was that Obama's strategy of turning out minority voters and winning enough white middle-class voters better represented the changing composition of the American electorate. After four years in office, Obama's campaign could not replicate the full enthusiasm it had enjoyed among minority and young voters, but it was still good enough to win the popular vote, 51 percent to 47 percent.

Obama's success came through minority and lower-income voters.[32] He ran better in affluent neighborhoods than had McCain. Romney's campaign reversed the hemorrhaging among middle-class and upper-income (mostly white) voters. His strategy to win these voters proved successful. There just were not enough of them to win the election. The campaign's belief that the minority vote for Obama in 2008 was an anomaly that could not be replicated underestimated a well-financed and well-organized machine that Obama and his strategists had built in the four years of his presidency.

Romney's loss took Republicans by surprise. Even the usually astute Karl Rove was caught off guard by the turnout of minority voters for Obama. There was not much consolation in the Republican camp after the loss, but Republicans had regained traction among white middle-class voters. It was a modest victory, certainly not enough to wash away defeat, but it provided a modicum of hope that the Republicans had not quite become the Federalists or Whigs of old—the defunct and forgotten parties of the past.

Democrats feared that the 2014 midterms were going to be bad, but they did not expect the thumping that Republicans gave them. Democrats hoped that the mobilization of women and minorities, and a list of good candidates, might offset the gains that Republicans were expected to make. It did not take much number-crunching of the 2012 exit polls to see that Republicans had some built-in turnout advantages as they entered the 2014 midterm elections.[33] House Democratic candidates in 2012 lost voters over the age of 45, and had barely won the 30- to 44-year-old vote. The under-30 youth vote accounted for 19 percent of all votes cast in 2012, while the over-65 vote made up 21 percent. Everyone knew that older voters turn out more than young voters in midterm elections, usually by about 19 percent. Older voters pay more attention to congressional elections and have deeper roots in their communities. Furthermore, even in the 2012 elections, the share of voters under 45 was falling, from 56 percent in 1992 to 45 percent in 2012.

But the generation gap was not the only problem facing Democrats. The white vote, especially the white middle-class vote, had shifted back to the Republicans. The gains Obama made in 2008 among middle-class and upper-income voters had been reversed. Class-warfare rhetoric had mobilized lower-income, young, and minority voters, but it should not have been surprising that the white middle-class and upper-income voters were turned off by it.

White voters are especially important in many Sun Belt states. In Southern states, Democratic candidates figured that they needed about 30–40 percent of the white vote and could count on 90 percent of the black vote. As races tightened, Democratic candidates found themselves hoping to snare 25 percent of the white vote. The white vote proved decisive for Republican candidates in 2014. Nationally, Republicans running for the House won 60 percent of the white vote.[34] Whites carried the election for Republican candidates in the South and the non-South. Outside the South, whites went Republican by an average of 8 points. In Southern states, the number of white voters marching to the Republican drumbeat was deafening.

In the Senate races in the South, Republican candidates won whites by an average of 42 points. Democratic Party reliance on minority voters was disastrous. The only Senate race in which the white vote for a Democrat was over 30 percent was in North Carolina, where Democratic senator Kay Hagan fared better, winning 33 percent of the white vote. Six years earlier when she ran for her seat, she had taken 39 percent of the white vote, including young white voters under 30, who broke for her by a two-to-one margin. In 2014, younger white voters went decisively for her opponent, Thom Tillis.

Democrats improved their overall margin among white voters in only three states: Minnesota, Oregon, and Mississippi. Not too much should be made of this, however. In Mississippi, Democratic Senate candidate Travis Childers grew the white vote from 8 percent in 2008 to 16 percent. Doubling the white vote in six years might have looked good if it were a skewed consultants' report, but Childers lost the election to Republican incumbent Thad Cochran. Sixteen percent of the white vote, even if it had doubled in eight years, still proved fatal.

Why have white voters deserted the Democrats? After his reelection, President Obama claimed that he had a mandate to help middle-class families having a hard time staying in the middle class. The 2014 elections showed that most middle-class voters were not buying it.[35] Most white voters were repulsed by class-warfare rhetoric. The slight economic recovery, evident in lower unemployment rates, has had only marginal perceived benefits for middle-class Americans. Older middle-class retirees have been hurt by low interest rates, which have suppressed returns on safe, fixed investments. Gambling on a soaring stock market goes against common sense for older middle-class investors. Low interest rates have boosted prices of assets like high-end real estate, but most middle-class and working-class Americans and small businessmen find access to capital or mortgages hard to get. Middle-class Americans see economic recovery as mostly benefiting the top 1 percent, the rarified elite in America. Democrats' call for higher income taxes alienated small-business people and professional middle-class Americans. Such rhetoric might not give the plutocrats on Wall Street or Silicon Valley second thoughts, but for many middle-class Americans carrying the brunt of income taxes, such rhetoric is scary, even if they are reassured that taxing the rich will not affect them.

Middle-class American voters in 2014 expressed their anxiety about the future. Nearly 80 percent of voters leaving the polls said that they believed the country was still in recession. These voters do not have great faith in the future, either. Nearly 50 percent do not believe that their children will do better than they have. They have lost faith in

Democratic promises of bettering the middle class, even while Democrats practice class warfare.

FUTURE POLITICS: WHITE AND MIDDLE-CLASS VOTERS

What does the desertion of white middle-class voters from the Democrats portend for the future of the Democratic and Republican parties? The loss of white middle-class voters in the 2014 midterms was disastrous for Democrats. Dismissing these results as just an off-year election would be a mistake. Presidential elections turn out minority and young voters, and this should help Democrats lower on the ticket, presuming that the party has a presidential ticket that draws enthusiasm from these voters. It is also true that in 2016 Republicans will have more congressional seats to defend. At this point, Republicans have a strong lock on Congress, and it is generally easier for incumbents to defend their seats.

The real problem Democrats face is the large numbers of white voters who are going to be around for a while. Everywhere Democrats look, there is an erosion of white voters willing to cast votes for them. It is not just that they have lost the middle-class white vote; they have lost the white working-class vote, once the backbone of the party. In 2014, over 60 percent of white non-college-educated voters went Republican. White working-class districts have been trending Republican for the last twenty years, and this trend is only increasing.

White working-class voters have been joined by white middle-class voters. Whites have become the backbone of the Republican Party, and this will benefit the GOP in the future. Whites are the vast majority in many states, including once-Democratic strongholds and key swing states. In New England and the upper Midwest, whites constitute the majority of the population. Whites make up 86 percent of the population in Iowa, and 93 percent of the population in West Virginia. In Colorado, a state that Democrats lost in 2014, whites make up 80 percent of the electorate, and in Kentucky, where Democrats lost another Senate race, nonwhites made up only 11 percent of the electorate in 2014 (and only 15 percent in 2008). In Colorado, Cory Gardner won middle-income voters with annual salaries between $50,000 and $100,000. This gave him the slim margin of victory.

Yet Republicans should not be sanguine about the future. Democrats have shown that they can nominate candidates, such as Bill Clinton in 1992 and Barack Obama in 2008, who can win the white middle-class vote. Democrats have to parse an uneasy coalition of the very wealthy and the poor, whites and minority voters. The identity politics of the past might be a failing strategy in the long term, but it remains a powerful strategy in the near future. Republicans, too, have created a volatile coalition: of religious voters in an increasingly secular society, and of white voters in a racially pluralistic society. Republicans stand as a pro-business party, while many lower-income white voters distrust Wall Street and big business.

Republicans yearn for a Reagan-like figure who will appeal to pro-business voters while winning lower-income voters. Yet the party's track record on presidential candidates since Reagan is poor. One only needs to remember Robert Dole, John McCain, and Mitt Romney. It makes for good discussions on blogs that Republicans can win those "missing" lower-income white voters to sustain their future, but getting disenchanted and disengaged eligible voters to turn out in large enough numbers to compensate for minority voters' support of their opponents is easier on paper than in reality.

Furthermore, there is no certainty that middle-class white voters will remain Republican. In the end, Republicans need to show voters that they have something real to offer in the way of solutions. Being an opposition party allows Republicans to criticize the Affordable Care Act, weak economic growth policies, and entitlements, and to play on national security threats. Republicans need to convince voters that they are not just the party of big business and instead represent the interest of average Americans who have struggled to make ends meet over the last decade. The GOP needs to show that it can govern, and for many Americans, a Republican-controlled Congress since 2014 has not been all that convincing in this regard. As Democrats are quick to point out, Congress's approval rating is much, much lower than President Obama's has been.

Appealing to white middle-class voters while attracting some upwardly aspiring minority and young voters can make Republicans into a majority party. Crafting policies, campaign strategies, and an agenda that cuts across racial-ethnic, gender, age, and socioeconomic lines is a formidable task for both parties. It is essential for Republicans, because on the presidential level, Democrats have shown that they can win the White House just on their base of minority and young voters.

What favors Republicans in the future, though, is that across all segments of the electorate, two issues stand out: jobs and economic growth. If Republicans can afford to become ensnarled in issues that play to the Democratic rhetoric of "the war on women" or class warfare, their appeal as a party of economic growth and job creation will benefit them. Republicans have a solid base in the white middle class. The test for them will be to keep this base and extend its reach to the larger electorate that is composed of minority voters, young voters, and nonreligious voters. To accomplish this means not alienating white and religious voters, while proving to the rest of the electorate that Republicans are not the party of rich white guys and religious fanatics.

If Republicans can put together a winning strategy that convinces voters that they are committed to a prosperous, strong, and equal-opportunity society, they can win. Many Americans are weary of class, race, and gender warfare. They prefer to live and let live in a country creating opportunities for everyone.

6

RELIGIOUS VOTERS

RELIGIOUS VOTERS—WHITE EVANGELICAL CHRISTIANS—REMAIN A critical bloc for the Republican Party. Catholic voters are important swing voters, and Jewish voters can play a key role in certain states. The question that Republican strategists are asking is, can the evangelical vote be expanded without losing other voters, especially in a secularized society?

- Religious voters are a central bloc in the GOP because of the high proportion of white evangelical Christian voters in Republican primaries and in state elections.
- Republican candidates are compelled to discuss social issues and express values in line with these voters because of their importance, especially in presidential primaries and statewide elections.
- At the same time, the majority of voters, especially younger voters, are secular, and many are "repulsed" by the so-called Religious Right.

This creates a dilemma for Republicans seeking to become a majority party. In 2014, successful Republican candidates deftly handled these issues. Whether these lessons can be translated into national presidential elections can begin to be answered by exploring what motivates religious and secular voters.

The Republican ascendancy that began in the late 1970s and continued through 2008 occurred with the rise of the so-called Religious Right. By mobilizing evangelical Protestants, traditional Roman Catholics, and Mormons, the Republican Party expanded its voter base and made the once-Democratic South into a GOP stronghold. Republican strategists found that social issues—abortion, the Equal Rights Amendment, and gay marriage—both attracted disenchanted Democrats to the GOP and brought new voters to the polls.

There were costs to this strategy, as successful as it was. The Religious Right became an easy target that allowed Democrats to attack Republicans as religious zealots, theocrats, and bigots. Social issues brought new voters to the polls, but also turned off other, more moderate voters, especially in the suburbs. The rise of the Religious Right also created fissures within the GOP between social conservatives and economic conservatives. These tensions were played out in often-heard complaints by social conservatives that the GOP establishment exploited the anxieties of religious voters in order to elect disingenuous candidates interested only in pushing a pro-business, low-tax agenda. The Religious Right also provided an opportunity for progressives to charge small-government Republicans with being hypocrites, demanding small-government policies when it came to economic and environmental regulation but big government in the bedroom.

Since George Washington's second administration, American political parties have always been composed of uneasy coalitions. The most apparent analogy for modern Republicans is the antebellum Whig Party, a coalition of evangelical Christian reformers, economic developers, manufacturers, pro-bank politicians, and slaveholders in the South. The coalition fell apart over slavery and the Whig Party collapsed.

Many Republicans understand that running just on social issues is not enough to win elections these days in most places, given a highly polarized electorate and an increasingly secular society. Social issues, on the other hand, cannot be ignored. Religious conservatives remain a prominent force in Republican politics, especially in presidential primaries. Forty percent of voters in Republican presidential primaries identify themselves as evangelical Christians. This imparts a disproportionate voice in the primaries to evangelicals, whom Republican candidates need to attract. Evangelical voters are especially important in the early primaries in states such as Iowa, followed by Super Tuesday primaries in the South. As a consequence, Republican presidential contenders must address social issues such as abortion and gay marriage, even though this distracts from focusing on economic and national security issues. It also means that candidates who focus primarily on social issues meant to appeal to evangelical and traditionalist religious voters emerge as major presidential contenders. One thinks of Rick Santorum and Mike Huckabee, both of whom won the Iowa caucus in their presidential bids.

If conservative religious voters were a big enough bloc to win a general election, Republicans would not have a political problem. Some Christian Right leaders, such as Ralph Reed, the first political director of the Christian Coalition and now director of the Faith and Freedom Coalition, maintain that there still exists an untapped potential for Republicans among evangelical Christians. Reed notes correctly that over 50 percent of evangelical Christians do not vote. If these evangelicals could be mobilized into voting, Republicans could become a majority party. This argument is similar to the one that Republicans could become a majority party if they tapped the "missing five million" whites who did not vote in 2012. Both arguments assume that the GOP can win elections by expanding its base among whites and evangelical Christian voters. Both arguments assume that this disinterested "nonvoter" can be mobilized to vote Republican. And both arguments face two problems: first, the white vote in itself was not enough to win the White House in the previous two presidential elections; and second, while white and evangelical Christian voters are critical to the Republican Party, neither the white nor evangelical Christian population is growing. America remains one of the most religious countries in the developed world, but large numbers of Americans, especially among the young, are secular. This means that not only are fewer Americans attending church regularly or identifying with organized religion, but their outlook is secular. Finally, it is hard for a party to appeal to nonvoters successfully without risking the loss of other voters. One is reminded of how William Jennings Bryan merged the Populists into the Democrats, pushed conservative Democrats to the Republicans, and created a Republican majority for thirty years.

The changing nature of religion in politics revealed itself all too clearly in the 2012 presidential election. For the first time in American presidential politics, not one of the candidates for president or vice president was a white Anglo-Saxon Protestant. On the Democratic side, incumbent Barack Obama was black; his running mate, Joe Biden, was Roman Catholic. The Republican challengers included Mitt Romney, a Mormon, and Paul Ryan, a Catholic.[1] The declining influence of white Anglo-Saxon Protestantism in politics was further apparent in 2014 when the Speaker of the House, John Boehner, was a Catholic; Senate majority leader Harry Reid was a Mormon; and the nine justices of the Supreme Court did not include a Protestant. This was a far different world than in 1776, when fifty-five of the fifty-six signers of the Declaration of Independence were white Protestants.

THE PASSION OF A YOUNG CHRISTIAN

Steven L. is a serious, well-considered young man, a second-year MBA student at a state university, and an ROTC student. Looking at him, one would not know that his father is a Korean American and his mother is white. He is polite, easygoing, and not effusive in conversation, although he smiles easily. Underlying his understated demeanor, though, is a deep faith as a nondenominational Christian, a loyal Republican, and a fierce American patriot. At heart, he is a warrior for his faith, his party, and his country.

Steven grew up in Southern California. He attended a Christian homeschool cooperative program with about seventy other children, before his parents enrolled him in a public high school with about 2,600 students. Steven found the adjustment from homeschooling to public school easy. He has three sisters, one older and two younger. All his siblings consider themselves Republicans, although his younger sister is more socially liberal than the rest of the family.

His father was born in Long Island, New York, but at the age of six the family returned to their native Korea. The family was in the utilities industry and was well-to-do. The patriarch of the family was his father's uncle. All of Steven's cousins grew up in Seoul, but they shared with Steven a love of James Bond and John Wayne. They were pro-American. His father did not grow up a Christian. He became a Christian while at the University of Oregon. There he met his future wife, the daughter of Christian missionaries who had spent most of their lives in the Sudan in the late 1950s through the 1970s. Steven's mother grew up in the Sudan, before she met her future husband at the campus ministry at Oregon.

One of his father's brothers also moved to Southern California. He married a Japanese American. "My family," Steven says, "is pretty culturally diverse and tolerant." He notes that a lot of Koreans have animosity toward the Japanese because of the atrocities committed in Korea during World War II, but this animosity was not seen in his extended family. He gets along with his two cousins, although they are liberal politically and vote Democratic. When asked why he thought he was a conservative and his cousins liberals, he said that they are both smart and want to be scientists, but as Asian-American teenagers, his cousins mostly want to fit into American culture. He said their views might change as they get older, but "who knows."

Steven's household was Christian and Republican. His parents were not active in the GOP, but at the dinner table they would talk politics. As a young boy growing up, he listened to talk radio, read conservative classics, and was deeply influenced by F. A. Hayek's *Road to Serfdom*. In high school he was not active in Republican Party politics. His greatest passion was wrestling.

Steven's first years in college were not political. He focused mostly on school and ROTC. He joined a local nondenominational evangelical church. Most of the nine hundred members of the congregation were young people. He became active in Republican Party politics during the Republican primary in 2012. He was anti-Obama but did not have strong opinions about any of the Republican contenders. He came to support Mitt Romney as the best candidate to defeat Obama. He now considers himself a libertarian-conservative, a "bit more socially conservative" than many of his libertarian friends. He believes that Christianity offers a "necessary and healthy foundation" for the country. He believes in a strong national defense and a restrained American foreign policy, but he is not opposed to American military intervention if necessary.

When asked why minority voters, of which he could be considered one, are so strongly Democratic, he observed that it is easy to generalize about minority voters. Hispanics are religious, while many Asian Americans, with the exception of Koreans, are not religious. What minority voters have in common, if a generalization can be made, is that family and tradition are important to them. Minority voters, he argues, can be won to the Republican side if the party emphasizes the importance of the free market and the importance of family in society. The problem with Romney for many minority voters was that he seemed to represent the political establishment in their native countries—rich and privileged. For Asian Indians, he says, "Romney represented the caste system they had sought to escape." He came across to them as "the guy in India who supported slavery through the caste system."

Steven believes that many young people are changing their views of Obama. He feels that Obama excited young voters because he was a "shiny new object" in politics and and they wanted to be part of something new. They were looking to be part of history. Obama was "anti-establishment and was taking on Hillary Clinton." He adds that it "became cool to wear an Obama shirt."

Steven believes that Republicans can win the youth vote in the future. The key, he maintains, is arguing for free market principles, quality education, fiscal responsibility, and a strong foreign policy based on "standing up for what's right." At the end of the day, "Americans will recognize evil for what it is." He thinks that Republicans need to convince young voters that the party favors change and reform. While many of his friends are nonreligious or even anti-religious, a large number of his friends are Christians concerned about social issues and anti-Christian attacks in the press and by politicians who are trying to "maliciously divide people." He asks, "Why are not these people okay with a mix of faith-based principles and religious institutions involved in charity and helping the poor?" His own church congregation volunteers a "huge" amount of time in community work through food and clothing drives, tutoring programs, and youth activities. A religious foundation, he stresses, is essential to a "good society." He concludes that what makes America truly exceptional is religious freedom. Republicans should not be afraid of standing up for religious freedom or defending "Judeo-Christian" values.

Steven is concerned about America's future, but he is committed to serving his country. "This is one of the most racially and culturally diverse countries in human history," he declares. "I want to defend our values from those who want to destroy it." This is his faith as a Christian American. "I am committed to four years' service in the military after I finish my MBA, and I am looking forward to it. After this, I might go into sales in the aerospace industry or an international defense consulting firm." He adds that he would like to have a family and children. "I don't have any racial preferences of whom I marry," he reflects. "My main interest in a partner will be their values."

AMERICANS IN A SECULAR AGE

Young Christians such as Steven see America becoming a more secular and religiously diverse society. In a massive study of American religious attitudes and affiliations released in May 2014, the Pew Research Center reported that the "Christian share of the U.S. population is declining, while the number of U.S. adults who do not identify with any organized religion is growing."[2] Comparing this study with an earlier 2007 study, Pew researchers noted a rapid decline in church membership that is occurring across denominations and among all age groups and races. Although Americans remain the most religious people in Western society, those who describe themselves as Christians dropped nearly 8 percent in just seven years from the first study. Roughly seven in ten Americans identify as Christians affiliated with an American denomination. At the same time, those describing themselves as atheists, agnostics, or nothing in particular have grown to 28 percent. The greatest loss among Christian denominations has been in mainline Protestant churches and Roman Catholics. Evangelical Christians have remained relatively stable.

About 44 percent of American adults have a different religious affiliation from the one they grew up with.[3] Nonetheless, many Americans remain deeply religious. About 76 percent of Americans, including some who identify as nonreligious, report that prayer is an important part of their lives. This percentage is about the same as it was twenty-five years ago. Furthermore, close to 40 percent of Americans reported in 2012 that they go to religious services about once a week. What has climbed, though, is the percentage of Americans who say that they seldom or never attend religious services. Most Americans (80 percent) believe in a higher being, but an increasing number over the last twenty-five years say they doubt the existence of God. The percentage of Americans who believe that the Bible should be taken literally has also declined from the late 1970s, to about 31 percent in 2012.

This coincides with a sharp decline in religious affiliation. Disaffiliation from organized religion is distributed across economic, gender, and educational lines. Most of this turn away from organized religion has occurred among whites. The share of blacks and Hispanics who are religiously unaffiliated has not changed much. Those who are not affiliated tend to be more secular, even though the majority of those unaffiliated still believe that religious institutions are a force for good in society. Three-quarters of those unaffiliated, however, believe that religious organizations bring people together and help strengthen communities. They just do not share the religious experience.

Millennials are especially apathetic toward Christianity. As a result, the median age of Americans affiliated with a denomination has risen. Christian participation is becoming more and more just for old people. Nonetheless, there are still 178 million Americans who identify themselves as affiliated Christians. Of these, about 36 million are mainline Protestants, belonging to the United Methodist Church, the

American Baptist Church, the Evangelical Lutheran Church, the Presbyterian Church (U.S.A.), and the Episcopal Church. American evangelical Christians number about 62 million. Their numbers in churches such as the Southern Baptist Convention, the Assemblies of God, Churches of Christ, the Lutheran Missouri Synod, and the Presbyterian Church in America have remained stable. The Roman Catholic share of the population has also remained relatively stable, with about 51 million Catholic adults in America.

More than a third of millennials are religiously unaffiliated. This is not to say, however, that many millennials are not religious. While Pew researchers correctly emphasize the decline of religiosity among this generation, a closer look at the survey shows that close to 50 percent consider themselves Christians affiliated with a church. Among those declaring themselves Christians, 16 percent are Roman Catholic, 11 percent are mainline Protestants, and 20 percent are evangelical Protestants. This religious orientation suggests that Republicans can attract the youth vote by not backing away from the importance of religious freedom and the importance that organized religion plays in American society.

Nearly a quarter of Generation Xers describe themselves as atheists or agnostics. They reflect a trend of American adults who are leaving their churches. Nearly one in five adults, across generations, who grew up Christian now identifies with no religion. This decline in religious affiliation is occurring across all regions. In the South today, 19 percent of adults list themselves as unaffiliated. In the Midwest, the number is 20 percent; in the Northeast it is 25 percent; and in the West, the most secular region in the country, it is 28 percent.

The greatest erosion of religious affiliation has occurred among whites. Close to a quarter of whites told Pew researchers that they do not belong or go regularly to church. But large numbers of blacks and Hispanics are also unaffiliated. College-educated Americans have become increasingly unaffiliated. Indeed, only 64 percent of college-educated adults remain churchgoing. Declines in religiosity have occurred among non-college-educated people as well, but the rate of this downward trend has been less rapid.

American Christianity appears to be in decline. The country is becoming more secular, and Protestants are no longer the majority of the population, at only about 47 percent. Only 15 percent of Americans identify themselves as belonging to mainline Protestant churches. Many Christians in America today express anxiety and anger about the growing secular culture. It's not just that the culture is changing; nor is it that there has been an exodus of youth away from organized religion. Instead, many Christians feel that their faith is under direct attack.

Christians tend to be more conservative on social issues. For example, the Pew study found that about 38 percent of evangelical Protestants oppose same-sex marriage, compared to about 31 percent of white Catholics and 33 percent of Hispanic Catholics. Black and Hispanic Protestants stand even more opposed to same-sex marriage, with 54 percent among black Protestants and 58 percent among Hispanic Protestants. Furthermore, the shift among Christians to Republican or Republican-leaning party identification has increased. By the time of the 2012 election, the number of Republicans among white evangelicals had increased, especially among the young. White evangelicals over 30 years of age who are Republicans stand at 69 percent, but even more significantly, white evangelicals under 30 declaring themselves Republican have increased. A similar increase was seen among Roman Catholics, old and young. Fifty-four percent of white Catholics under 30 called themselves Republican, compared to only 40 percent who labeled themselves Democrats. Catholics over 30 split 49 percent Republican to 43 Democrat. This movement toward the Republican Party marked an 8 percent increase from 2008 for Catholics over 30 and an even more significant shift among young Catholics, a gain for the Republicans of 13 percent from 2008.

Across-the-board party identification toward the Republican Party has increased from 2008. Although 52 percent of those under 30 described themselves as Democratic or Democratic leaning in 2012, there was a decided shift of 4 percent within this age cohort declaring themselves Republican. For white evangelicals, this shift was even higher, especially among those under 30, who increased by 15 percent. A similar shift occurred among young Catholics. Older evangelical, mainline

Protestants and Catholics shifted Republican on average by about 5 percent.

The Jewish vote accounts for about 2 percent of the popular vote. In 2012, Romney won 30 percent of this vote, up 8 points from what McCain received in 2008, when he took only 22 percent. Romney made inroads among Jews but did not equal George H. W. Bush's 35 percent in 1988, Reagan's 39 percent in 1980, or Eisenhower's high mark in 1952, when he won 40 percent, the highest percentage of any modern Republican presidential candidate since World War II. Republican gains in 2012 among Jews arguably reflected an anomaly in an election year with generally low turnout among all voters.[4]

The Jewish vote, although a small percentage of the total electorate, is especially important in states such as Florida. Obama won Florida by only a 0.87-point margin, or 74,000 votes out of 8.4 million cast. In 2012, pro-Israel Jewish groups flooded the state with anti-Obama TV spots. Whether these ads paid off in Florida with Jewish voters is arguable. The Florida Jewish vote for Romney matched national exit polls, which gave Obama 66 percent and Romney 30 percent of the Jewish vote. Whatever the case, by 2014 there was a marked shift among Jews away from the Democratic Party. Gallup pollsters found that among all Jewish voters (those affiliated with a synagogue or not), there was a 5-point drop in Jews declaring themselves Democrats.

Sixty-one percent of Jews identified themselves as Democrats, still a sizeable bloc within the Democratic coalition. A 5-point drop in Democratic affiliation is significant, however, especially when this decline was even higher, 10 percent, among "very religious" or "moderately religious" Jews. This means that among religious Jews, Democrats have a small share of the vote. Like other voters, Jews rank economic and job creation as their major concerns, but foreign policy issues, U.S.-Israel relations, and the Iran nuclear deal in 2015 have been particular concerns for Jewish voters, especially the more religious.[5]

This shift toward Republicans among Christians and Jews is significant. Democratic strategists maintain that Americans are becoming more liberal, but a close look at Pew Research shows otherwise. The majority of Americans, except for 49 percent of millennials, describe themselves as "patriots." Older Americans—the Gen X, Boomer, and Silent generations—expressed overwhelming patriotic sentiments, ranging from 64 percent to 84 percent. Millennials were most supportive of gay rights (61 percent), but only 37 percent of Gen Xers said they supported gay rights, compared to 33 percent of boomers and only 32 percent of the Silent Generation. Even more revealing were those who thought of themselves as environmentalists. Only a surprising 32 percent of millennials described themselves as "an environmentalist," while around 40 percent of their elders labeled themselves this way.

Republicans should not back away from a view that churches and community religious institutions remain essential to community cohesiveness. As Robert D. Putnam, a Harvard University sociologist, shows in great detail, the single biggest factor in helping the poor better their lives is religion. Religion is important for the rich and the poor.[6] Compared to their non-churched peers, youth involved in religious organizations take tougher courses in high school and get higher grades and test scores. Children involved in religious organizations are less likely to drop out of high school.

"Controlling for many other characteristics of the child, her family, and her schooling," Putnam writes, "a child whose parents actually attend church regularly is 40 to 50 percent more likely to go on to college than a matched child of non-attenders."[7] More college-educated parents attend church than their non-college-educated counterparts. Putnam's argument is not that going to church regularly induces moral principles, which he would not deny, but that organized religion provides a social system and community support. A single woman experiencing alcohol or drug addiction will find a real safety net in a support system of caring congregations, ministers and priests, and pastoral counselors. This religious community enables a poor single mother to improve her life emotionally, socially, and economically. A Republican candidate who recognizes the importance of religion held by the majority of Americans, and that these religious beliefs embody compassion, not just zealotry, can win over both religious and nonreligious voters.

Religious voters cannot be ignored by Republicans, nor should they be ignored by Democrats, for that matter. Much of the Republican base is religious, while more of the Democratic base is secular. Those who are unaffiliated (six out of ten) describe themselves as Democrats. Over a third describe themselves as "liberals," while only 20 percent say they are conservative. Yet neither party is composed purely of religious or secular voters.

RELIGIOUS VOTERS IN AN AGE OF ANXIETY

While social trends for minorities, women, and youth give cause for optimism, the trends for conservative religious Americans do not. This should cause anxiety for the GOP, as the number of these voters appears to be decreasing as a proportion of the electorate, at least if present trends hold in the long run. Today, religious voters have a significant impact on Republican primaries and in general elections. A look at the exit polls in 2012 reveals the importance evangelical voters have in key primary states.

In February 2016, caucuses and primaries were held in Iowa and New Hampshire. In Iowa, 38 percent of the voters were evangelical; in New Hampshire, 12 percent identified themselves as evangelical. These were followed by a wave of primaries in March. A quick glance of self-identified evangelical voters in 2016 primary states in order of their election dates shows the importance of the religious vote:

Alabama: 47 percent evangelical.
Minnesota: 23 percent evangelical.
North Carolina: 35 percent evangelical.
Virginia: 23 percent evangelical.
Mississippi: 50 percent evangelical.
Michigan: 28 percent evangelical.
Ohio: 31 percent evangelical.
Florida: 24 percent evangelical.
Illinois: 20 percent evangelical.
Missouri: 37 percent evangelical.[8]

Of course, not all evangelical Christians will vote Republican. The exit polls in 2012 included all voters, Republican and Democrat, white, black, and Hispanic. African-American evangelicals tend to vote Democratic. Still, the importance of the evangelical Christian vote in presidential primaries is profound.

The influence of the religious vote raises important issues for Republicans if they are going to become a majority party: does appealing to religious voters—that is, those voters who primarily cast their votes based on religious values—turn off voters less interested in social issues? An even more important question: is there an untapped well of evangelical Christians who are not voting but, if mobilized, could be enough to win elections for GOP candidates?

Any discussion of religious voters needs to understand that many traditional Christians are anxious about their place in American society. In the late 1970s, Republican strategists translated a similar anxiety among religious Americans into votes. Traditional Catholics, evangelical Christians, and Mormons felt under attack. Supreme Court decisions banning prayer in school and supporting the legalization of abortion were especially upsetting. Rising divorce rates and heavy drug and alcohol use also suggested dysfunction or moral decay. The rise of the radical feminist movement, critical of "stay-at-home" mothers and traditional marriage, furthered this sense of alienation. Republican candidates played upon these anxieties to mobilize these voters. Evangelical voters, once Democrats, became Republicans. Evangelical disillusionment with Jimmy Carter played a role, too. Roman Catholics, once the lynchpin of the Democratic Party, are now divided nearly 50–50 between Republicans and Democrats.

The anxiety Christians felt about their place in American society and politics never fully abated, but many believed that they had found a voice in the Republican Party. The relationship between the party and religious voters was always an uneasy one. The connection seemed strongest in the 1980s, when Jerry Falwell's Moral Majority, Pat Robertson's *700 Club*, and many Catholic bishops and clergymen took stands that resonated with the Republican Party. As time passed, there was special resentment against George H. W. Bush, who never appeared comfortable with the Religious Right. Complaints were heard frequently from leaders in the Religious Right that Republicans were taking their votes for granted. Furthermore, a strong sentiment prevailed in traditional and evangelical Christian circles for a retreat from party politics.

This sentiment was captured in 1996 in a special issue of *First Things*, edited by Rev. Richard Neuhaus, a leading spokesman for traditional Catholicism. In the introduction to the special issue, "End of Democracy," Neuhaus asked his readers "whether we [traditional Christians] are reaching the point where conscientious citizens can no longer give moral assent to the existing regime." He asked readers to consider the idea that "the government of the United States of America no longer governs by the consent of the governed."[9] This perspective that government, elected representatives, and public officials no longer represented the values or the interests of traditional Christians remained a strong undercurrent within conservative circles, especially after the 2008 election, when Democrats won the White House and Congress. Some religious conservatives appeared to feel that they were a saved remnant living in Caesar's corrupt Rome. It was not a pervasive belief among conservative religious leaders, who continued to call upon their followers to vote, yet a view prevailed among many Christians to render unto Caesar what was his and concentrate their efforts on attaining the kingdom to come.

Feelings of being under attack have intensified among Christians in the last eight years. The Supreme Court's decision to recognize a constitutional right for gays to marry in *Obergefell v. Hodges* (2015) came as a blow to conservative Christian activists. This decision was cheered by many progressive pundits, who claimed that the Religious Right had lost the "cultural war." The Supreme Court's decision was just one in a series of setbacks in what religious conservatives see as a war against their faith and beliefs. Religious monuments have been removed from public places; Christian business owners have been fined for refusing to extend services to gay couples intending to marry; and corporate leaders have been forced to step down because of their support for traditional marriage. Across the country, American college and university students who express Christian faith have come under criticism. InterVarsity Christian Fellowship, an evangelical Christian group, has been forced off many campuses for its opposition to gay marriage.

The clash over rights—religious freedom, civil rights, and equal protection under the law—is not easily resolved. Most Americans believe that a business owner should sell to anyone who wants the product. Segregationists' resistance to serving or providing public accommodations to blacks cannot be forgotten. Customers have constitutional rights not to be discriminated against. A business owner cannot discriminate against a customer because of race, gender, age, or sexual orientation. Under the law, selling a good is different from participating in an activity—let's say a wedding party, for example. The distinction between offering a product for sale and participating in an activity that is against one's religious or moral principles, however, is blurry. Does a wedding planner who is black have to sell or participate in a wedding celebration of Ku Klux Klan members who insist that white supremacy be the theme of the wedding? Does a Holocaust survivor or Orthodox Jewish event planner have to offer services to a neo-Nazi group planning a celebration of Adolf Hitler's birthday? Constitutional principles of freedom of conscience and free association can conflict with civil liberties and the equal protection clause.

Such issues have raised anxiety among religious Americans. Capturing this anxiety by keeping and extending their religious base will mean striking a delicate balance between Republicans who proclaim themselves to be defenders of constitutional rights and voters who are upset with how the constitution has been interpreted.

As University of Notre Dame political scientist David Campbell warns, efforts by conservatives to promote religious freedom in opposition to gay rights and other social issues have the potential to galvanize nonreligious voters. He observes that many millennials have been repulsed by the Religious Right.[10]

Some leaders of the Religious Right maintain that evangelical voters are an untapped resource. Presidential candidate Mike Huckabee argued in the *Christian Post* that if 10 percent more evangelical voters had gone to the polls, Obama would not have won the 2012 election. Huckabee posited that there are about 80 million evangelical

Christians, but only 20 million actually voted in 2012. An even smaller number, 10 million, he emphasized, vote in the midterm election and primary elections, where they could have a disproportionate influence. "What would happen," he asks, "if, instead of half of those voters being registered, 75 percent of them were? And what would happen if, instead of half of them voting, 75 percent of them voted? If 10 percent more Evangelicals had voted in the last presidential election, we would have a different president than the one we have right now." The Providence Forum, a conservative religious website, echoed this view a short time later by pointing out the same figures. From these numbers, the Forum concluded, "If every Christian would register to vote and then do so, candidates who share their beliefs and values would win the presidency in a landslide." Of course, this assumes that all Christians would vote conservative. Progressives can make a similar argument that not all Hispanics, blacks, or secular voters—the current Democratic base—are registered either. Barry Goldwater also made similar arguments about unregistered conservatives in 1964. Goldwater no doubt did win extra conservative votes, but in the process he lost moderates and the election in a landslide.[11]

The argument that evangelical Christians could be a decisive voice in American politics is based on polling done by George Barna, a Christian pollster, who claims that Christian pastors are not encouraging their congregations to vote. He jokingly told the Family Research Council's Values Voter Summit, "The great theologian, Woody Allen, once said this, success is 80 percent just showing up. And frankly, if we don't show up, then I'll tell you what happens. Government does whatever it wishes to do. When we show up, government does what we sent it to do."

Other religious conservatives feel less sanguine about the capacity of evangelical voters to propel the party into majority status. Well-known radio commentator Michael Medved, a conservative Jew, challenges the notion that "victory lies with the hordes of disillusioned Christian evangelicals for whom today's GOP isn't nearly conservative enough."[12] Medved bolsters his argument with data from polling conducted by Ralph Reed's Faith and Freedom Coalition, which looked at Obama's

2012 victory in the key swing states of Florida and Ohio. Reed, a leading spokesman for the Christian Right, found that evangelical turnout in these states ranged between 75 percent and 80 percent, the highest turnout of any segment of the electorate. These evangelical Christian voters went overwhelmingly for Mitt Romney, a Mormon, belying any argument that evangelical Christians would refuse to vote for a Mormon.

Medved notes further that the evangelical vote for George W. Bush in 2004, a Republican victory, constituted 23 percent of the electorate, 3 points lower than the turnout (26 percent) of evangelicals in 2012. Medved questions whether the turnout of evangelicals can get much higher and whether the "missing" 50 percent of evangelical Christians can be registered and would vote Republican. Although Medved does not break down the evangelical vote itself, many African Americans identify themselves as evangelicals, and they make up about 6 percent of the evangelical population. There is no reason to assume that these black evangelicals would vote overwhelmingly Republican.

Past politics undermines the argument that evangelical Christians can carry a presidential candidate to the Promised Land. The experience of presidential candidates in the Iowa caucuses in 2008 and 2012 reveals some of the problems of this strategy. In 2008, presidential candidate Mike Huckabee targeted evangelical voters. The strategy worked. He won Iowa with 34.4 percent of the vote. Nonetheless, his five main rivals won more than 65 percent of the combined vote.

Four years later, as a plethora of Republican candidates descended on Iowa to contest the first caucus in 2012, Rick Santorum, a conservative Catholic running largely on social issues, sought to repeat Huckabee's strategy. Targeting traditional Catholics and evangelical Christians, he spoke repeatedly, tirelessly, and heatedly about the importance of Christian morality and values in American society. He, too, won the Iowa caucus. Yet behind the headlines of his victory stood the reality that Santorum won only thirty-four more votes than Mitt Romney, who did not emphasize social issues in his Iowa campaign. Altogether, Santorum's main rivals—Mitt Romney, Ron Paul, and Newt Gingrich—outpolled him, close to 60 percent to his 24.6 percent.

Winning the Republican caucus in Iowa with a heavy evangelical vote was not enough to win the nomination for Huckabee in 2008 or Santorum in 2012. In fact, in combined votes, neither Huckabee nor Santorum won the majority of voters in Iowa. What the Iowa caucuses and primaries show, and what the inability of Huckabee or Santorum to win the final presidential nomination shows, is that while evangelical voters constitute an important bloc in Republican primaries and are essential in a general presidential election, they are not enough to win the White House for a Republican candidate who makes social issues the primary focus of a campaign. Evangelical voters play a more significant role in statewide elections, especially in off-year midterms. A review of the previous presidential elections and the 2014 election shows the strengths and weaknesses of conservative religious voters.

CHRISTIAN VOTER MOBILIZATION IN REPUBLICAN ELECTIONS

Devout Christian voters carry their moral concerns into the voting booth, but religious beliefs play a varied role in shaping political attitudes in unexpected ways. Religion matters for these voters on critical issues. Before exploring the role religion plays in the voting booth, it is important to note that conservative religious voters list the economy and job growth as their top two concerns.

Polls conducted by Pew Research in 2010 and 2014 reveal nuances in religious voters.[13] Asked how religion affects their views on immigration, the environment, government, hunger, poverty, abortion, and same-sex marriage, voters told Pew researchers that the answer depended upon the particular issue. Immigration, the environment, hunger, and poverty are good examples of issues in which religion plays a minimal role. About half of those who hear about immigration in church told Pew researchers that their clergy are favorable toward immigrants, and close to 65 percent said their clergy encourage environmental protection. An even higher number (88 percent) report that their priests and clergy talk about hunger and poverty in America. Yet on these issues, churchgoing voters do not pay much attention to the clergy.

Religion informs many voters' views on same-sex marriage and homosexuality, abortion, and capital punishment. These issues stand in sharp contrast to views about immigration, the environment, and welfare. In 2010, 35 percent of Americans, based on the survey, declared that religion was the major influence on their views of same-sex marriage. Of these, 60 percent who oppose gay marriage are influenced by religious views. Forty-five percent of abortion opponents say religion exerts the most important influence on their thinking. About a third of those opposed to the death penalty are informed by religious beliefs. Only 10 percent of Americans cite religion as influencing their thinking about government assistance to the poor.

What this polling suggests is that religious conservatives hear what they want to from their clergy. Religious voters appear to ignore messages from the pulpit about immigration, the environment, and public assistance, while accepting what they hear in opposition to same-sex marriage, abortion, and capital punishment. These positions can be viewed as "conservative" beliefs, with the exception of capital punishment. However these social issues are placed within the ideological spectrum, churchgoing Americans are filtering messages from their religious leaders.

At the same time, many conservative religious voters believe that religion and politics do mix. That this had become particularly true by 2014 was revealed in a Pew Research survey conducted that year. In that survey, nearly 60 percent of Republican or Republican-leaning respondents said they believed that churches should express views on social and political issues, an 11 percent rise since 2010. The call for churches to speak out on political issues was even higher among evangelical Protestants, 66 percent of whom called for churches to be engaged with these issues. Black Protestants shared this belief, at 60 percent. Catholics and mainline Protestants were more divided on the role of the church in politics. In fact, both groups split down the middle on whether churches should be talking about these issues.[14]

Not only do religious voters believe that churches should be talking about political issues, but there is a rising sentiment that political leaders need to talk about religious values. Pew Research found that from the 2010 survey to the 2014 survey there had been an increase in the number of Americans who believe that political leaders need to talk more about their religious faith. Now about 44 percent of Americans want leaders to talk about religious values. Nearly 70 percent of evangelical Protestants say that political leaders are offering too little expression about religious faith and prayer. This contrasts with only about a quarter of Americans who believe there has been just about the right amount of religious speech from politicians.

Many Americans are declaring that religion and politics mix, and they believe that candidates elected to office should have strong religious views. The number of people holding these views is surprising, given the general view that America is becoming increasingly secular. Over 83 percent of evangelical Christians and nearly 60 percent of white Catholics believe that it is important for members of Congress to have strong religious views. This desire for politicians to hold strong religious beliefs coincides with a general belief that religion is critical to a well-ordered society. More than 56 percent of Americans believe it is a "bad thing" that religion is losing influence in America. The belief that secularization is bad for American society is held by 77 percent of evangelical Christians, as well as by the majority of mainline Protestants (66 percent), black Protestants (65 percent), and Catholics (61 percent). Even the religiously unaffiliated, who see the influence of religion declining in America, are divided evenly on whether secularization is a good or bad thing.

This has consequences for both political parties. Roughly half of American adults (47 percent) see the Republican Party as friendly toward religion, while 30 percent say that the GOP is neutral. This is not the case for Democrats. Only 29 percent of Americans see the Democratic Party as friendly toward religion, and 25 percent describe Democrats as unfriendly toward religion. Democrats are viewed as the party hostile to religion. Obama is increasingly seen as unsympathetic toward religion. Nearly 30 percent say that the administration is unfriendly to religion, a sharp increase from the 17 percent who held this view in 2009 and higher than the 23 percent who held this view in 2012. Within two years, the view that Obama is unfriendly toward religion shot up by 6 points, a bad trajectory for any president. Religious voters might be declining slightly in influence, but it is still not good to be perceived as the anti-Christian party or president, as are the Democrats and Obama.

Religion is important to many Americans in their lives and politics. Yet exaggerating the importance of religion in how people vote would be misleading. Among the things that concern religious Americans, religious issues rank fairly low. Whether religious or unaffiliated, evangelical Protestant or mainline Protestant, Catholic or Protestant, voters tend to rank the most important issues that concern them the same. Ninety percent of Americans say that the economy and jobs are their top concern. Seventy-eight percent rank healthcare, 73 percent rank terrorism, 69 percent rank budget deficits, and 68 percent rank taxes as "very important."

These are primarily economic and national security issues. Talk of a cultural war can distort what is most concerning to American voters. Although social issues should not be dismissed as unimportant, they rank low as priorities that concern Americans. Immigration ranked tenth on the list of concerns (about 58 percent ranked it as a "very important" concern). Abortion and same-sex marriage ranked last on the list of Americans' thirteen major concerns. These issues fell slightly behind "the environment," at 57 percent. Less than a majority (43 percent) ranked abortion as a "very important" issue, and only 32 percent saw same-sex marriage as "very important." This Pew survey was conducted shortly after the 2014 election and before the Supreme Court declared same-sex marriage a constitutional right. In the end, economic and national security issues outweigh social issues in the minds of most American voters. Politicians in both parties should keep this in mind when going after the religious vote.

Evangelical Protestants might not march to the polls in large enough numbers to guarantee that Republicans win every election, but their vote remains essential to any success. Mainline Protestants and Roman Catholics have tended to vote Democratic in every postwar election, with a couple of exceptions. Democrats cannot count on always getting the Catholic vote, but Catholics have been consistent in favoring Democratic presidential candidates in the post–World War II period. Even in 1952, when Dwight D. Eisenhower won in a landslide election, the majority of Catholics (56 percent) voted for his opponent, Democrat Adlai Stevenson.[15] They did not desert Stevenson in 1956 either, giving him 51 percent of their vote. Democratic margins for Catholic voters shot up with John F. Kennedy heading the ticket in 1960, but since 1980 they have played a role as swing voters. White Catholics today lean Republican by about the same margin as all whites (50 percent to 41 percent). Hispanic Catholics lean Democratic, 58 percent to 25 percent. Mormons are overwhelmingly Republican, at 70 percent, just a little more than Jews who identify themselves as Democrats (61 percent).

Religious identity in politics is best indicated by church attendance. Americans who attend church regularly will be most informed in the voting booth by their religion. Gallup began tracking church attendance in voting behavior in 2000, which showed a clear correlation between weekly church attendance and Republican affiliation. Since 2000, those who attend church regularly have voted Republican in ranges of 55 percent (2008) to 63 percent (2004).

Because evangelical Christians tend to vote Republican, they are an important part of a coalition made up of pro-business conservatives and religious conservatives. It does not always make for an easy coalition, either in political campaigns or in trying to govern. On national, state, and local issues, elected Republicans can find themselves accused of being RINO (Republican In Name Only), part of the Republican establishment, and fostering "crony capitalism" if they pursue legislative compromise at the expense of social issues, which religious voters often believe cannot be compromised. Either one is for or against abortion, gay marriage, or myriad other cultural issues. Elected officials in safe congressional or state legislative districts can afford to take strong, uncompromising positions on these issues, offering red meat rhetoric to their constituents. National and statewide candidates facing a divided electorate on these issues have to offer voters more nuanced positions. Such positions need not be unprincipled, but can rather be pragmatic. Hard-core activists provide the troops that knock on doors, distribute literature, make phone calls, and staff campaign offices. These activists are important. Convincing them that "principled pragmatism" is what they should look for in a candidate is critical to winning elections.

The main issue facing the GOP in the future as its looks to become a majority party is whether the George W. Bush 2004 campaign, which relied heavily on mobilizing evangelical voters, can be replicated in the future. The bare Republican presidential victory in 2000 convinced the George Bush/Karl Rove/Dick Cheney team that in order to win reelection in 2004, evangelical voters needed to be mobilized.[16] Rove believed that they had not been mobilized in 2000 and blamed the near-death experience on 3 million evangelicals who failed to show up. Ralph Reed, a leading strategist on the Christian Right, was hired to reach evangelical Christian voters. Nine battleground states were targeted through Reed's Social Conservative Outreach program. Chairpersons were selected in these battleground states with specific targets for voter registration, recruiting committed volunteers, and reaching like-minded voters. Churches and pastors were contacted to conduct voter registration drives and to speak out on abortion and marriage issues.

The results were impressive. More than 350,000 evangelical Christians volunteered for the Bush campaign (out of 1.4 million total volunteers). On Election Day, the campaign drew 3.5 million more evangelical voters than had shown up in 2000. These voters came out for Bush, who won 78 percent of the evangelical vote. An estimated 6 million new evangelical voters from 2000 (including those who had voted for Al Gore in 2000) pulled the Republican lever. It was an impressive victory, which suggested that evangelical Christian voters offered a path to electoral success.

In the 2012 presidential election, Republican candidate Mitt Romney won 76 percent of the "Born-Again/Evangelical" vote. This percentage equaled Bush's vote in 2004 and upped McCain's 73 percent share of the evangelical vote in 2008. At the same time, Obama's share of the evangelical vote declined a full 6 points, from 26 percent in 2008 to 20 percent in 2012. A good portion of Obama's evangelicals were African Americans. Monday-morning quarterbacks after the election pointed out that while Romney's share of the evangelical Christian vote rose, the numbers of evangelicals turning out to vote had declined. Romney's share of the pie was larger, Richard Griffin declared in his conservative RedState blog, but he had "a bigger slice of a smaller pie." Griffin was quick to note the share of the evangelical vote declined by 5 or 6 points in certain states, including Indiana, Kansas, and Ohio. He observed that the evangelical turnout or rise in Republican support among evangelicals came in reliable red states and declined in purple or blue states.[17]

Griffin attributed this decline to Romney's lame efforts to reach grassroots evangelical Christians. Instead, Griffin argued, the Romney campaign had gone to the top and talked to religious leaders, hoping that it would trickle down to the grassroots faithful. In 2004, the Bush campaign mobilized evangelicals to recruit other evangelicals. In the end, "the faithful were never convinced of [Romney's] sincerity on the issues they care about," Griffin declared, adding, "I know this because I was one of the unconvinced in an important swing state and my mega-church was filled with others like me." He concluded that the "laziness of the Romney campaign on the Church issue contributed to the difference between being the President of the United States and being another failed candidate like George Romney [Mitt's father, who tried unsuccessfully for the Republican nomination] before him."

The remark about Mitt Romney's father was an un-Christian jab, but the argument raised a critical issue. The Romney campaign understood from the outset that it was going to be a tight race. Incumbent presidents are rarely defeated for a second term. The Romney campaign believed that Independents were critical to his election. In the end, Romney won Independents by 5 points nationwide, and in some critical states, such as Ohio, by as much as 10 points. Nonetheless, he lost the general election, including the key state of Ohio.

Griffin concluded that evangelicals did not turn out in the numbers they have in the past, and when they did they were unenthusiastic. He wrote, "The thing to remember about religious voters is that unlike any other voting segment, they believe that history has already been written and they understand that even when someone terrible is elected, it is God's will. This is a mindset that allows many people to sit out an election in a way that a union member or NRA supporter never could."

This observation about the capricious character of religious voters was strangely reminiscent of Whig Party strategist Thurlow Weed, who complained about religious voters in 1844. His party's candidate, Henry Clay, lost the 1844 election. Evangelical Christians in New York voted for the anti-slavery Liberty Party instead of Whig candidate Henry Clay, handing the election to James K. Polk. Evangelicals disliked Clay as a slaveholder, a drinker, a gambler, and a womanizer. Once in the White House, Polk initiated a war with Mexico to expand slave territory. By standing on principle and refusing to vote for Henry Clay, a slaveholding, dueling, hard-drinking politician who nonetheless opposed the expansion of slavery, Christian voters gave the election to the "greater of two evils." After the election, Thurlow Weed, a Whig politician, complained that the trouble with religious voters is that they are fickle. When Weed helped found the Republican Party in the 1850s, he made certain that evangelicals played a subordinate role.

The issue today for Republicans is not whether Christian voters are "fickle," but whether there are enough evangelical Christian voters to build an entire campaign. If there are, can these untapped voters be persuaded to vote Republican? And for every evangelical Christian won, are other votes lost? It is doubtful, frankly, that evangelical voters are a large enough constituency to win presidential elections for Republicans. Christian evangelical, Catholic, and mainline Protestant voters cannot be ignored, however. Evangelical Christians play an especially important role in midterm elections, as evidenced in 2014. Based on polling from the Faith and Freedom Coalition, white evangelicals made up 23 percent of the electorate in 2014, and they voted 82 percent Republican.[18] Combined with other conservative religious voters, Catholics, and Mormons, Christian pollsters maintain, their share of the religious conservative vote exceeded that of the African-American, Hispanic, and youth vote. The Faith and Freedom Coalition concluded, "They [the Religious Right] will be equally vital in 2016." Glen Bolger, who conducted the survey, declared, "Voters of faith—Protestant and

Catholic—are the foundation of the GOP. Without their overwhelming support, there is no GOP majority."

Pew Research exit polls confirmed the importance of traditional religious voters in helping the Republican wave that swept over Congress in 2014. This vote proved critical to Republicans winning the House, the Senate, governorships, and state legislatures. Conservative Christians were helped in 2014 by the lower turnout of Democratic-base voters—millennials, Hispanics, and African Americans. In the last two presidential elections, Democrats were able to offset the white Christian vote, as well as the white vote in general, by turning out their base.

The share of the white evangelical Protestant vote and the white Catholic vote is falling. Social and cultural changes in American society have created intense anxiety among Christian conservatives. Republican candidates tapped into this anxiety in 2014. Republican candidates, however, finessed social and cultural issues by focusing on the economy, job creation, and, to a lesser degree, national security. Republican candidates running in red states did not back down from their conservative views on social issues, but they did not make social issues the focus of their campaigns.

Winning the evangelical vote and the traditional Catholic and Mormon vote is directly related to winning the white vote. Republicans need to maintain their base among white voters. Mobilizing white voters, however, should not come at the expense of galvanizing Hispanic and black voters, either in general or midterm elections. Hoping that minority or young voters will not turn out as they did when Obama won in 2008 or 2012, or that turnout will fall in future midterm elections, is not a good strategy.

In the end, Americans want a well-ordered, prosperous society. Even with secularization, most Americans believe that religion is important to a well-ordered society. Close to half of those surveyed who listed themselves as religiously unaffiliated questioned whether the decline in religious influence in America was a good thing.

Just as religious revivals have come and gone in America, usually spending themselves after moments of enthusiasm, secularization is by no means a linear advancement. The social trend is toward secularization, but with every social trend comes anxiety and resistance. Republicans, if they are to become a majority party, need to direct current cultural and social anxiety among traditional Christians into political advancement. In the end, despite all the concerns that traditional Christians will retreat from politics, forming a remnant of true believers in a corrupt and evil world, this retreat seems unlikely. Christian conservatives will remain engaged, and whatever the stresses, they will likely remain Republicans. They are a force in the party now and they represent part of the future. Conservative Christians are just not the entire future for a party seeking majority status.

7

POLARIZED ELECTORATE

REPUBLICANS SEEKING MAJORITY STATUS FOR THEIR PARTY FACE A highly politicized and ideologically motivated electorate. Americans marching to the polls, whether Democrat or Republican, are steadfast in their political views. They vote for one party or the other along straight party lines. Fewer voters split their ballots. The share of self-identified moderates has declined. Democratic voters, for the most part, consider themselves liberals, while most Republicans consider themselves conservatives. One result of this polarization is that candidates are encouraged to play to their core base through microtargeting aligned voters. The problem for Republicans is that their core base is not quite large enough to win the White House, as shown in the previous two presidential elections.

To become a majority party in this polarized climate, Republicans should understand the following:

- A voter's political belief is not set in stone. Ideological orientations can change with specific events, changing socioeconomic status, and age.

- Republicans cannot run national campaigns or state races based on mobilizing core voters. They need to reach out to Independents and moderates.
- Moderate-Independent voters still constitute the plurality of voters. Republican candidates, especially on the national level, should NOT write off these voters. This does not mean that Republicans should moderate their views; they need to articulate that they are principled, but understand that the voters want their representatives to be able to govern.
- Republicans should stand as educational reformers and advocates for civic education. Republicans are not alone in this concern for the decline of civic literacy in America. This should be a bipartisan issue for all Americans, whatever their political affiliations. Republican thought should be at the vanguard in calling for educational reform.

Both political parties, Republican and Democratic, face a central paradox of the American electorate today: voters going to the polls are more engaged in politics in general, more consistent in their voting, and highly ideological. At the same time, Americans suffer from massive ignorance about American institutions, how they work, our nation's history, and even the meaning of national holidays such as Independence Day on July 4. Americans suffer from a sharp decline in what is called "civic literacy." This paradox, in which many voters are especially well informed and consistent in their voting for ideological reasons, while at the same time a larger number of Americans are deeply ignorant about the foundational principles of American democracy, has profound implications as to whether Republicans can become a majority party, but it also has serious consequences for a healthy democracy in the future.

The consequence of a highly polarized electorate allows little room for political candidates to win over voters who consistently vote for one political party. These ideological voters self-identify as "conservative" or "liberal," and they stick to their beliefs in the voting booth. These voters, a growing number in both parties, refuse to split their tickets or switch parties. Estimates place 40 percent within each party as highly polarized. This polarization encourages political candidates to play to their base and not move to the center after winning their party nominations. In the past, the general rule of politics, especially presidential politics, was that a successful candidate would win their party's nomination by appealing to the ideological base, and then move to the center to win the general election; now that is increasingly becoming a strategy of the past.

Successfully mobilizing the base and then conducting a campaign around it was the key to George W. Bush's reelection campaign in 2004, and to Barack Obama's successful reelection in 2012. Both campaigns sought to mobilize and expand their base support, while offering perfunctory rhetoric favoring bipartisanship. More typical of the older strategy—appealing to the base to win his party's presidential nomination, and then moving to the center to attract Independent voters—was Mitt Romney's unsuccessful presidential campaign in 2012. In fighting for his party's nomination during a long-drawn-out and competitive primary, Romney moved to the right on many issues, as seen most readily in his views on immigration. Challenged by rivals such as Rick Perry, then the governor of Texas, who had taken a strong stance in favor of "controlling the border," Romney suggested he was in favor of deporting undocumented immigrants. His campaign understood the toxicity of mentioning a pathway to citizenship for these undocumented immigrants, or a general amnesty.

In the general campaign, Romney's strategy was to hold on to his base while appealing to Independents. This strategy meant pressing issues such as tax reform that appealed to his base, while downplaying or avoiding more divisive issues such as abortion or gay marriage. He tempered rhetoric that might be construed as mean-spirited or personally directed at his rival, President Obama. The Obama campaign, on the other hand, undertook a scorched-earth campaign that directly attacked Republican policies, Romney the candidate, the man, and his family. The Obama strategy was based solely on winning his base, while basically writing off moderate Republicans or swing Independent voters.

Many congressional races, like presidential contests, are about winning only the base and not potential crossover voters (arguably voter volatility in 2016 may change this strategy for Democrats and Republicans alike). Having won election primarily by winning the ideological base of their parties, congressional representatives stick to their ideological confines when it comes to crafting, proposing, and voting on legislation. The consequence is gridlock in Congress. It is all about appealing to base supporters, avoiding ideological deviation and any accusation of selling out to the other side, thereby betraying basic principles. In this atmosphere, a representative portrayed as a "sellout" finds it useless to suggest that passing legislation is by nature a messy, sausage-making business, or that he or she believes in "principled pragmatism." Moral absolutes and democratic politics are not easily reconciled. By its nature, politics is the practice of compromise, and for those given to moral absolutes, compromise means betrayal of principle. With voter polarization, we live more and more in a political world of moral absolutes.

Moral absolutes find an uneasy place in the actuality of politics, but this should not belie the importance for a candidate and a party in maintaining core principles. Some issues can be compromised in the legislative process. Ronald Reagan understood this during his presidency. He was willing to compromise on some issues to achieve larger goals. Compromise should not mean "me-too-Republicanism," but principled pragmatic leadership. Americans are looking for serious leaders who articulate clear principles, achieve legislative success, and address the serious problems facing the nation, domestically and internationally, in the twenty-first century. If Republicans can stand by principle and show that they can govern, they will enhance their capacity to become a majority party in the future.

HOW AMERICAN VOTERS BECAME POLARIZED

The American political structure erected by those who wrote the U.S. Constitution was built around the concept that good government entailed principle and compromise. The founders sought a constitutional order to protect liberty, property, and individual rights, and a governing system that prevented rash, ill-thought-out legislation and encouraged political compromise. They feared political parties, popular democracy, and centralized government. Contrary to these sentiments, the national politics that emerged has been that of intense partisan conflict, the continual expansion of suffrage, and the expansion of federal power.

The proper role of the federal government gave rise in George Washington's administration to the early formation of political parties. Although not well formed, these early political parties were based on uneasy coalitions of sectional, economic, and religious interests. A narrowly based sectional party, such as John Adams's Federalist Party, with its strength lying only in New England, inevitably faced extinction. The rise of the Republican Party in the mid-1850s, following the collapse of the Whig Party, proved to be the one exception to a regionally based party. Because of the Republican Party's anti-slavery position, it became a party of the North, without a base in the South. Its feeble attempt to build the party in the South during the Reconstruction period that followed the Civil War failed. The South became a Democratic stronghold until after World War II.

While the two dominant parties, Democratic and Republican, offered voters clear policy choices, both parties were built around uneasy coalitions of divergent economic and cultural interests. Voters, though, were driven less by socioeconomic or ideological divisions than by ethnic and religious alignments. The New Deal Democratic Party coalition, which emerged under Franklin Roosevelt in the 1930s, brought together a coalition of Northeast urban voters, largely Catholic, union members in the North, and white voters in the South. The New Deal coalition dominated national politics throughout the early 1960s with Lyndon Johnson's Great Society. Southern white voters began to desert the Democratic Party on the presidential level beginning in the early 1950s. Republican appeals to small government, low taxes, conservative cultural values, and a strong national defense began to erode the strength of the Democratic Party in the South, especially with the emergence of white suburban voters. The turning point came when Richard Nixon actively pursued a Southern strategy in 1968 and 1972.

The process of winning white voters to the Republican cause was accelerated in Ronald Reagan's presidential campaign in 1980.

The Democratic Party's support of black civil rights played a role in the loss of the South, although many scholars attribute too much importance to "race" as the single cause of the rise of the Republican Party in the South. The erosion of the Democratic Party vote had begun well before the rise of civil rights protests in the 1960s. After 1960, upper-income groups switched to the Republican Party. This coincided with demographic changes in the South, particularly the tremendous growth of suburbs outside major Southern cities and the large influx of Northerners to the South. These suburban voters were concerned with issues such as low taxes, anti-unionism, and family values, and they moved into the Republican Party. Others brought their party with them from the North. As political scientists Byron Shafer and Richard Johnston demonstrate, it was economics, not race, that won the South for the Republicans. The burgeoning suburban middle classes went Republican in 1980 and the elections that followed because of promises of tax cuts and a smaller federal government.[1]

The Democrats' loss of the South to the Republican Party and the breakup of the New Deal coalition set the context for ideological polarization within the electorate. Discussion among political scientists and media pundits of the cause and extent of this polarization is extensive and complex. One school, represented by Morris P. Fiorina in *Cultural War? The Myth of a Polarized America* (2006), argues that polarization is found mostly inside the Washington, D.C., Beltway, in the halls of Congress, and in the media elite. American voters, Fiorina and his coauthors argue, are not polarized along ideological lines. American voters are mostly moderate centrists. Congress is polarized, however, and sparking this polarization are the cultural warriors within the Republican Party. The argument is that Republican congressional representatives have been voting along strict party lines since the late 1990s. Democrats have responded with more partisan voting, but even here, congressional Democrats are given to more moderation in casting their votes. Fiorina's argument is backed by extensive political science literature looking at congressional roll calls. The argument that Republicans have drifted more to the right and have become more partisan in Congress drives conservatives up the wall. They are quick to point out that the Democratic Party moved further to the left after 1972 and is no longer the party of Franklin Roosevelt's New Deal liberals.

Without entering into the weeds of congressional roll calls, the more important question is whether the electorate itself is polarized ideologically. Political scientist Alan I. Abramowitz explores exactly this question in *The Disappearing Center: Engaged Citizens, Polarization, and American Democracy*, published shortly after the election of 2008. In a close analysis of voting behavior, Abramowitz shows that the American electorate is deeply polarized, a trend that began well before Obama's election.

Abramowitz argues that political polarization has occurred both among the elite and the American people. Polarization among the electorate paralleled the ideological divisions within the electorate and among political leaders. This polarization has increased political participation and voter consistency at the polls, but it is reshaping American politics by ensuring gridlock.

Polarization occurs along ideological lines, with one notable exception: African Americans. Whether they identify themselves as liberals, conservatives, or moderates, religious or nonreligious, they consistently vote Democratic. They are not ideological voters. Whites, on the other hand, vote mainly along ideological lines, across socioeconomic status. The fire line for white voters is along religious lines and not class lines. Voters who attend religious services tend to be Republican. The exception to this behavior is black voters, who cast their ballots Democratic, whether they are religious or not.

Partisan polarization is evident in the voting public and is no longer confined to a small group of party leaders or media elites. Engaged voters see important differences between the parties. In 2004, for example, 75 percent of Americans believed that there were profound differences between the parties.[2] In the 2006 midterm House and Senate elections, over 90 percent of voters identified or leaned toward one party or the other. No longer did most Americans believe that their vote was between Tweedledee and Tweedledum. Although many Americans still have little or no interest in politics, many voters do.

Ideological voters make up about 40 percent of the electorate. Politically engaged Democrats overwhelmingly call themselves liberals (82 percent), while 91 percent of Republican voters self-identify as conservatives. Many voters place themselves in the moderate category, but self-described moderates tend to vote consistently for one party over the other. Thus, while moderates remain the largest grouping (45 percent) within the electorate, conservatives constitute about 34 percent, while liberals make up about 21 percent, according to voter surveys in 2006. Some more recent polls suggest an uptick in self-identified liberals, but the important takeaway for Republicans is that their base is conservative and hard-core Republican. Hispanic and young voters place themselves on the liberal side of the spectrum. Voters' attitudes change, however, given specific events and based on socioeconomic status, family relations, and age.[2]

There is a sharper divide in how liberals and conservatives see American corporations. Most Republicans (60 percent), and conservatives by an even higher margin (67 percent), view American corporations favorably. Generally, the American public has a favorable view of corporations, about half, while 43 percent have an unfavorable view of American business. A closer look at the Pew survey reveals some surprising results when broken down by age cohort. Those between the ages of 30 and 49 and those over 66 have the most favorable views of American corporations (about 50 percent in each age group). Not far behind on the favorability rating are those young Americans between the ages of 18 and 29. Forty-eight percent view American corporations favorably, while 43 percent of this age group do not. The age group most unfavorable to corporations are those aged 50 to 64. Only 45 percent of this age cohort are favorably disposed toward corporations, while 49 percent view corporations unfavorably. This is the only age cohort that has a more unfavorable than favorable view. Republicans should remember this in their campaigns. Nonetheless, contrary to Democratic attacks on business, most Americans like American business.[3]

In a more recent study conducted in 2015, Pew found that this ideological divide continued.[4] The survey found that ideological division has intensified. Democrats still held an 11-point advantage, with about 32 percent of voters identifying themselves as Democratic or Democratic-leaning, and about 23 percent identifying themselves as Republican or Republican-leaning.

The number of those describing themselves as Independents has increased so much that more voters—39 percent—now identify as Independents than as Democrats or Republicans. Independents, though, often vote for one party over the other, so this category can be deceiving. What is important is that many voters now see themselves as Independents. This is a good sign for Republicans, in that these voters are up for grabs. A good candidate can persuade them to overcome their voting tendency if they usually vote Democratic or confirm their tendency to vote Republican.

This polarization within the engaged public is having pronounced consequences in elections. State election returns in 2008 and 2012 reveal that many states were not at all competitive. Obama and McCain won many states by landslide votes. For example, in 2008, Obama won California, New York, and Illinois by close to 25 points each; Michigan by 16 points; and Pennsylvania by 10 points. All in all, Obama won 28 states, carrying 21 of these states by more than 10 points. Only 4 states carried by Obama were by less than a 5-point margin. A similar pattern appeared with Republican candidate John McCain, who carried 22 states, of which 15 were won by 10 points or more. Only 2 of his state victories were won by 5 points or less. Furthermore, Republicans, although they lost the election, increased their margin of the popular vote in the red states of Oklahoma, Arkansas, Louisiana, and Tennessee.

The 2012 election proved no different. Obama carried 10 states by margins ranging from 36 points (Vermont) to 8 points (Minnesota). He overwhelmed the popular vote in California, Connecticut, Delaware, District of Columbia, Hawaii, Illinois, Maine, Maryland, Massachusetts, Michigan, Minnesota, New Jersey, New Mexico, New York, Oregon, Rhode Island, Vermont, and Washington.

The 2012 election showed just how widespread polarization is within the electorate. Moreover, the returns reveal the advantage Democrats have in the most populous states with large electoral votes. Given these wide margins, Republicans face headwinds in future presidential elections. But another observation is also in order: the importance of key swing states. In key battleground states, only 3–7 points decided the election for either candidate. Obama won Florida by 1 point, Ohio by 2, Virginia by 3, Wisconsin by 7, Colorado by 4, Iowa by 6, Nevada by 6, and New Hampshire by 6. Romney won North Carolina by 3, the only battleground state he carried. Given the highly polarized electorate in most states, presidential campaigns focus on key states. Even in these states, the Obama campaign focused on mobilizing its base. Romney's campaign, too, sought to mobilize its base while reaching out to Independent voters. The Republican campaign did pretty well among Independents, but not well enough to win the White House for Romney.

Congressional campaigns show a similar polarization. There are fewer marginal districts up for grabs. As Abramowitz shows, the number of marginal districts that can swing either way fell from 208 to 156 from 1992 to 2004. This decline cannot be attributed solely to redistricting, in which Republicans and Democrats carved up districts to be safe for their party candidates. Redistricting has exerted only a minor effect on competiveness in House districts. On the contrary, because of population movement, immigration, and party realignment within the electorate, partisan voters live around those of the same party: Republicans surrounded by Republicans, and Democrats surrounded by Democrats. The obvious result of this polarization is that, once elected to Congress, representatives tend to be more partisan. This partisanship, however, is apparent not only in so-called "safe districts" but also in representatives elected from marginal districts. They vote straight liberal or straight conservative on most pieces of legislation in Congress. Representatives in the House and the Senate have moved further and further apart on policy issues, ensuring gridlock.

On almost every issue, engaged voters are polarized, whether it be taxes, economic policy, national security, foreign policy, healthcare, energy, or the environment. In the 2008 presidential campaign, Obama supporters were significantly more liberal and McCain supporters more conservative. The sharpest divide was over the Iraq War, but differences were also seen regarding health insurance, abortion, and gay marriage. Obama supporters were highly opposed to the Iraq War, were pro-choice, and were for gay marriage. Among likely voters, 73 percent of Obama supporters were liberals when scored on an eight-item political ideological scale, versus close to 70 percent of McCain supporters who were conservative on policy issues. In this way, liberal and conservative voters have become more consistent in their attitudes. If a voter is conservative on one issue, they tend to be conservative on other issues; similarly with liberals. This used to not be the case for most voters.

The ideological divide can be broken down by groups. Democratic voters are less likely to be white; less likely to be married; and less likely to be Christians. Married, white Christians, now making up less than half of all voters and less than one-fifth of voters under 30, are most likely to be Republican. Although Christians are a declining proportion of the electorate, married individuals constitute the large majority of the electorate, and whites make up over 70 percent of the electorate.

The primary question of why this ideological polarization has occurred is not fully explored in the surveys. Political scientists such as Morris P. Fiorina and journalist Ronald Brownstein maintain that polarization is an elite phenomenon encouraged by political leaders and activist interest groups, especially those on the right.[5] They point specifically to the interjection of social issues such as abortion and gay rights that have been used by Republicans to mobilize grassroots, single-issue voters who are culturally conservative. Abramowitz and Pew researchers show that ideological polarization runs deep within both parties, but they do not explore specifically why voters have been polarized.

Any answer to this question should begin with the role of the federal government in creating a good society. Both progressives and conservatives agree that serious social and economic problems confront the nation today. Progressives tend to view government programs as the best way of ameliorating these problems. This entails the enlargement of government regulation, welfare entitlements, and social engineering through federal bureaucracies. Conservatives, on the other hand, while not dismissing the idea that government has an important role in defending the nation, ensuring the rule of law, and maintaining a safety net for the elderly, the disabled, and those who find themselves temporarily unemployed, look first at local communities, voluntary associations, and free markets to promote the general welfare, political liberty, and economic well-being. They fear power, the domination of some people over others. Power, they hold, is a natural aspect of government and can be made legitimate only through a compact of mutual consent. If left unconstrained, as the founders believed, government power degenerates into tyranny. The proper role of government is to serve as a referee in adjudicating various sectional, economic, and social interests. The coercive powers of government should remain weak, while the adjudicating powers of government should be uncorrupted by special economic, social, or political interests.[6]

Ideological polarization, as Abramowitz and Pew Research surveys show, has increased political participation within the electorate. The engaged electorate tends to be more politically involved in campaigns, contacting friends and neighbors to vote for their candidates, participating in political activities, and being concerned about the outcomes of elections. Abramowitz shows that polarization has inspired voter turnout. A record-number of Americans, 123 million, went to the polls in 2004, an increase of 18 million over 2000, marking a 63.8 percent turnout.[7] Yet turnout steadied and even fell slightly in 2008 and 2012. In 2008, 131 million people voted, but this was only a 63.6 percent turnout, slightly less than in the 2004 election. In 2012, 132.9 million people voted, but this was only a 61.8 percent turnout.

Turnout has increased in presidential primaries. In 2000, about 33 million Americans voted in the presidential primaries; in 2008, the number increased by 24 million to 57 million. Turnout increased in every major subgroup—blacks, Hispanics, women, and youth—within the electorate. While this turnout did not reach the proportions of nineteenth-century presidential elections, sometimes nearing 90 percent, it reversed a downward trend in voter turnout that had been occurring throughout much of the twentieth century. Of course, there are some great anomalies in the twentieth century. In 1960, Chicago turnout exceeded 98 percent citywide and was more than 100 percent in a number of precincts. The dead seemed to be so enamored with Democratic candidate John F. Kennedy that they appeared to rise from their graves to go to the polls.

Most people will see a rise in voter turnout as a good thing in a democracy. In this respect, polarization makes a favorable contribution to a vibrant democracy. Polarization, however, has a downside. Candidates hoping to appeal across party lines face a barrier in attracting swing voters. Instead, campaign strategy within a polarized electorate turns to attracting co-partisans, ignoring potential crossover voters. Even in critical swing states in presidential races, campaigns focus on core supporters. The polarized nature of political campaigns increasingly appears even in marginal congressional districts. Congressional representatives from marginal districts vote increasingly along straight party lines, thereby ensuring polarization in the House.

Polarization also increases opportunities for demagoguery within American politics. Ideological voters want to frame every issue as a matter of principle, scrutinize every candidate for deviation, tend to look for politicians who "tell it like it is," and are willing to attack "the establishment." Fiery language framed in sound bites, which convey coded messages that tap into voter discontent about serious and complicated issues, will find appeal among informed ideological voters, as well as among less well-informed voters who share anxieties and hostility to politics-as-usual. A thin line separates campaign rhetoric from demagoguery. Good campaign rhetoric should appeal to the head and the heart; demagoguery appeals only to base passions. William Jennings Bryan, who won the Democratic Party nomination in 1896 after his famous "Cross of Gold" speech, tended toward demagoguery. He portrayed the financial interests and "gold bugs" in his party who supported a gold standard as "crucifying mankind on a cross of gold." The language was eloquent, but it portrayed opponents as Pontius Pilates, willing to have all humanity suffer so wealth could be maintained. Such rhetoric precluded serious discussion of a complicated monetary issue. Bryan, a born crowd-pleasing rabble-rouser, did not want discussion; he wanted electoral arousal.

Demagoguery is also found in today's politics: in denunciations of undocumented immigrants crossing the Mexican-American border as rapists and criminals, as one Republican candidate declared in the 2016 primaries; or in incessant Democratic accusations against Republicans for waging a "war on women" or attempting to suppress the black vote. Such language appeals to elements within the ideological cores of the Republican and Democratic parties. To suggest that such campaign language is demagogic is not to dismiss these issues, and such negative language in campaigning is not new in American politics. Americans understand that political campaigns are a "blood sport" that encourages politicians to paint their opponents in insidious ways. "Gotcha" is an old game that dates to the founders. Slurs and false accusations were common in the 1790s, and Aaron Burr killed Alexander Hamilton in a duel for suggesting privately that Burr was a traitor. Americans understand that in a campaign rally, a candidate won't have time for a full exploration of complex issues, but the vilification of opponents cannot be healthy for democracy.

THE DECLINE OF CIVIC LITERACY IN AMERICA TODAY

While voter turnout has ranged around 60 percent in the last two presidential elections, a single striking point remains true: large numbers of adult Americans do not vote.[8] About 30 percent of the eligible citizenry did not register to vote in 2012. Democrats declare that this is voter suppression by Republicans. Allowing easier online registration, relaxing rules regarding voter ID, and other measures, Democrats argue, will increase voter turnout. Maybe, but it is worth noting that over seven in ten Americans (74 percent) favor photo IDs to vote and less than a quarter (23 percent) oppose voter identification.[9] Whites overwhelmingly favor voter ID (78 percent); but nonwhite (67 percent) and black Americans (65 percent) also favor such laws. What is not considered, however, is that many Americans just do not care about voting. A comparison of turnout in states that have different voting policies is informative. Pennsylvania does not have an easy voting process and makes voting by absentee ballot difficult, whereas Washington state uses only mail-in ballots. In Washington, every registered voter is automatically sent a mail-in ballot. But turnout is not substantially higher in Washington. The failure to return a ballot shows low motivation, not lack of access.

This disengagement coincides with a general decline in civic literacy in contemporary America. The framers of the Constitution built into the American political system a number of anti-majoritarian features, including equal representation of nonpopulous states in the Senate, the presidential veto, lifetime appointment of federal judges, and a divided government. Based on their reading of history and seventeenth- and eighteenth-century political thought, they feared pure democracy, in which the people ruled directly. They had personal experiences with mob rule, before and during the American Revolution. Mobs could not be controlled. The delegates distrusted popular democracy, yet sought to create a representative republic based on popular sovereignty. James Madison and Alexander Hamilton made a sharp distinction between *popular and direct* democracy and *republican* government. They justified their suspicions of direct democracy by their study of human nature and historical experience. As Hamilton told Washington after the Philadelphia convention, "Man, after all, is but Man." They remained suspicious of the passions of the people, but upheld an Enlightenment faith in the ultimate rationality of the people. The trick was to design a political system where passions could be expressed without doing real harm and preventing solutions to real problems. As a result, delegates at the Philadelphia Constitutional Convention in 1787 constructed a political order that delicately balanced democratic and republican values; centralized authority and states' rights; local and regional interests; and executive, legislative, and judicial powers. Nonetheless, they held great faith in the capacity of the people to govern themselves through representative government.

At the foundation of a representative government was a well-informed and educated electorate. Thus they placed great emphasis on a "virtuous" citizenry that was well educated in the moral and founding principles of representative (republican) government. They did not expect that every voter would understand the intricacies of monetary, financial, military, or foreign policy, but they believed a virtuous people should have a general grasp of basic civics—the nature of American political institutions, the founding principles of good government and a well-ordered society. The framers' concept of the electorate was limited mostly to white men and excluded many, including women and African

Americans, from voting. They retained property qualifications for voters and officeholders because they doubted that the propertyless cared about the long-term interests of society. They believed in public education. An informed citizenry, the founders believed, was essential to the success of this new experiment in representative government.

Not only are large numbers of Americans politically disengaged, they are shockingly ignorant about the basics of American history and democratic institutions. This does not mean they are dumb, but many are civic illiterates. In 2011, *Newsweek* asked 1,000 U.S. citizens to take the official U.S. citizenship test.[10] The results shocked even cynical journalists. Only 29 percent could name the vice president of the United States. Seventy-three percent could not correctly say why we fought the Cold War. Close to half (44 percent) were unable to define the Bill of Rights. Reviewing the results, Jacob Hacker, a Yale political scientist, observed that we have a political culture in which wired activists on the left and the right dominate debate—surrounded by a swamp of general ignorance within the rest of the public. Many Americans take part in civic activities—voting, attending local political or school meetings, or volunteering for a political party or candidate. Yet many Americans, close to a third, remain uninvolved or uninformed about political issues and disengaged from political activity.[11]

This translates into an ignorance of current political issues.[12] For example, fewer than 25 percent of Californians answered in one poll that they "knew much" about the Affordable Care Act. In another survey conducted by the Pew Research Center in 2011, most Americans did not know whether Republicans or Democrats controlled the House or the Senate; only four in ten could identify John Boehner as the then House Speaker; and roughly three in ten correctly answered that the federal government spends more on Medicare than on scientific research, education, or interest on the national debt.[13] In fact, slightly more than a third (36 percent) said that the interest on the debt is greater than total government expenditures. On the other hand, over half of Americans in the polls correctly identified Mark Zuckerberg as the founder of Facebook. Many Americans know more about popular culture and its icons than they do about politics.

Not all the news is dismal, however. Most Americans knew that No Child Left Behind was about education, who the leader of Libya was at the time, and the current unemployment rate, and possessed a general knowledge of economics and politics. They knew (77 percent) that the federal deficit is larger than it was in the 1990s, and 64 percent knew that there is an unbalanced trade deficit.

Young Americans are especially ignorant about American history. In 2011, the National Assessment of Education Progress, conducted by the U.S. Department of Education, found American students to be less proficient in their nation's history than in any other subject.[14] Only 12 percent of high school seniors passed the exam, with many failing to answer simple questions. The scores were a little higher among eighth graders and fourth graders, but not anything to write home about. Only 20 percent of fourth graders and 17 percent of eighth graders passed the exam, which asked basic multiple-choice questions about the American Revolution, Abraham Lincoln and the Civil War, World War II, and why *Brown v. Board of Education* was important. In another survey, conducted in 2007 by the Intercollegiate Studies Institute, a conservative organization, only 50 percent of college seniors passed a civic literacy exam.[15] The exam included basic questions such as identifying the document where this phrase comes from: "We hold these truths to be self-evident, that all men are created equal." A majority could not correctly identify the Declaration of Independence. Over fourteen thousand college seniors were tested at over fifty universities and colleges. Seniors at some of America's most elite institutions were the worst performers. In fact, Cornell University seniors were the worst performers on the test. Many Cornell students are from New York state, one of the states that abandoned mandatory U.S. history for high school graduation decades ago to make way for other topics in the new politically correct curriculum.

TOCQUEVILLE'S WARNING ABOUT SOFT DESPOTISM

The decline in civic literacy presents a major cultural and social problem for American democracy itself. The warnings of a French visitor to

America before the Civil War about the erosion of an active citizenry should be echoing in the ears of every American citizen. In 1831, Alexis de Tocqueville came to America to report on the fledgling democracy. He was impressed by its vibrancy, its individualist ethos, and the opportunity this new nation presented to its citizens. He warned that the seeds of destruction of this new democracy lay in a centralized administrative state—government bureaucracies—that would ultimately subvert democracy. In the second volume of *Democracy in America* (1840), he declared that the greatest threat to the American experiment in liberty lay in an apathetic citizenry. He shared with his readers one major trepidation about America's future: Americans, as a people, were so egalitarian in their outlook, individualistic in their spirit, and materially competitive that he worried about the decline of what he described as "civil spirit" in the new nation. Democracy worked, he declared, only if citizens remained involved in democratic political culture. He warned that if Americans became too absorbed in their personal lives, too materially oriented, and inordinately focused on their economic advancement in place of civic involvement, America would be left only with the guise of democracy.

If this occurred, he predicted, Americans would be left with a "soft despotism," in which citizens become involved in their individual "petty pleasures" and selfish interests. In this corrosive culture, democratic government is subverted by an administrative bureaucratic sovereign state. Tocqueville bears quoting in detail on this point: "After taking each individual in this fashion, . . . the sovereign [government] extends its arms about society as a whole; it covers its surface with a network of petty regulation, complicated, minute, and uniform—through which even the most original minds and vigorous souls know not how to make their way past the crowd and emerge into the light of the day."

There is a general anxiety, especially pronounced among grassroots Republicans, that the bureaucratic state has emerged as a "soft despotism." Since the late 1960s, Americans have expressed a growing distrust of the federal government. Today, trust in America's institutions and its leaders has reached an all-time low. In a recent poll conducted by Gallup in June 2015, Americans expressed little confidence in institutions, with the exception of the military, small business, and the police.[16] The military received the highest confidence, with 72 percent of Americans expressing a great deal or quite a lot of confidence in it. This was followed by small business with 67 percent and the police with 52 percent. The rest of American institutions fell below a majority expressing any degree of confidence: church and organized religion came in with a 42 percent confidence rating; the presidency stood at 32 percent; and the Supreme Court was at 32 percent. Lowest on the confidence scale were television news (21 percent), big business (21 percent), and Congress, not cracking 10 percent.

Republican candidates can take the easy way by playing on this public distrust, but Americans are looking for a positive message from leaders. Americans are optimistic by nature. There is deep patriotism within the American public. They are looking for leaders who can govern; who convey a faith in the nation's future; and who believe that the country's best days are not behind us. Running against Washington and "politics-as-usual" is standard fare in American politics. But the most successful leaders articulate people's anxieties while offering a message of hope and reform. Republicans look back nostalgically to Ronald Reagan as the exemplary politician who captured public anxiety while delivering an optimistic message. There is not going to be another Reagan in the future, however. Like Franklin Roosevelt before him, Reagan emerged at a certain time and place in history. This is not to say that Republicans cannot find candidates who capture the anxious mood of the country, or who appeal to their partisan base while capturing wavering Democratic voters disgusted with the tone of politics, their party leadership, and the direction of the country.

Republicans should learn from the past and Reagan's political skills. The problems the country faces today are not those of the 1980s. The electorate is different from what it was thirty-five years ago. New solutions and a new reform agenda are called for in the twenty-first century. If the Republican Party convinces the public that it can govern, that it offers reform, and that it is the party of the future, it will emerge as the majority party.

NOTES

INTRODUCTION

1. Wendy Wang, "The Rise of Intermarriage," Pew Research Center (February 10, 2012).
2. This discussion of contemporary urban America draws from Joel Kotkin, "The Peril to Democrats of Left-Leaning Urban Centers," http://www.new geography.com/content/005018-the-peril-democrats-left-leaning-urban -centers.
3. Nate Silver, "There Is No 'Blue Wall,'" *FiveThirtyEight* (May 17, 2015), http://hotair.com/archives/2015/05/12/nate-silver-no-the-democrats-dont -have-a-lock-on-an-electoral-college-majority/.
4. Reid Wilson, "The Blue and the Grey: Why Democrats Need to Rebuild Their Bench" (August 16, 2015), http://morningconsult.com/2015/08/the -blue-and-the-grey-why-democrats-need-to-rebuild-their-bench/.

CHAPTER 1

1. Christy Hoppe, "Greg Abbott Tops Wendy Davis in Texas Governor's Race," *Dallas Morning News,* November 4, 2014.
2. Uri Dadush et al., *Inequality in America: Facts, Trends and International Perspectives* (Washington, D.C., 2012), p. 53.
3. Dadush et al., *Inequality in America*, p. 52.
4. Joseph B. Williams, "College of Tomorrow: The Changing Demographics of the Student Body," *U.S. News,* September 22, 2014; Mark Hugo Lopez, "Women's College Enrollment Gains Leave Men Behind," Pew Research Center, March 6, 2014; Daniel Borzelleca, "The Male-Female Ratio in College," http://www.forbes.com/sites/ccap/2012/02/16; "Black Student Graduation Rates Remain Low, but Modest Progress Begins to Show," *Journal of Blacks in Higher Education* (January 22, 2013).
5. "UCLA Study Reveals Growing Gap Among Hispanic College Students," October 2008, http://diverseeducation.com/article.
6. National Center for Education Statistics, *Digest of Education Statistics, Department of Education* (Washington, D.C., 2012).

7. Dadush et al., *Inequality in America: Facts, Trends and International Perspectives*, p. 53.

8. U.S. Census Bureau, "Women in the Workforce" (Washington, D.C., 2010).

9. For an important voice in this area, see Arthur C. Brooks, *The Conservative Heart: How to Build a Fairer, Happier and More Prosperous America* (New York, 2015).

10. Pew Research Center, "2014 Party Identification Detailed Tables," http://www.people-press.org/files/2015/04/4-7-Party-ID.

11. Pew Research Center, "A Deep Dive into Party Affiliation: Sharp Differences by Race, Gender, Generation, Education," http://www.people-press.org/2015/04/07/.

12. Michael Medved, "The 'War on Women' Failed in 2012," *Wall Street Journal*, April 17, 2014.

13. Jeffrey M. Jones, "Gender Gap in 2012 Is Largest in Gallup's History," www.gallup.com/poll/158588/gender-gap-2012.

14. Margie Omero and Tara McGuinness, "How Women Changed the Outcome of the Election," https://www.americanprogress.org/issues/women/report/2012.

15. Samuel P. Jacobs, "With the Help of Women, Obama Wins Second Term," http://www.reuters.com/article/2012/11/07.

16. Emma Brockes, "Why Obama Won the Women's Vote," *Guardian*, November 7, 2013.

17. Polling can be found at http://www.gallup.com/poll/1576/abortion.aspx; http://www.gallup.com/poll/1183999/more-americans-pro-life-than-pro-choice-first-time.aspx; http://www.rasmussenreport.com/public_content/politics/current_events/abortion/46_are_pro=choice__43_pro_life; http://www.norc.org/PDFs/GSS%20Reports/Trends%20m%; http://www.quinnipiac.edu/news-and-events/quinnipiac-university-poll/national/release; and http://www.lifenews.com/2013/11/04polling-data-consistently-shows-women-are-pro-life-on-abortion/.

18. Amanda Marcotte, "Why Did Romney Lose? Conservatives Blame Single Women," http://www.slate.com/blogs/xx-factor /2012/11/09.

19. In Virginia the female vote was 54 to 45, in Wisconsin 57 to 42, and in Iowa 59 to 40 for Obama over Romney. Melina Henneberger, "Why Romney Lost the Women's Vote," *Washington Post*, November 7, 2012.

20. Andrew Dugan, "Women in Swing States Have Gender-Specific Priorities," http://www.gallup.com/pol/158069; CNN, "Romney, Obama Court Women in Final Weeks," http://www.com.201/10/25.

21. John Cassidy, "What's Up with White Women? They Voted for Romney, Too," November 8, 2012, http://www.newyorkercom/news/john-cassidy.

22. This discussion draws from Cassidy, "What's Up with White Women? They Voted for Romney, Too."

23. *New York Times*, "The Campaign Against Women," May 19, 2012.

24. Geoffrey Cowley, "GOP Lawmakers Escalate Their War on Women," MS-NBC, May 18, 2013.

25. Isabel V. Sawhill, "2014 Midterms: Women Voters Care About More Than Reproductive Rights," http://www.brookings.edu/blog/fixgov/post/2014/10/2014.

26. Jennifer Rubin, "The GOP's Problem with Women," *Washington Post,* May 20, 2013.

27. Stephen Collinson, "How the 'War on Women' Is Changing," http://www.cnn.com/2014/4/10/27; and Jay Newton Small, "The Surprising Struggles of Mark Udall to Win Colorado Women," http://www.time.com/354159/mark-udall-war-on.

28. Ashe Show, "2014 Midterms Are a Proving Ground for the 'War on Women' Narrative," http://www.washingtonexaminer.com/2014-midterms-are-pro.

29. Shane Goldmacher, "Can Democrats Win a 'War on Women' Debate Against a Woman?," October 22, 2014.

30. http://www.nbcnews.com/politics/elections/2014/IA/senate/exitpoll.

31. John Harwood, "Taking Their Umbrage Where They Can Get It: Democrats Reprise 'War on Women' Case Against Republicans," *New York Times,* September 19, 2014; Emma Margolin, "North Carolina Readies New Abortion Lims as GOP War on Women Expands," MSNBC, http://www.msnbc.com/thomas-roberts/north-carolina-readies-new-abortion-limits; Nia-Malika Henderson, "Groups Use 'War on Women' Strategy to Bolster Hagan in N.C. Senate Race," http://www.washingtonpost.com/blogs/she-the-people/wp/2014/06/18/groups-use-war-on-women-strategy-to-bolster-hagan-in-n-c-senate-race/.

32. Andrew Johnson, "Grime's 'War on Women' Problem," *National Review,* April 11, 2014.

33. Christina A. Cassidy, "In Georgia Senate Bid, Nunn Talks Economy to Women," Yahoo News, October 18, 2014, http://news.yahoo.com/georgia-senate-bid-nunn-talks-economy-women-164915008—election.html.

34. http://www.dailykos.com/story/2014/09/05/1327329/-AR-Sen-Ladies-Tom-Cotton-R-Is-Not-On-Your-Side.

35. John Wagner, "In Md. Governor's Race, Larry Hogan Pushes Pocketbook Issues, But Foes Push Back," *Washington Post,* August 14, 2014.

36. *OnTheIssues,* "Larry Hogan on Abortion," http://www.ontheissues.org/Governor/Larry_Hogan_Abortion.

37. Jeff Quinton, "Pro-Life Issues and the Republican Candidates for Maryland Governor," and other postings on http://www.quintonreport.com.

38. Quoted in John Wagner, "In Md. Governor's Race, Larry Hogan Pushes Pocketbook Issues, But Foes Push Back," *Washington Post,* August 14, 2014.

39. Jay Root, "Wendy Davis Lost Badly. Here's How It Happened," *Washington Post,* November 6, 2014.

40. Christy Hoppe, "Greg Abbott Tops Wendy Davis in Texas Governor's Race," *Dallas Morning News,* November 4, 2014.

41. Neil Stroka quoted in Robert Draper, "The Great Democratic Crack-Up of 2016," *New York Times,* May 12, 2015.

42. Quoted in Robert Draper, "The Great Democratic Crack-Up of 2016," and http://www.realclearpolitics.com/articles/2014/11/11/the_other_gop_wave_state_legislatures__124626.html#ixzz3aRO0AKX0.

CHAPTER 2

1. Steven Mufson and Juliet Eilperin, "Baltimore Riots Put Obama Strategy for American Cities Under Closer Scrutiny," *Washington Post,* May 4, 2015.
2. U.S. Census Bureau, "QuickFacts from the U.S. Census Bureau" (Baltimore, 2015), http://quickfacts.census.gov/qfdstates.
3. Excellent portraits of demographic changes in America are found in William H. Frey, "The Major Demographic Shift That's Upending How We Think About Race," *New Republic,* December 1, 2014, and his more expansive *Diversity Explosion: How New Racial Demographics Are Remaking America* (Washington, D.C., 2015).
4. Frey, *Diversity Explosion: How New Racial Demographics Are Remaking America,* p. 10.
5. These and the following figures are taken from Asian American Justice Center, "Behind the Numbers: Post-Election Survey of Asian American and Pacific Island Voters in 2012," April 2013.
6. Frey, *Diversity Explosion: How New Racial Demographics Are Remaking America,* p. 214.
7. Frey, *Diversity Explosion: How New Racial Demographics Are Remaking America,* p. 218.
8. These statistics are drawn from Frey, "The Major Demographic Shift." Further statistics on racial intermarriage and racial identification can be found in U.S. Census reports in 2010, httip://www.census.gov/prod/cen2010/brief/c201Obr-11.pdf.
9. Richard Alba, *Blurring the Color Line: The New Chance for a More Integrated America* (Cambridge, MA, 2009), pp. 205, 224.
10. Alba, *Blurring the Color Line: The New Chance for a More Integrated America,* pp. 3, 6–7; and Frey, *Diversity Explosion: How New Racial Demographics Are Remaking America,* pp. 193, 195.
11. This discussion of migration to Sun Belt states relies on Frey, *Diversity Explosion: How New Racial Demographics Are Remaking America,* especially chapters 4–7, pp. 65–148.
12. Mark Hugo Lopez, "The Hispanic Vote in the 2008 Election," Pew Research Center, November 7, 2008; and Mark Hugo Lopez, "Latino Voters in the 2012 Election," Pew Research Center, September 7, 2012.
13. Asian American Justice Center, "Behind the Numbers: Post-Election Survey of Asian American and Pacific Island Voters in 2012," April 2013. Statistics in the next two paragraphs from same source.
14. Mark Hugo Lopez, "Latino Voters in the 2012 Election," Pew Research Center (September 7, 2012).
15. Figures on the increased minority vote and decreased white vote in Nevada are found in Frey, *Diversity Explosion: How New Racial Demographics Are Remaking America,* p. 234.
16. Frey, *Diversity Explosion: How New Racial Demographics Are Remaking America,* p. 234.
17. Lopez, "Latino Voters in the 2012 Election."
18. http://www.rasmussenreports.com/public_content/politics/current_events/immigration/immigration_update and http://www.pollingreport.com/im

migration.htm; NBC/Wall Street Journal poll cited in Laura Makler, "Majority of Republicans Back Legal Status for Immigrants," *Wall Street Journal*, August 3, 2015; Miriam Jordan, "Poll: Most Say Let Immigrants Stay," *Wall Street Journal*, June 5, 2015.

19. Asian American Justice Center, "Behind the Numbers: Post-Election Survey of Asian American and Pacific Island Voters in 2012," April 2013.

20. Jeffrey M. Jones, "Half of U.S. Hispanics Identity as Political Independents," Gallup, July 2, 2012; M. J. Lee, "Poll: Half of Hispanics Independents," *Politico*, July 2, 2012.

21. "Behind the Numbers: Post-Election Survey of Asian American and Pacific Island Voters in 2012."

22. Clemént Doleac, "The Voto Latino, Towards a More Independent Movement," Council on Hemispheric Affairs, January 23, 2015.

23. Peter Jamison, "Korean Americans Hate Gay Marriage Most, New Poll Reveals," *SF Weekly News*, July 20, 2010.

24. Figures are from Jens Manuel Krogstad, "More Hispanics, Blacks Enrolling in College, But Lag in Bachelor's Degrees," Pew Research Center, April 24, 2014; and "Mark Hugo Lopez, "Among Recent High School Grads, Hispanic College Enrollment Rate Surpasses That of Whites," Pew Research Center, September 8, 2013.

25. C. N. Lee, "New Horizons for Learning," http://education.jhu.edu/PD/new horizons/strategies/topics.

26. Daniel Halper, "Avoiding the Trump Trap on Immigration," *Weekly Standard*, July 22, 2015, http://www.weeklystandard.com/blogs/avoiding-trump-trap -immigration_995242.html.

27. Ester Yu-His Lee, "Latinos Voted Democrat 2-1, But Shifted Republican in Some Key Races," http://thinkprogess.org/immigration/2014/11/06.

28. U.S. Census Bureau, *Income and Poverty in the United States* (2012). For homeownership, see "Social, Economic and Housing Statistics," *U.S. Census Bureau News*, January 29, 2015.

29. U.S. Department of Labor, "Labor Force Characteristics by Race and Ethnicity, 2011," Report 1036, August 2012; and Richard Alba, *Blurring the Color Line*, pp. 96–105.

30. Centers for Disease Control, *National Statistics Reports* (January 15, 2015).

31. Sean P. Cunningham, *Cowboy Conservatism: Texas and the Rise of the Modern Right* (Lexington, KY, 2010).

32. "New Mexico's Governor: Susana Martinez Shows How Republicans Might One Day Woo Latinos," *Economist*, December 17, 2011.

33. Harry Bruinius, "Mia Love, The First Black Republican Woman in Congress, Is 'Solid Gold' for GOP," *Christian Science Monitor*, November 5, 2014; George Will, "Utah's Mia Love Battles Stereotypes," *Newsweek*, September 24, 2012.

CHAPTER 3

1. John Della Volpe, "Survey of Young America's Attitudes Toward Politics and Public Service," Institute of Politics, Harvard University, 2014.

2. Michael Medved, "The 'War on Women' Failed in 2012," *Wall Street Journal*, April 17, 2014.

3. "Millennials in Adulthood," Pew Research Center, May 7, 2014: Scott Keeter, "Young Voters in the 2008 Election," Pew Research Center, November 13, 2008; Kevin Robillard, "Election 2012: Youth Vote Was Decisive," *Politico*, November 7, 2012; "Voter Turnout among Young Women and Men in the 2012 Presidential Election," *Circle*, May 2013; "Young Voters Supported Obama Less, but May Have Mattered More," Pew Research Center, November 26, 2012; Institute of Politics, Harvard University, "Survey of Young Americans' Attitude toward Politics and Public Service," October 29, 2014; John Sides, "Democrats have a Young People Problem, Too," *Washington Post*, March 10, 2014; David Leonhardt, "Why Teenagers May Grow Up Conservative," *New York Times*, July 8, 2014; Stanley B. Greenberg, *America Ascendant* (New York, 2016).

4. Volpe, "Survey of Young America's Attitudes Toward Politics and Public Service."

5. Author interview, May 18, 2014.

6. Louis Jacobson, "Are There More Welfare Recipients in the U.S. than Full-Time Workers?," January 28, 2015, http://www.politicalfact.com/punditfact /statements; "Welfare Statistics," http://www.statisticbrain.com.welfare-stat istics.

7. Peter Baldwin, *The Narcissism of Minor Differences: How America and Europe Are Alike* (New York, 2009), pp. 97–121.

8. Educational Testing Service, *America's Skills Challenge: Millennials and the Future* (Princeton, NJ, 2015).

9. Wendy Wang, "Record Share of Americans Have Never Married," Pew Research Center, September 9, 2014.

10. For the economic consequences of single parenting, see Robert D. Putnam, *Our Kids: The American Dream in Crisis* (New York, 2015).

11. Fred Siegel and Robert Doar, "De Blasio's Welfare Reform Reversal," *City Journal* (Spring 2015).

12. Lydia Saad, "Generational Differences on Abortion Narrow," Gallup, March 12, 2010, http://www.gallup.com/poll/126581; and "Abortion," Gallup, 2015, http://www.gallup.com/poll/1576.

13. This discussion draws upon Robert Wuthnow, *After the Baby Boomers: How Twenty- and Thirty-Somethings Are Shaping the Future of American Religion* (Princeton, NJ, 2009), especially pp. 157–79.

14. Paul Taylor, "Six Take-Aways from the Census Bureau's Voting Report," Pew Research Center, May 5, 2013; The Center for Information and Research on Civic Learning and Engagement, "Voter Turnout Among Young Women and Men in the 2012 Presidential Election," May 2013.

15. Michael Winerip, "Boomers, Millennials and the Ballot Box," *New York Times*, October 28, 2012; Volpe, "Survey of Young America's Attitudes Toward Politics and Public Service."

16. Volpe, "Survey of Young America's Attitudes Toward Politics and Public Service."

17. Paul Taylor, *The Next America: Boomers, Millennials and the Looming Generational Showdown* (New York, 2015), p. 44.
18. Taylor, *The Next America: Boomers, Millennials and the Looming Generational Showdown*, pp. 61–63.
19. "The Generation Gap and the 2012 Election," Pew Research Center, November 3, 2012, http://www.people-press.org/2011/11/03.
20. Taylor, *The Next America: Boomers, Millennials and the Looming Generational Showdown*, pp. 63–64.
21. David Plouffe, *The Audacity to Win: The Inside Story and Lessons of Barack Obama's Historic Victory* (New York, 2009), pp. 21, 32, 48, 51–52; and John Heilemann and Mark Halperin, *Game Change: Obama and the Clintons, McCain and Palin, and the Race of a Lifetime* (New York, 2010), p. 107.
22. Susan Mach, "Winning the Youth Vote for Obama: A Conversation with Jonathan Kopp," *Communication for Social Change*, 2010, http://www.communicationforsocialchang.org/mazi-articles.php?i+393.
23. Celia Bigelow, "Romney Lost OH, PA, and VA Because of the Youth Vote," *Townhall.com*, November 16, 2012, http://townhall.com/columnists/celiabigelow/2012/11/14/romeny_lost-oh-pa.
24. Amanda Ruggan, "Young Voters Powered Obama's Victory While Shrugging Off Slacker Image," *U.S. News*, November 8, 2008.
25. Center for Information and Research on Civic Learning and Engagement, "The Youth Vote in 2012," May 10, 2012. Stacy Techer Khadaroo, "The Untold Story of Obama's Youth Vote Victory," *Christian Science Monitor*, November 15, 2012, http://www.csmonitor.com/USA/DC-Decoder/2012/11115/The-untold-story-of.
26. "Youth Vote Critical to Obama's Reelection," *Huffington Post*, November 30, 2012, http://www.huffintonpost.com/college.
27. Pew Research Center, "Young Voters Supported Obama Less, But May Have Mattered More," November 26, 2012.
28. Joceyln Killey, "As GOP Celebrates Win, No Sign of Narrowing Gender, Age Gaps," Pew Research Center, November 5, 2014.
29. College Republican National Committee, "Grand Old Party for a Brand New Generation," 2013; Katie Glueck, "Report: How GOP Lost Young Voters," *Politico*, June 2, 2013.
30. "This 21-Year-Old Is Trying to Become a Major Player in Conservative Politics. So Far It Seems to Be Working," *National Journal*, 2015, http://www.nationaljournal.com/politics/this-21-year-old-is-trying.

CHAPTER 4

1. "Midterm Elections' Turnout," *USA Today*, November 5, 2014.
2. Rob Gurwitt, "Baby Boomers' Impact on Elections," http://www.governing.com/generations/government-management/gov-baby-boomer-impact-on-elections.html; Frank Newport, Jeffrey M. Jones, and Lydia Saad, "Baby Boomers to Push U.S. Politics in Years Ahead," Gallup, January 23, 2015.

3. Material here and in next three paragraphs is from: Dionne Searcey and Robert Gebeloff, "America's Seniors Find Middle-Class 'Sweet Spot,'" *New York Times*, June 14, 2015; Sandra L. Colby and Jennifer M. Ortman, "The Baby Boom Cohort in the United States: 2012 to 2060," United States Census Bureau, May 2014; Kelvin Pollard and Paola Scommega, "Just How Many Baby Boomers Are There?," Population Reference Bureau, April 2014; and Frank Newport, Jeffrey M. Jones, and Lydia Sadd, "'Baby Boomers' Politics vary Significantly by Age," Gallup, January 23, 2014.

4. Jim Harter and Sangeeta Agrawal, "Many Boomers Reluctant to Retire," Gallup, January 20, 2014.

5. Dennis Jacobs, "More Nonretirees Expect to Rely on Social Security," Gallup, April 30, 2012.

6. Rob Gurwatt, "Baby Boomers' Impact on Elections," September 2012, http://www.governing.com/generations/government-management/gov-baby-bo omer-impact-on-elections.

7. Frank Newport, Jeffrey Jones, and Lydia Saad, "Baby Boomers to Push U.S. Politics In the Years Ahead."

8. Sylvia Ann Hewlett, Laura Sherbin, and Karen Sumberg, "How Gen Y and Boomers Will Reshape Your Agenda," *Business Review* (July–August 2009).

9. Statistics here, and in next paragraph, from Dave Johnson, "These Charts Show the Baby Boomers' Coming Health Crisis," *Time*, May 11, 2015.

10. Social Security and Medical Board of Trustees, "A Summary of the 2012 Annual Reports," Social Security, http://www.ssa.gov/oact/trsum/index.html.

11. Paul Taylor, *The Next America: Boomers, Millennials, and the Looming Generational Showdown* (New York, 2014), p. 137.

12. Administration on Aging, "A Profile of Older Americans: 2011," http://www.aoa.gov/aoarrot/aging_statistics/Profile/2011/3.aspx.

13. Taylor, *The Next America: Boomers, Millennials, and the Looming Generational Showdown*, pp. 174–75.

14. Taylor, *The Next America: Boomers, Millennials, and the Looming Generational Showdown*, p. 59. For a major study of boomer retirement expectations before the recession, see AARP, *Baby Boomer Envision Retirement II* (May 2004).

15. Drew Deilver, "5 Facts About Social Security," Pew Research Center, October 16, 2013.

16. "Public Opinions on Social Security," National Academy of Social Insurance, January 2013, https://www.nasl.org/learn/social-security/public-opinion.

17. Nicoletta Batini, Giovanni Callegari, and Julia Guerreiro, "An Analysis of U.S. Generational Imbalances: Who Will Pay and How?," International Monetary Fund, April 2011.

18. Richard W. Evans, Laurence J. Kotlikoff, and Kerk L. Phillips, "Game Over: Simulating Unsustainable Fiscal Policy," *National Bureau of Economic Research Working Paper Series*, March 2012.

19. Richard Eskow, "Social Security, Ten Years from Now," *Huffington Post*, May 12, 2015.

20. Emily Brandon, "The Baby Boomer Vote: Sandwiched Again," *U.S. News*, November 18, 2008.

21. Voter registration was high among the 45- to 54-year-old cohort, at over 73 percent. U.S. Census Bureau, "Voting and Registration in the Election of November 2008," July 2012.

22. Wisconsin (57 percent to 42 percent); Virginia (51 percent to 46 percent); Ohio (53 percent to 45 percent); Florida (52 percent to 47 percent); and Colorado (56 percent to 42 percent). *New York Times,* "Election Results 2008," December 9, 2008.

23. Pew Research, "The Generation Gap and the 2012 Elections," November 2011, http://www.people-press.org/2011/11/03.d.

24. It was a decided shift in older voters. Voters aged 45–64 went Republican, 51 percent to 47 percent. For those over 65, even more voted for Romney, 56 percent to 44 percent. Roper Center, "How Groups Voted in 2012," 2012, http:www.ropercenter.ucon.edu.

25. Dan Eggen, "Direct Mail Still a Force in Campaigns," *Washington Post,* October 12, 2012.

26. In Virginia, Romney won the 45- to 64-year-old vote, 53 percent to 46 percent. Four years earlier, Obama won this block by 3 points. In Ohio, Romney won this age group by 4 points, 51 percent to 47 percent. In 2008, this age group gave Obama a 7-point margin in his favor. In Florida, the 45- to 64-year-old vote broke for Romney as well, 52 percent to 48 percent, just about the reverse of what it had been for Obama in 2008 against McCain. Romney took the 45- to 64-year-old vote by 5 points in North Carolina, 3 points in Colorado, and 6 points in Iowa—all reversals from the 2008 election. *Washington Post,* "Exit Polls 2012: How the Vote Has Shifted," November 6, 2012.

27. Ronald Brownstein, "Election Reinforces Divide Between Millennials, Baby Boomers," *National Journal,* November 8, 2012.

28. Susan Page, "A Defining Gap: Seniors for Romney, Millennials for Obama," *USA Today,* July 30, 2012.

29. Exit poll figures are from CBS News, http://www.cbsnews.com/elections /2014.

30. Jocelyn Kiley, "As GOP Celebrates Win, No Sign of Narrowing Gender, Age Gaps," Pew Research Center, November 5, 2012.

31. Brad Bannon, "Hate Political Gridlock? Blame It on the Boomers," *U.S. News,* October 17, 2013.

CHAPTER 5

1. Paul Taylor, *The Next America: Boomers, Millennials, and the Looming Generational Showdown* (New York, 2014), pp. 2–5.

2. Taylor, *The Next America: Boomers, Millennials, and the Looming Generational Showdown,* p. 9.

3. Pew Research, "The Lost Decade of the Middle Class," August 22, 2012, http://www.pewsocialtrends.org/2012/08/22/the-lost-decade-of-the-middle-class/.

4. "The African American Middle Class," *Black Demographics,* 2010, http:// blackdemographics.com/households/middle-class/.

5. Dante Chinni, "Small Gains with Black Voters Could Boast the GOP in 2016," *Wall Street Journal,* June 28, 2015.

6. Jason M. Breslow, "The State of America's Middle Class in Eight Charts," *PBS Frontline,* July 9, 2013, http://www.pbs.org/wgbhpages/frontline/bus iness-economy.

7. Richard Moran, "America's Four Middle Classes," Pew Research Center, July 29, 2010.

8. Libby Kane and Andy Kierz, "How Much You Have to Earn to Be Considered Middle Class in Every State," *Business* Insider (April 2, 2015); Donald J. Boudreaux and Mark J. Perry, "The Myth of a Stagnant Middle Class," *Wall Street Journal,* January 24, 2013.

9. Figures on house size and numbers of television sets are taken from U.S. census data. A discussion of work hours needed to purchase refrigerators, televisions, and dishwashers can be found in Don Bondtreaux, "The Future: Back to the Past," http://cafehaek.com/2012/11.

10. "Health Expenditures—Total of GDP in the United States," http://www .tradingeconomics.com, 2013.

11. Jeffrey M. Jones, "U.S. Parents' College Funding Worries Are Top Money Concern," Gallup, April 20, 2014.

12. U.S. Department of Education, National Center for Education Statistics, *Digest of Education Statistics* (Washington, D.C., 2013).

13. https://www.debt.org/students/.

14. https://www.insidehighered.com/news/2015/04/13/aaup-full-time-faculty -salaries-22-percent-year.

15. Crissinda Ponder, "Saving Money Remains Low Priority in the U.S.," bankrate.com, November 14, 2014.

16. http://www.statista.com/statistics/246234/personal-savings-rate-in-the -united-states/.

17. G. E. Miller, "A Personal Savings Rate by Country Comparison," 2011, http://www.20somethingfinance.com/a-personal-savings-rate-by-country -comparison; and "United States Personal Savings Rate, 1959–2015," http://www.tradingeconomics.com/united-states/personal-savings.

18. Nancy Hellmich, "Retirement: A Third Less Than $1,000 Put Away," *USA Today,* April 1, 2014.

19. Employee Benefit Research Institute, "How Confident Are Americans About Retirement?," 2015; Rich Morin, "More Americans Worry About Financing Retirement," Pew Research Center, October 22, 2012, http://www .pewresearch.org/staff/rich-Morin/. For understanding the relationship between public service employee unions and the pension problem, see Daniel DiSalvo, *Government Against Itself: Public Union Power and Its Consequences* (New York, 2015).

20. Ti Chen, "American Household Credit Card Debt Statists: 2015," https:// www.nerdwallet.com/blog/credit-card-data.

21. Ellie Ismaildou, "The New Greece May Be in the U.S.," *Market Watch,* June 30, 2015, http://marketwatch.com/story/these-lurking-debts; Jonathan Todd, "America Is Facing a Pension Time Bomb," March 23, 2015, http:// www.nerdwallet.com/blog/category/cities/economics.

22. Martin Neil Baily and Barry P. Bosworth, "U.S. Manufacturing: Understanding Its Past and Its Potential Future," *Journal of Economic Perspectives* (Winter 2014): 3–36.

23. Sean Trende, "The Case of the Missing White Voters, Revisited," June 21, 2013; "Does GOP Have to Pass Immigration Reform?" June 25, 2013; "The GOP and Hispanics: What the Future Holds," June 28, 2013; and "Demographics and the GOP, Part IV," July 2, 2013, http://www.realclearpolitics.com./articles/2013.

24. Trende, "Demographics and the GOP, Part IV," July 2, 2013, http://www.realclearpolitics.com./articles/2013.

25. The GOP and Hispanics: What the Future Holds," June 28, 2013; and "Demographics and the GOP, Part IV," July 2, 2013, http://www.realclearpolitics.com./articles/2013.

26. Sean Trende, "Yes, the Missing Whites Matter," July 12, 2013, http://www.realclearpolitics.com./articles/2013.

27. Ronald Brownstein, "Republicans Can't Win with White Voters Alone," *Atlantic*, September 7, 2013.

28. Alan I. Abramowitz and Ruy Teixeira, "'Missing Voters' in the 2012 Election," *Crystal Ball*, July 25, 2013, http://www.centerforpolitics.or/crystalball/articles.

29. "GOP Pollster Explains Why Republicans Need Record Minority Support to Win in 2016," February 24, 2015, http://www.huffingtonpost.com/2015.

30. Karl Rove, "More White Votes Alone Won't Save the GOP," *Wall Street Journal*, June 26, 2013.

31. Roper Center, "How Groups Voted in 2008," 2008, http://www.ropercent.uconn.edu.

32. Roper Center, "How Groups Voted in 2008."

33. David Wasserman, "The GOP's Built-in-Midterm Advantage," *Cook Political Report*, May 31, 2013.

34. Jennifer Agiesta and Jesse J. Holland, "Why GOP Won: Shifting White Votes Hurt Democrats," November 6, 2014, http://www.aol.com/article/2014/11/06.

35. Jon Kotkin, "The Demographics That Sank the Democrats in the Midterm Elections," *Forbes*, December 11, 2014, http://www.forbes.com/sites/joelkotkin/2014/11/2015.

CHAPTER 6

1. Paul Taylor, *The Next America: Boomers, Millennials, and the Looming Generational Showdown* (New York, 2014), pp. 4–6.

2. Pew Research Center, *America's Changing Religious Landscape* (May 12, 2015).

3. Taylor, *The Next America: Boomers, Millennials, and the Looming Generational Showdown*, pp. 126–38; and Robert Wuthnow, *After the Baby Boomers: How Twenty- and Thirty-Somethings Are Shaping the Future of American Religion* (Princeton, NJ, 2007).

4. "America's Changing Religious Landscape," Pew Research Center, May 12, 2015. Pew Research data cited in next few paragraphs is from this same source.

5. Jewish voting patterns are found at https://www.jewishvirtuallibrary.org /jsource/US-Israel/jewvote.html. For the switch in Jewish voters toward Republicans, see Josh Kraushaar, "How Obama's Foreign Policy Is Hurting Hillary Clinton's White House Chances," *National Journal,* July 16, 2015, http://www.nationaljournal.com/against-the-grain/how-obama-s-foreign -policy-is-hurting-hillary-clinton-s-white-house-chances-20150714.

6. Robert D. Putnam, *Our Kids: The American Dream in Crisis* (New York, 2015), pp. 191–226.

7. Putnam, *Our Kids: The American Dream in Crisis,* p. 224.

8. Evangelical voters were not identified in every state. See http://elections.nbc news.com/ns/politics/2012/all/president/#.VcuX2flH5l0.

9. Quoted in Gregory L. Schneider, *The Conservative Century: From Reaction to Revolution* (Lantham, MD, 2009), pp. 182–83.

10. Quoted by Albert R. Hunt, "Will Nonreligious Reshape U.S. Politics?," May 17, 2012, http://www.bloombergview.com/articles/2015-05-17.

11. Napp Nazworth, "Huckabee: If 10 Percent More Evangelicals Had Voted, Obama Would Not be President," *Christian Post,* September 27, 2014, http:// www.christianpost.com/news/huckabee; "Your Vote Matters," *Providence Forum,* June 29, 2015, http://www.providenceforum.or/yourvotematters.

12. Michael Medved, "Invisible Armies of Evangelicals Cannot Deliver Victory in 2016," *USA Today,* May 18, 2015, http://www.usatoday.com/story /opinion/2015/05/18/christian-evangelicals-elections-demographics -medved-column/26474707/.

13. Pew Research Center, "Few Say Religion Shapes Immigration, Environmental Views," September 17, 2011, http://www/pewforum.org/2010/09/17; and Pew Research Center, "Religion in Public Life," September 22, 2014, http://www/pewforum.org/2014/09/22/section-1-religion-in-public-life/.

14. Pew Research data here and on the following pages is from "America's Changing Religious Landscape," Pew Research Center, May 12, 2015; "How the Faithful Voted: 2012 Preliminary Analysis," Pew Research Center, November 7, 2012; "How the Faithful Voted: 2014 Preliminary Analysis," Pew Research Center, November 5, 2014; Pew Research Center, "Religion in Public Life," September 22, 2014, http://www/pewforum.org/2014/09/22/ section-1-religion-in-public-life/.

15. Election figures here and in the next paragraph are found in Gallup Research, "Election Polls: Historical Trends," http://www.gallup.com/polls/9460/elec tion-polls-vote-groups. Also see http://cara.georgetown.edu/presidential%20 vote%20only.pdf; "Election Polls—Presidential Vote by Groups; Gallup Historical Trends," Gallup, http://www.gallup.com/poll.

16. Richard Griffin, "What Went Wrong in 2012? The Case of the 4 Million Missing Voters," November 14, 2012, http://www.redstate.com/diary /giffenelection/2012/2/11.

17. Griffin, "What Went Wrong in 2012?" Griffin material on ensuing pages is from this same source.

18. "Evangelical Vote Played Decisive Role in GOP Wave in 2014," *Faith and Freedom News*, November 12, 2014, http://ffcoalition.com/blog/2014-11-05 /evangelical-vote-2014-election.

CHAPTER 7

1. This argument is spelled out in great quantitative detail in Byron E. Shafer and Richard Johnston, *The End of Southern Exceptionalism: Class, Race, and Partisan Change in the Postwar South* (Cambridge, MA, 2006).
2. Alan I. Abramowitz, *The Disappearing Center: Engaged Citizens, Polarization and American Democracy* (New Haven, CT, 2010), p. 79.
3. Hannah Fingerhut, "Millennials' Views of News Media, Religious Organizations Grow More Negative," Pew Research Center, January 4, 2016; "Views of Banks, Large Corporations, Small Business Improve Since 2010," Pew Research Center, December 21, 2015.
4. Pew Research, "A Deep Dive into Party Affiliation," April 7, 2015, http:// www.people-press.org/2015/04/07.
5. Morris P. Fiorina et al., *Culture War? The Myth of a Polarized America* (New York, 2006); and Ronald Brownstein, *The Second Civil War: How Extreme Partisanship has Paralyzed Washington and Polarized America* (New York, 2007).
6. Donald T. Critchlow, *American Political History: A Very Short Introduction* (New York, 2015).
7. Alan I Abramowitz, *The Disappearing Center*; turnout figures are drawn from John E. Silvia and Tim Quinlan, "Presidential Elections in America: A Primer," Wells Fargo Securities, August 4, 2015.
8. https://www.census.gov/prod2010pubs/p.20-562.pdf.
9. "Voter Identification Laws," *Washington Post* (poll), August 13, 2012, http:// www.washingtonpost.com/page/21010/-2019.
10. Andrew Romano, "How Ignorant Are Americans?" *Newsweek*, March 20, 2011.
11. Quoted in Aaron Smith, "Civic Engagement in the Digital Age," Pew Research Center, April 25, 2013, http://www/pewinternet.org/2013/04/25 /civic-engagement.
12. Gregory Ferenstein, "Most Americans Unaware of [Insert Issue Here]," *TechCrunch*, June 25, 2014, http://www/techcrunch.com/2014/01/25/most -americans-are-unaware-of-insert-issue-here/.
13. Pew Research Center, "Well Known: Clinton and Gadhafi: Little Known: Who Controls Congress," March 31, 2011, http://www/people-press.org /2011/03/31well-known-clinton-and-gadhafi.
14. Sam Dillon, "U.S. Students Remain Poor at History, Tests Show," *New York Times*, June 14, 2011.
15. "Failing Our Students, Failing America," http://www.americancivicliteracy .org/2007/summary.
16. Gallup, "Confidence in Institutions," June 2–7, 2013, http://www.gallup .com/poll/1597.

INDEX